CSR, Sustainability, Ethics & Governance

In recent years the discussion concerning the relation between business and society has made immense strides. This has in turn led to a broad academic and practical discussion on innovative management concepts, such as Corporate Social Responsibility, Corporate Governance and Sustainability Management. This series offers a comprehensive overview of the latest theoretical and empirical research and provides sound concepts for sustainable business strategies. In order to do so, it combines the insights of leading researchers and thinkers in the fields of management theory and the social sciences – and from all over the world, thus contributing to the interdisciplinary and intercultural discussion on the role of business in society. The underlying intention of this series is to help solve the world's most challenging problems by developing new management concepts that create value for business and society alike. In order to support those managers, researchers and students who are pursuing sustainable business approaches for our common future, the series offers them access to cutting-edge management approaches.

CSR, Sustainability, Ethics & Governance is accepted by the Norwegian Register for Scientific Journals, Series and Publishers, maintained and operated by the Norwegian Social Science Data Services (NSD)

More information about this series at http://www.springer.com/series/11565

Joanna Dyczkowska • Andrea Szirmai
Madarasine • Adriana Tiron-Tudor
Editors

Development of Integrated Reporting in the SME Sector

Case Studies from European Countries

Springer

Editors
Joanna Dyczkowska
Department of Costing, Tax Management and Controlling
Wroclaw University of Economics and Business
Wroclaw, Poland

Andrea Szirmai Madarasine
Department of Accountancy
Budapest Business School
Budapest, Hungary

Adriana Tiron-Tudor
Faculty of Economics and Business Administration
Babes-Bolyai University
Cluj Napoca, Romania

ISSN 2196-7075 ISSN 2196-7083 (electronic)
CSR, Sustainability, Ethics & Governance
ISBN 978-3-030-81902-6 ISBN 978-3-030-81903-3 (eBook)
https://doi.org/10.1007/978-3-030-81903-3

This Springer imprint is published by the registered company Springer Nature Switzerland AG.
The registered company address is: Gewerbestrasse 11, 6330 Cham, Switzerland

Foreword

In proposing the Corporate Sustainability Reporting Directive ('the CSRD'), the European Commission ('the Commission') has announced its intention to overhaul the corporate reporting system in the European Union ('the EU') such that sustainability reporting will assume equal importance to that of financial reporting. In so doing, corporate reporting will then be aligned with and support the EU's policy objectives, including 'net zero' emissions, that is, carbon neutrality. EU Sustainability Reporting Standards, including ones tailored to the needs and capacities of small and medium-sized enterprises ('SMEs'), will be developed by the European Financial Reporting Advisory Group ('EFRAG'). The Commission has instructed EFRAG to build on existing standards and frameworks when developing these standards.

This book is, therefore, particularly relevant and timely. It represents a valuable contribution to the literature on integrated reporting ('IR'). It examines the level of IR development in six European countries (Germany, Hungary, Italy, Poland, Romania, and the UK) and explores the prerequisites for IR implementation in the SME sector. In so doing, it enhances our understanding as to the incidence and practice of IR among SMEs across Europe as well as the potential influence IR might have on the form and content of the sustainability reporting standards to be developed by EFRAG. IR can serve as the basis for such standards.

The CSRD does not require non-listed SMEs, which constitute the great majority of business enterprises, to produce sustainability reports. Rather, they can volunteer to produce such reports, and it is in the European public interest that they do. SMEs are naturally concerned to ensure that the benefits of reporting exceed the costs. The infusion of IR into the sustainability reporting standards in a proportionate manner promises to enable SMEs to report in a succinct manner to their stakeholders and, through integrated thinking that IR promotes, help them be more strategic and successful.

EFAA is especially interested in this book and the other deliverables of the INTEREST project since the sustainability agenda presents a significant challenge and opportunity for small and medium-sized accountancy practices (SMPs). SMPs have a key role to play in helping SMEs prepare sustainability reports, just as they currently do financial reports, and so will greatly benefit from the insights presented.

EFAA, London, UK Paul Thompson

Introduction

The following book examines the level of integrated reporting development in six European countries (Germany, Hungary, Italy, Poland, Romania, and the UK) and explores the prerequisites for IR implementation in the SME sector.

Integrated reporting has gained momentum since the International Integrated Reporting Council (IIRC) published its first IR Framework in 2013 with the intention of facilitating the emergence of integrated thinking and reporting. The IIRC (2013a, p. 33) emphasized that an aim of an integrated report was to communicate concisely about 'how an organization's strategy, governance, performance and prospects, in the context of its external environment, lead to the creation of value in the short, medium and long term'.

Revitalization of the IR Framework in 2021 led to the extension of an integrated report's primary purpose by drawing attention to the fact that value may be created but also preserved and eroded (IIRC 2021, p. 5). Changes in value over time manifest in increases, decreases, or transformations of the capital induced by the organization's activities, relationships, and interactions (IIRC 2021, p. 16). The designation of the IR framework has not altered. It is still primarily dedicated to the private sector and companies of any size. However, the IR principle-based guide does not explicitly explain how and to what extent SMEs should follow the framework.

The potential benefits of IR are not explicitly convincing for SMEs. On the one hand, they may perceive integrated reporting as a long and complex process that requires a considerable change in an enterprise's structure, processes, and thinking (Stent and Dowler 2015). However, researchers argue that these changes are not revolutionary but incremental (Dumay and Dai 2017; Guthrie et al. 2017; Stubbs and Higgins, 2014). This means that they do not affect the enterprise's values and beliefs but mostly the resources, structures, and collaboration between people instead of working in silos (Argento et al. 2019). The other problems that SMEs encounter are information system deficits resulting in a lack of access to the relevant data, administrative burdens, and high preparation costs (Arena and Azone 2012;

Gerwanski 2020). All these factors may discourage SME managers from voluntarily reporting non-financial issues.

On the other hand, some positive signals are worth considering, for instance, The BlackSun report (2014) summarizing the second research project results with IIRC Pilot Programme organizations. The document delivers compelling evidence on the IR benefits perceived by the newcomers on the IR route. The early adopters of IR highlighted a better understanding of how they created—or destroyed—value and the benefits from data quality improvement. They also highlighted that moving towards IR positively influenced their relationships with stakeholders and enabled them to better understand the enterprise's strategy and longer term objectives. The pilot programme participants noticed that IR implementation connected their departments breaking down silos and broadened perspectives. Most of them admitted that they either considerably altered what they measured or had plans to do so in the future. These arguments speak in favour of IR or at least open a discussion on opportunities and risks as well as the cost and benefits related to IR implementation.

SMEs are often labelled as the 'lifeblood', 'backbone', and 'powerhouse' of the global economy. According to the EUROSTAT report published on March 26, 2021, the overwhelming majority (99.8%) of EU-27 businesses were represented by SMEs employing fewer than 250 persons. In 2018, SMEs' economic weight regarding their contribution to employment and value added was as follows: 65% of the EU-27's non-financial business economy workforce and 52.8% of the value added. In comparison to SMEs, large enterprises (with 250 or more persons employed) amounted to 0.2 % of the total number of enterprises, but their economic weight was relatively higher: 35% of the EU-27's non-financial business economy workforce and 47.2% of the value added (EUROSTAT, 2021)

The situation and opportunities of SMEs considerably differ from that of larger companies. The distinctive feature is not only size but also the specific nature of SMEs, which does not allow for the same practical application of tools, business models, and interpretative schemes that prove adequate for larger enterprises.

Firstly, SMEs values are built on founder-manager beliefs, skills, and initiatives (Cohen, 2013). SMEs may also be affected by the family 'footprint' in management or the owner's direct leadership resulting in a lack of detachment between ownership and control. Control in SMEs is often private, independent, and autonomous, whereas planning and budgeting processes are mostly unstructured (Cohen 2013). The owner's strategic role may directly influence the decisions with their own beliefs and personal relationships, which, in turn, significantly impact the company's choices in terms of social commitment and sustainability. On the other hand, as Cohen (2013) states, SME simple structure enables fast, agile, and flexible decision making.

Secondly, SMEs are contingent on market conditions and clients, and in terms of community, they are locally oriented and connected (Cohen 2013). Smaller companies are deeply rooted in the local territory as a rule. On the one hand, a genuine relationship with the local community may be beneficial for both sides. On the other hand, a solid commitment to local matters and networks may divert attention from other stakeholders and their reasonable expectations.

Thirdly, SMEs often have a direct and personal relationship with employees, customers, and suppliers, due to the small number of employees involved in the company's activities. Such a situation favours relationships based on trust and reciprocity both between owners and employees and between these and external stakeholders. Therefore, SMEs generally do not have a structured method to communicate their CSR initiatives. Further, because in most cases, they live these initiatives as an integral part of their activity that does not require external evidence.

Fourthly, SMEs have a limited pool of resources available, whether these are organizational, financial, know-how, or skills. These constraints often press entrepreneurs to adopt a short or medium-term strategic outlook, as the lack of a sufficiently stable and solid resource base does not allow for longer term planning and investments.

Finally, Cohen (2013) emphasizes a different character of SMEs' culture: direct, informal, and with much entrepreneurial spirit and specificity of human resources reflected in multi-skilled and multi-tasks, flexible, and engaged employees (Cohen 2013, p. 15).

SMEs are vulnerable to changing business conditions and any market perturbance. The economic disruption unleashed by COVID-19 has affected SMEs both on the supply and demand sides. Enterprises faced logistical challenges related to the disruption of transportation and labour shortages. SMEs also experienced a deep decline in sales due to lockdowns, the shutting down of several global value chains in affected industries, and a drop in consumer confidence (Juergensen et al. 2020).

IR may provide a catalyst for a more cohesive reporting system in SMEs and help them legitimize business activities in the difficult times after the COVID-19 pandemic. On the one hand, traditional reporting is too complex to communicate material matters to stakeholders, and, therefore, it lacks relevance. Moreover, it is based on backwards-looking information, and there arise questions about who might be the recipients of such information. Both investors and managers need useful information. Therefore, it would be better for them to access financial data in real time to make informed decisions.

On the other hand, enterprises interact with heterogeneous stakeholders who have various information needs and expectations. IIRC (2021, p. 11) highlights that an integrated report's primary goal is to clarify providers of financial capital how an organization creates, preserves, and erodes value over time. Indeed, in the revisited version of the IR framework, the IIRC has not changed its position that other stakeholders such as employees, customers, suppliers, business partners, local communities, legislators, regulators, and policymakers may benefit from an integrated report; however, still, they are not treated as the primary group of interest. This approach has been met with criticism of IR Framework privileging shareholders over stakeholders and sustainability (Flower 2015). Indeed, IIRC adopts the instrumental perspective of stakeholder theory in IR and assumes that an enterprise has no interest in all stakeholders' welfare, but rather it should use the opportunities that result from stakeholder management for reaching corporate objectives (Speziale 2019).

Presently, SMEs have become increasingly aware of the importance of non-financial reporting (NFI) reflecting social and environmental aspects of business impact. They are trying to signal considerably more about their sustainability activities (Ashton et al., 2017). Furthermore, they are strongly encouraged to disclose such information. EFAA (2018), for instance, draws attention to the potential benefits of voluntary NFI disclosure to SMEs, their stakeholders, and the wider public.

IR goes a step further and may change SMEs' mindset about what constitutes successful business by introducing integrated thinking, which is 'the active consideration by an organization of the relationships between its various operating and functional units and the capitals that the organization uses or affects' (IIRC 2021, p. 3). Therefore, investors can use integrated reports to make more informed decisions about capital allocation, and SMEs can manage critical risks and opportunities, build confidence among stakeholders, and improve future performance. IIRC (2021) distinguishes between the six capitals: natural, human, manufactured, social and relationship, intellectual, and financial; however, SMEs are not required to report against all of them, but to ask themselves the questions of which and how might each be material to them.

It should be emphasized that IR concept is not only for reporting but also for management (Pozolli and Attolini 2014). It helps directors and managers create a complete view of the whole system which creates, preserves, or destroys the value by existing relations, business activities, and outputs. Besides, IR can satisfy banks and financial institutions' information needs, which are typically significant stakeholders for SMEs (Pozolli and Attolini 2014). IR will provide them with information on how an enterprise's strategy contributes to value creation, which gives insights into how the organization can achieve its objectives, including financial ones and be a reliable debtor.

This book contributes to the literature by providing valuable insights into non-financial reporting practices of SMEs operating in countries of various regulatory frameworks and differentiated IR implementation progress. The research on IR implementation in SMEs is presently narrow and explorative than evidence-based (Kaya and Türegün 2014; Del Baldo 2015, 2017, 2018; Amirrudin et al. 2019; Gerwanski 2020; Muslichah et al. 2019, 2020). Much more research can be found concerning the development of sustainability reporting in SMEs (Arena and Azzone 2012; Cohen 2013; Langwell and Heaton 2015; Massa et al. 2015; Shields and Shelleman 2017; Caputo et al. 2017; Agostini et al. 2018; Moneva and Hernandez-Pajares 2018; Bergmann and Posch 2018; Girella et al. 2019a; Steinhöfel et al. 2019; Rossi and Luque-Vílchez 2021; Rodríguez-Gutiérrez et al. 2021). This study fills the research gap and provides a cross-sectional overview of SMEs' reporting practices considering their specific regulatory environment. The authors of chapters outline unique circumstances that accompany each SMEs' business activity in various countries, considering political, economic, social, cultural, and technological conditions. The book also makes a practical contribution by providing several observations and recommendations for SMEs regarding IR implementation, taking an international perspective of three West European countries and three Central Eastern European countries (CEECs).

Each chapter of the following book is dedicated to one country and is structured as follows. The first part provides general economic statistics about the SME sector. The second section overviews the corporate regulatory reporting environment in a particular country that may impact and shape IR development. The third part analyses national constituencies enabling or constraining IR, including political, economic, social, cultural, and technological factors. The following section presents the empirical evidence on IR. It reflects SMEs' experience in non-financial reporting and indicates the best practices that refer to both medium-sized and large companies (in case of a lack of evidence for the SME sector) since their experience may constitute a good benchmark for SMEs to start the IR implementation journey. The last section includes conclusions and remarks based on each country evidence regarding implications for IR implementation in SMEs.

References

Agostini, M., Costa, E., & Bagnoli, C. (2018). The role of small and medium practices in the sustainability reporting of Italian small and medium enterprises. In L. C. Carvalho & E. Truant (Eds.), *Maintaining sustainable accounting systems in small business* (pp. 1–23). Hershey, PA: IGI Global.

Amirrudin, M. S., Abdullah, M., Abdul Aris, N., & Mohammed, N. F. (2019). Are SMEs ready for integrated reporting? The Malaysian experience of accountability. *International Journal of Financial Research, 10*(5), 301–312.

Arena, M., & Azzone, G. (2012). A process-based operational framework for sustainability reporting in SMEs. *Journal of Small Business and Enterprise Development, 19*(4), 669–686.

Argento, D., Culasso, F., & Truant, E. (2019). From sustainability to Integrated Reporting: The legitimizing role of the CSR manager. *Organization and Environment, 32*(4), 484–507.

Ashton, W., Russell, S., & Futch, E. (2017). The adoption of green business practices among small US midwestern manufacturing enterprises. *Journal of Environmental Planning and Management, 60*(12), 2133–2149.

Bergmann, A., & Posch, P. (2018). Mandatory sustainability reporting in Germany: Does size matter? *Sustainability, 10*(11), 3904.

BlackSun, (2014). *Realizing the benefits: The impact of Integrated Reporting.* Retrieved April 3, 2021 from https://integratedreporting.org/wp-content/uploads/2014/09/IIRC.Black_Sun_Research.IR_.Impact.Single.pages.18.9.14.pdf

Caputo, F., Veltri, S., & Venturelli, A. (2017). A conceptual model of forces driving the introduction of a sustainability report in SMEs: Evidence from a Case Study. *International Business Research, 10*(5), 39–50.

Cohen, E. (2013). *Sustainability reporting for SMEs: Competitive advantage through transparency*. New York: Routledge.

Del Baldo, M. (2015). Is it time for integrated reporting in small and medium-sized enterprises? Reflections on an Italian experience. In S. O. Idowu, C. S. Frederiksen, A. Y. Mermod, & M. E. J. Nielsen (Eds.), *Corporate social responsibility and governance. Theory and practice* (pp. 183–209). Heidelberg: Springer International Publishing Switzerland.

Del Baldo, M. (2017). The implementation of integrating reporting <IR> in SMEs: Insights from a pioneering experience in Italy. *Meditari Accountancy Research, 25*(4), 505–532.

Del Baldo, M. (2018). Integrating reporting in SMEs. Issues and perspectives from Italy. In S. O. Idowu, C. Sitnikov, D. Simion, & C. Bocean (Eds.), *Current issues in corporate social responsibility. An international consideration* (pp. 195–215). Heidelberg: Springer.

Dumay, J., & Dai, T. (2017). Integrated thinking as a cultural control? *Meditari Accountancy Research, 25*(4), 574–604.

EFAA. (2018). *Survey of non-financial reporting requirements for SMEs in Europe*. European Federation of Accountants and Auditors for SMEs. Retrieved April 4, 2021 from https://www.efaa.com/cms/upload/efaa_files/pdf/News/20181119_NFRbySMEsReport-FINAL.pdf

EUROSTAT. (2021). *Key figures on European business. Statistics illustrated*. 2021 Edition (March 26), Retrieved April 3, 2021 from https://ec.europa.eu/eurostat/documents/3217494/12601271/KS-01-20-363-EN-N.pdf/57086a1d-ba26-a397-85b6-f28d08f28426?t=1616747084138

Flower, J. (2015). The integrated reporting council: A story of failure. *Critical Perspectives on Accounting, 27*, 1–15.

Gerwanski, J. (2020). Managers' incentives and disincentives to engage with integrated reporting or why managers might not adopt integrated reporting: An exploratory study in a nascent setting. *Qualitative Research in Accounting & Management, 17*(4), 553–558.

Guthrie, J., Manes-Rossi, F., & Orelli, R. L. (2017). Integrated reporting and integrated thinking in Italian public sector organizations. *Meditari Accountancy Research, 25*(4), 553–573.

IIRC. (2021). *The international <IR> framework*. International Integrated Reporting Council. Retrieved April 4, 2021 from https://integratedreporting.org/wp-content/uploads/2021/01/InternationalIntegratedReportingFramework.pdf

Juergensen, J., Guimón, J., & Narula, R. (2020). European SMEs amidst the COVID-19 crisis: Assessing impact and policy responses. *Journal of Industrial and Business Economics, 47*, 499–510.

Kaya, C. T., & Türegün, N. (2014). Integrated reporting for Turkish small and medium-sized enterprises. *International Journal of Academic Research in Accounting, Finance and Management Sciences, 4*(1), 358–364.

Langwell, C., & Heaton, D. (2016). Using human resource activities to implement sustainability in SMEs. *Journal of Small Business and Enterprise Development, 23*(3), 652–670.

Massa, L., Farneti, F., & Scappini, B. (2015). Developing a sustainability report in a small to the medium enterprise: Process and consequences. *Meditari Accountancy Research, 23*(1), 62–91.

Moneva, J. M., & Hernandez-Pajares, J. (2018). Corporate social responsibility performance and sustainability reporting in SMEs: An analysis of owner-managers' perceptions. *International Journal of Sustainable Economy, 10*(4), 405–420.

Muslichah, M., Wiyarni, W., & Nursasi, E. (2019). The effect of knowledge, perceived usefulness and social norms on intention to prepare integrated reporting in SMEs. *International Journal of Business and Social Research, 9*(4), 13–25.

Muslichah, M., Wiyarni, W., & Nursasi, E. (2020). Model of the integrated reporting for SMEs. *Journal of Sustainability Science and Management, 15*(2), 146–161.

Pozzoli, M. & Attolini, G. (2014). *Is Integrated Reporting Suitable for SMEs?*, Retrieved April 3, 2021 from https://www.ifac.org/knowledge-gateway/contributing-global-economy/discussion/integrated-reporting-suitable-smes

Rodríguez-Gutiérrez, P., Guerrero-Baena, M. D., Luque-Vílchez, M., & Castilla-Polo, F. (2021). An approach to using the best-worst method for supporting sustainability reporting decision-making in SMEs. *Journal of Environmental Planning and Management, 280*, 111844.

Rossi, A. & Luque-Vílchez, M. (2021). The implementation of sustainability reporting in a small and medium enterprise and the emergence of integrated thinking, *Meditari Accountancy Research* (in print).

Shields, J. F., & Shelleman, J. M. (2017). A method to launch sustainability reporting in SMEs: The B Corp Impact Assessment framework. *Journal of Strategic Innovation and Sustainability, 12*(2), 10–19.

Speziale, M. T. (2019). Theoretical perspectives on purposes and users of integrated reporting: A literature review. In S. O. Idowu & M. Del Baldo (Eds.), *Integrated reporting, CSR, sustainability, ethics & governance* (pp. 13–59) Springer Nature Switzerland AG.

Steinhöfel, E., Galeitzke, M., Kohl, H., & Orth, R. (2019). Sustainability reporting in German manufacturing SMEs. *Procedia Manufacturing, 33*, 610–617.

Stent, W., & Dowler, T. (2015). Early assessments of the gap between integrated reporting and current corporate reporting. *Meditari Accountancy Research, 23*(1), 92–117.

Stubbs, W., & Higgins, C. (2014). Integrated reporting and internal mechanisms of change. *Accounting, Auditing and Accountability Journal, 27*(7), 1068–1089.

Contents

List of Figures

List of Tables

Chapter 5

Chapter 6

SMEs and <IR>: An Introduction

Luca Brusati, Caterina Fuso, and Andrea Garlatti

1 Beyond Financial Reporting

A reliable, accurate and comprehensive assessment of corporate performance is of paramount importance for both the internal and external stakeholders of any firm, as it allows them to take informed decisions and manage their relationships properly. It is not only a bulwark for the protection of investors and the efficient functioning of financial markets, but also a tool to make management accountable vis-à-vis the interests of different categories of stakeholders. For this reason, firms are required by law to report their financial performance through annual financial statements and periodic financial reports based on detailed accounting standards. In addition to these documents, though, in recent decades companies have been required to report upon a wide variety of non-accounting information.

The more and more frequent introduction of non-financial reporting obligations can certainly be ascribed to the need to address stakeholders' expectations, which are increasingly diverse, and to a growing interest for corporate social responsibility, not only by business counterparts, but also by investors, regulators and civil society at large. The undeniable cultural evolution that involves a greater attention by public opinion to corporate performance, and in particular to the positive and negative externalities companies generate, entails a practical consequence: the need to develop new reporting standards suitable to highlight how companies create value over time, taking into account that traditional balance sheets are no longer adequate

L. Brusati (✉) · A. Garlatti
Udine University, Udine, Italy
e-mail: luca.brusati@uniud.it; andrea.garlatti@uniud.it

C. Fuso
Deloitte Tax & Consulting, Luxembourg, Luxembourg
e-mail: cfuso@deloitte.lu

J. Dyczkowska et al. (eds.), *Development of Integrated Reporting in the SME Sector*, CSR, Sustainability, Ethics & Governance,
https://doi.org/10.1007/978-3-030-81903-3_1

for this purpose. In other words, it is clear by now that traditional financial statements are unable to capture important components of corporate performance: they fail to shed light on aspects that are increasingly important for the ability of companies to create value and that, therefore, investors, credit institutions, financial analysts and other stakeholders are more and more often willing to know.

In addition to financial and manufactured capitals, which are relatively easy to quantify, each company underpins its long-term viability on intangible resources a well, such as intellectual capital, human capital, social and relational capital, and natural capital (IIRC, 2021). Traditional balance sheets are unsuitable to report on these capitals, since they were conceived with reference to an industrial economy based almost exclusively on tangible capital and labour. For this reason, there is a need to develop new performance measurement and disclosure standards, designed to account for the intangible components of the company's capital.

"CSR reporting" and, more recently, "sustainability reporting" are trendy names used to label the processes meant to assess and disclose corporate performance vis-à-vis its long-term commitment to sustainable development and societal expectations at large, so as to secure accountability towards both internal and external stakeholders. In other words, the aim of this kind of report is to make the sustainability of an organization's activities transparent to all its stakeholders and provide a comprehensive, unbiased representation of its performance, including both positive and negative impacts generated by its operations (Bernow et al., 2019; Romero et al., 2014). To date, there is no single definition of "CSR reporting" and "sustainability reporting", as there is no agreed-upon definition of "CSR" (Dahlsrud, 2008) and "sustainability" (Starik & Kanashiro, 2013). Indeed, these terms are generically used to describe any practice of reporting the economic, social and environmental impacts of a company, in line with the so-called triple bottom line approach (Elkington, 1994; Jeurissen & Elkington, 2000).

On the other hand, the result of corporate activities is increasingly intangible; not only because service firms are increasingly important compared to manufacturing ones, but also because, on top of creating products and services to be sold on the market, any company produces other outcomes, positive or negative, which are an integral part of the value—or disvalue—created by that company (Fig. 1). For this reason, there is an urgent need to define more appropriate reporting standards to measure and disclose the intangible dimension of the value created by a company, which escapes the logic of the market and does not find satisfactory representation in traditional financial statements.

It is precisely to meet the above requirements that integrated reporting (<IR>) was developed. To date, this framework is the most advanced approach available to conceptualize and communicate how strategy, governance patterns, business model, relations with stakeholders, past performance and future prospects, risks and opportunities allow a company to create value in the short, medium and long term. In other words, <IR> provides internal and external stakeholders with a comprehensive understanding of the interconnectedness of several types of resources, spanning financial, physical and intangible assets, such as social and intellectual capital,

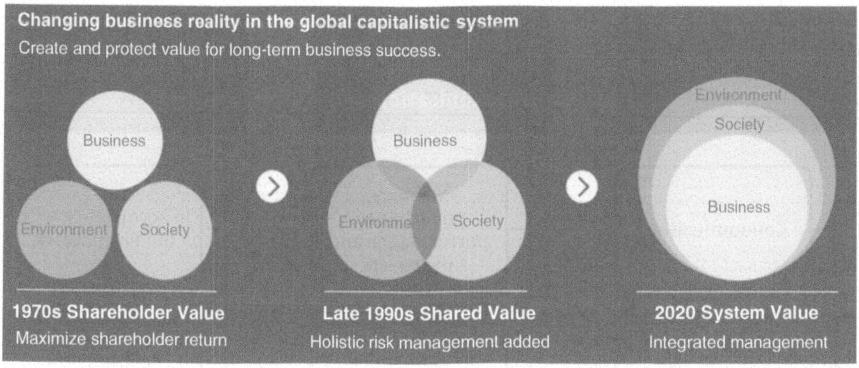

Fig. 1 Changing focus for management practice: 1970 to 2020. Source: IIRC (2019: 11)

environmental, social and governance parameters, key performance and risk indicators, business strategy and performance (de Villiers et al., 2014).

The peculiarity of <IR> lies in the fact that it is not meant to provide yet another disclosure requirement, aimed at adding cumulatively to the contents of pre-existing documents. Instead, it is an advanced form of reporting aimed at promoting an integrated representation of the company that decides to implement it, so as to help internal and external stakeholders understand how tangible and intangible assets, as well as the financial, social and environmental profiles of managerial decisions, interact with one another and affect the ability of the company to generate value (Eccles & Krzus, 2010). In this respect, <IR> goes beyond CSR and sustainability reporting: it reflects the need to emphasize the connectivity of information, so as to explain, in a single document, how the company creates value in the long term, not just to present a hodgepodge of financial and non-financial data, as it is the case with other non-financial reporting standards (English & Schooley, 2014) (Fig. 2).

More specifically, the International Integrated Reporting Committee (IIRC) in its discussion paper *Towards Integrated Reporting. Communicating Value in the 21st Century* defines the integrated report as a document "bringing together the material information about an organization's strategy, governance, performance and prospects in a way that reflects the commercial, social and environmental context within which it operates. It provides a clear and concise representation of how an organization demonstrates stewardship and how it creates value, now and in the future. Integrated reporting combines the most material elements of information currently reported in separate reporting strands (financial, management commentary, governance and remuneration, and sustainability) in a coherent whole, and importantly:

- Shows the connectivity between them; and
- Explains how they affect the ability of an organization to create and sustain value in the short, medium and long term" (IIRC, 2011).

The core purpose of <IR> is to capture a company's process of value creation by acknowledging and communicating that this very process is contingent on its ability

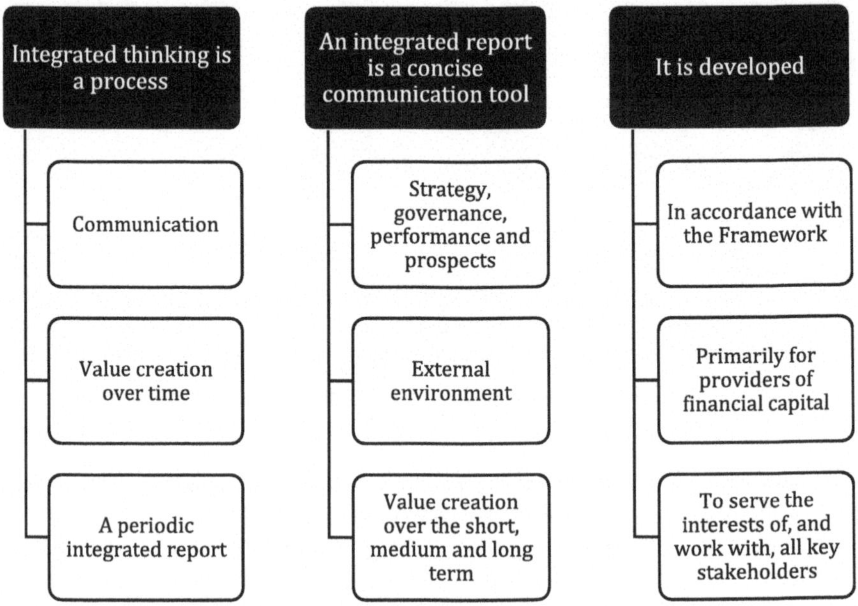

Fig. 2 Integrated reporting in a nutshell. Source: IIRC (2013a)

to develop and sustain specific critical assets and relationships with internal and external stakeholders. As a result, the report shall provide a clear picture and explanation of the way in which key sustainability issues have been incorporated into the company's operations, policies and overall business strategy. Importantly, the process of integrated thinking underpinning <IR> analyses the business journey of value creation from end to end, in a way that goes beyond a mere short-term perspective. This holistic perspective allows both internal and external stakeholders to better understand the financial implications of key social and environmental aspects and outcomes that traditional reporting standards cannot capture.

The integrated report can, therefore, be seen as a particular form of business report characterized by the emphasis on the following aspects:

- a multi-capital approach, according to which value is created through six capitals, i.e. financial, manufactured, intellectual, human, social and relationship, and natural capitals (IIRC, 2013a: 11, 2C);
- connectivity between information and the capitals to represent how an organization creates value over time;
- a combination of quantitative and qualitative information;
- a communication prepared with the purpose to explain how an organization creates value over time, to investors and to any interested stakeholder, including employees, customers, suppliers, business and technology partners, local communities, government agencies, policymakers and interest groups (NIBR, 2018).

The IIRC framework underpinning <IR> adopts a principle-based approach, i.e. aims to strike a balance between flexibility and compliance requirements, so as to take into account the many variables introduced by the specific characteristics of individual businesses and, at the same time, ensure a sufficient level of comparability among them. On this matter, <IR> guidelines do not require the inclusion of predefined key performance indicators, nor the use of specific measurement metrics. Therefore, those responsible for the preparation of an integrated report should examine the specific circumstances of the organization to highlight:

- the most material aspects;
- the way in which these aspects are disclosed, including the adoption of generally accepted methods of measurement and representation; if the information in an integrated report is similar to, or based on, other information published by the firm, then the report must be prepared on the same basis or be easily reconcilable with that information.

2 Value Creation in SMEs

As it holds true for any kind of business, small and medium enterprises (SMEs) create value in different ways: they interact on a regular basis with several internal and external stakeholders, including customers, by answering their demand for goods and services, employees, by providing them with desirable, fair and due working environments and conditions, and suppliers, investors, regulators and civil society, by participating in the job creation process, paying taxes and trying to meet societal expectations. Value is created, transformed or destroyed through a firm's business model, which takes inputs and transforms them to produce outputs and outcomes that, over the short, medium and long term, create or destroy value for the firm itself, its stakeholders, society and the environment.

The distinctive features of SMEs, which stand out and differentiate them from large enterprises not only in size, but also in nature, do not allow for the application of the same tools, business models and interpretative schemes that prove to be meaningful for larger enterprises and which, as such, are used to explain their management and performance. As Tilley (2002) pointed out, it would be a mistake to understand SMEs as "little big firms": their features are different in many respects and can be summarized in at least five points, which directly affect the functioning patterns of these companies, and consequently the way they report on their performance:

- The first specificity concerns the family footprint of the company's management and the direct leadership by the owner, thus not entailing, as a rule, any meaningful distinction between ownership and control (Gnan et al., 2015). As a result, the strategic role of the owner directly affects corporate decisions with his or her own beliefs and personal relationships, which, in turn, significantly influence the company's choices also in terms of social commitment and sustainability.

- The second peculiarity involves the rootedness of SMEs in local communities. On the one hand, this feature represents a positive element for linking any commitment to a genuine relationship with the territory and its community; on the other hand, it does not always open the company to external stakeholders, both in communicating its commitment to social responsibility and in seizing the opportunities for strategic partnerships with new stakeholders. In SMEs, social and environmental sustainability is often considered a consequence of personal bonds with employees, customers and suppliers; as such, it does not require targeted, formalized communication of corporate commitments vis-à-vis the community, the environment or the stakeholders relevant to the company. The role of personal relationships in the conduct of business, resulting from the small number of employees involved in corporate activities, favours dynamics based on trust and reciprocity, both between owners and employees and between the latter and external stakeholders, such as customers, suppliers and the community (Campopiano et al., 2012; Perrini, 2006). In other words, SMEs generally lack a structured approach to CSR, also because in most cases they consider these initiatives as an integral part of their activity that does not need external evidence. Instead, it would be important for them to succeed in getting their initiatives out of their restricted business context, also using various forms of networking with other companies to share resources and experiences.
- Another feature concerns the role of human resources, which are often the primary channel to leverage other relevant audiences. Employees are the primary stakeholders of SMEs: as such, they are the target of many initiatives aimed at achieving gender equality, work–life balance, etc. (Coppa & Sriramesh, 2013). As some companies already do, the focus should be on employee engagement, to make them real co-promoters of the organization in the community, thus harnessing their ability to communicate the values of the company in which they work. This is potentially a major asset for SMEs: they should learn to exploit it with different forms of communication, ranging from the most structured to the most informal level. Providing staff with adequate, consistent information on corporate performance, sharing the results achieved through the adoption of CSR strategies, measuring and reporting on employees' satisfaction, and promoting health and safety on the workplace, skills development and equal opportunities or favouring work–life balance are all high-impact tools: they can make each employee feel a team member, part of a virtuous process, motivated to communicate the commitments and values of the company to the outside world, also adopting individual behaviours consistent with these principles.
- A fourth peculiarity of SMEs is the limited pool of resources they have available, be they organizational, financial, know-how or skills. Even though empirical evidence suggests that entrepreneurial SMEs tend to adopt more formal strategic planning approaches, while conservative ones adopt more incremental approaches (Gibbons & O'Connor, 2005), resource constraints often force entrepreneurs to adopt a short- or medium-term strategic outlook, or even a purely reactive posture, as the lack of a sufficiently stable and solid resource base does not allow for longer-term planning and investments (Gibson & Cassar, 2005).

- Finally, SMEs are also characterized, as mentioned above, by the informality of their decision-making and performance control systems. Informality nurtures the capital of relationships based on trust rather than contractual obligations, which gives them a high degree of flexibility and responsiveness to the external environment, resulting in a possible competitive advantage over larger competitors featuring a higher degree of formalization and rigidity (Giovannoni & Maraghini, 2013).

Although the ecosystem of SMEs is extremely heterogeneous, some factors related to the value creation process are cross-cutting among this class of enterprises. The report *Creating Value for SMEs through Integrated Thinking* (IFAC, 2017) provides a comprehensive list of these factors. Obviously, SMEs need financial capital, which is essential for their survival at any stage of their life cycle, and can be provided in the form of equity, debt or a mix of both by different investors, such as family members, friends, venture capitalists, crowdfunding platforms and the financial markets. In order to create and sustain value in the long term, though, SMEs shall not rely on financial capital only, but on the continued availability, quality and price of a full range of other resources and relationships as well: those that the IIRC framework (IIRC, 2021) defines as the "capitals" of the "multi-capital model" to stress the very fact that value is not confined to financial capital alone but is stored in many other types of assets. The way these factors are valued, managed and combined by each organization in its particular context, i.e. its business model, is what defines it distinctively (Fig. 3).

The multi-capital model outlined by the IIRC framework to describe value creation in a holistic perspective identifies six types of capital, which are briefly described below.

- Financial capital: equity, debt, subsidies, grants and other financing instruments available to SMEs and to be allocated for the production and/or distribution of goods or services.
  - Debt: listing of the credit guidelines used; measurement of the level of indebtedness (financial leverage, EBITDA, etc.);
  - Equity: illustration of aspects such as the number of shares, year-end price and performance during the year, issues of new shares, buybacks and dividend policy;
  - Economic performance: inclusion and illustration of the main indicators, such as turnover, operating profit margin, net profit, ROE, ROS and ROA.
- Manufactured capital: tangible assets and infrastructure owned or rented by, or otherwise accessible to an SME for the supply of goods or services. In this respect, current and future projects must be described in such a way as to allow:
  - An assessment of their current value and expected remuneration;
  - The indication of the most significant investments in intangible assets;
  - The provision of specific data on the labour factor (total labour costs, average hourly costs, etc.).

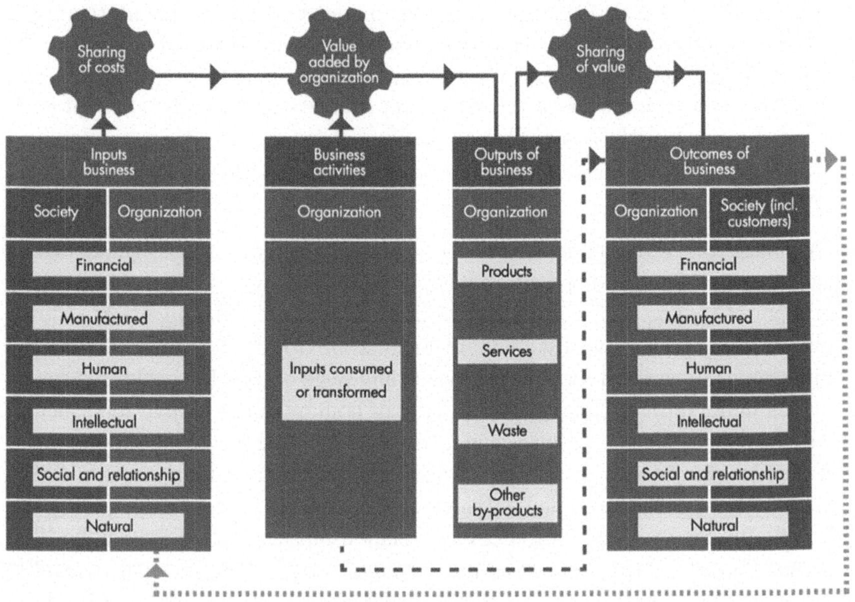

Fig. 3 Business model in a multi-capital perspective. Source: IIRC (2013b: 9)

- Human capital: skills, experience and motivation of employees and management, which are of paramount importance for the long-term sustainability and growth of any SME. In particular, the following aspects shall be highlighted:
  - Diversity and discrimination: percentage of women among employees and in management positions, percentage of employees belonging to minorities, etc.;
  - Benefits and compensation: medical insurance, agreements with commercial establishments, etc.;
  - Workplace safety: number of work-related accidents, compliance with safety standards, etc.;
  - Training: total investment in training, average number of training days per employee, etc.;
  - Stability of the relationship with the workforce: turnover, rate of absenteeism, number of employees registered with trade unions, etc.
- Social and relationship capital: a company's brand recognition and reputation, comprising its relationships with and embeddedness in the community where it is located, those with its customers, suppliers, business partners, competitors and other actors in the value chain, such as government agencies or interest groups.
- Intellectual capital: intangible assets that include goodwill, intellectual property (such as patents, trademarks, copyrights, software, rights and licenses) and organizational capital (such as implicit know-how, systems, procedures and

controls), which are essential for a SME's distinctive positioning and competitive advantage.

- Natural capital: disposal that an SMEs have of environmental resources, which can either be harnessed to generate value or be affected by the company's operations and that thus have to be managed accordingly. Externalities can be positive or negative and can ultimately increase or decrease the value created by the organization. Corporate stakeholders therefore need information on externalities to assess their impact and allocate resources accordingly. To this end, the following information should be featured by an integrated report:
  - Careful analysis of the environmental impact of the company's operations;
  - Activities performed and results achieved during the reporting period, benchmarked against the activities and results of previous years;
  - Formulation, implementation and disclosure of appropriate environmental performance indicators (CO_2 emissions, energy consumption, efficiency in water usage, amount of waste, environmental spills).

If these capitals are clearly identified and effectively managed, they have the potential to unlock value over time and to increase their ability to sustain it in the future. Obviously, not all capitals are equally relevant in all organizations; although most SMEs interact in some way with all forms of capital, these interactions can be secondary or so indirect that they are immaterial for the purposes of <IR>. Nevertheless, since value is created over different time horizons, for different stakeholders and through different capitals, maximizing just one capital without considering or underestimating the others will most probably fail to unlock sustainable value. For example, maximizing financial capital, such as profit, at the expense of human capital (e.g. through inappropriate human resource management policies and practices) is unlikely to maximize value in the long run, whereas an SME who has invested in training to develop its workforce in specific areas such as quality management will expect to see higher productivity and greater efficiency on the factory floor (IFAC, 2017). In other words, a sound management of all capitals may well generate a virtuous circle of value creation.

3 <IR> for SMEs: Opportunities and Challenges

Even though <IR> is an approach to corporate performance disclosure that can be implemented by any kind of business, regardless of its size, the most advanced reporting tools are traditionally implemented, by obligation or choice, by large companies. On the one hand, the significant impact of their activities on society increases the audience and sensitivity of stakeholders; on the other hand, precisely because of their size, these companies have greater resources—financial, technological, human, etc.—to allocate to reporting exercises.

Not surprisingly, the companies that have joined the IIRC Pilot Programme, aimed at testing and disseminating <IR> practices, are all large and often publicly listed. Looking at the broader issue of CSR reporting, though, a communication from the European Commission effectively summarizes the state of the art in Europe: "More and more companies are disseminating social and environmental information. SMEs often communicate this information informally and on a voluntary basis" (EC, 2011).

Available surveys on the current status and future prospects in non-financial reporting show contrasting results. On the one hand, companies state that CSR is a necessary prerequisite to become reliable partners. On the other hand, they tend to neglect the monetary quantification of the activities implemented and to overlook systematically negative results, to the detriment of transparency and credibility (Murillo & Lozano, 2006). SMEs, in particular, highlight the phenomenon of the so-called sunken CSR (Perrini, 2006), i.e. a corporate behaviour in line with the principles of social responsibility but not organized, explicitly defined or communicated to stakeholders as such. Interestingly, evidence shows that SMEs, which are part of global production chains, show greater attention to CSR communication, driven by the demands of large multinational companies (Vázquez-Carrasco & López-Pérez, 2013).

<IR> may provide a valuable means for SMEs to enhance the understanding and management of their value creation process, as well as to account for and disclose their performance to interested parties. For this reason, companies of any size have a stake in understanding the phenomena that could generate value and communicating their objectives, activities and results to both internal and external stakeholders. James (2013a) hypothesizes that SMEs may have naturally a higher degree of integrated thinking than their large counterparts, due to their intrinsic nature (i.e. they are dynamic, creative and flexible entities with low organizational complexity). Thanks to integrated thinking, <IR> can significantly improve the planning, management and disclosure of both SMEs' day-to-day operations and long-term mission by adopting a holistic perspective, encompassing its consumption of and impact upon all capitals that are critical for the company's value creation. <IR> enables SMEs to acquire a better appreciation of their strategies and of the impact of the objectives they pursue, as well as to understand the degree of integration between financial and non-financial performance. This process also helps them get a better grasp of the potential implications that external forces have on the firm itself, and consequently to design appropriate risk mitigation strategies, even more important taking into account the limited volume of resources that SMEs can rely upon to tackle external threats.

As a process meant to describe both positive and negative aspects, as well as significant challenges that must be tackled, <IR> allows SMEs to increase trust, reputation and visibility among their stakeholders. As a result, <IR> implementation encourages the development of a culture of accountability, along with better targeted management control systems, which further support data monitoring and quality.

Even in SMEs, where there are fewer people sharing the load, barriers unintentionally arise, if only because people do not have the opportunity to stop, think and share information in a deliberate way, and enterprise resource planning systems are not developed enough to make up for this (IFAC, 2017). Integrated thinking is instrumental in overcoming compartmentalization and allowing for a smoother flow of information among business units, thus facilitating the development of smarter cross-functional thinking. Thanks to <IR>, SMEs have the chance to optimize their information base and develop an integrated understanding of the value-adding process pursued by the firm.

SMEs are in many cases assessed against their recent financial performance, which can pose an obstacle to long-term value creation. Yet, investors and other stakeholders, such as employees and potential clients or business partners, are equally interested in aspects that go beyond the mere financial data, such as the company's vision and mission, its strategy and its revenue model, which all concur to the achievement of its goals. By simplifying the language, avoiding the use of technical jargon and displaying quantitative data graphically, <IR> gives SMEs the chance to reach a broader range of users and ensures that key information is both intelligible and meaningful.

James (2013b) suggests that, in the context of SMEs, <IR> can be beneficial to both intra-firm assets—e.g. improving strategic decision-making and risk management, and deepening employee loyalty—and external strategic factors—e.g. enhancing brand value and reputation, easing investor credit and lowering the cost of capital. Moreover, <IR> improves risk management as the company evaluates risks in a holistic, inter-functional perspective (Manes-Rossi et al., 2017); in particular, integrated thinking mitigates reputational risk, as the dialogue it triggers within the company and with its stakeholders allows it to track changes in expectations and beliefs and to align its strategy and actions accordingly (Bebbington et al., 2008).

The articulation of corporate strategies in goals and projects and the timely monitoring of progress they elicit help tackle challenges and harness opportunities more readily and with limited capital. Moreover, thanks to integrated thinking it is not uncommon to achieve cost savings in business operations, to identify solutions suitable to improve products and services and to reap competitive advantage in terms of greater operational effectiveness, brand differentiation and innovation. In broader terms, an integrated view of the value creation process facilitates the development of an innovation culture in SMEs and highlights their growth orientation (Macias & Farfan-Lievano, 2017).

Employees prefer to work for companies with a good reputation; the growth of respect, esteem and confidence in the company triggered by <IR> may lead to higher talent attractiveness and retention rates, along with better opportunities for professional growth and personal development. As a result, other things being equal the firms engaging in <IR> can benefit from a lower cost of labour, greater employee loyalty and increased productivity thanks to higher employee focus and overall motivation (Mio et al., 2016).

Finally yet importantly, by providing better insights into corporate performance and prospects <IR> enhances relationships with capital providers, resulting in more accessible (Cheng et al., 2014) and less expensive (Dhaliwal et al., 2011) sources of finance. Investors can benefit in particular from information related to:

- the quality of the report, which reflects the quality of management;
- clear and concise information that can enable a comprehensive evaluation of the firm regarding credit access;
- a straightforward representation of strategies, risks and opportunities, which can have a direct impact on capital;
- an overview of the business model and of its connection with the strategy, which allows to understand how the company generates cash flows and how it creates value;
- interdependencies between internal and external resources and the strategic partnerships the company has built;
- how operational and market risks are identified, managed and mitigated;
- the priority objectives actions pursue and their continuous monitoring;
- the procedures and the processes used to make strategic decisions;
- the prospects and the longer-term corporate viability and resilience, thanks to dynamism and flexibility.

Whereas it is clear that non-financial reporting requirements for SMEs are growing (EFAA, 2018), empirical evidence on the strategies that SMEs are or are not adopting to cope with the increasing needs for non-financial information is still limited. In 2016, a systematic review of research articles surveying the field of <IR> revealed that out of fifty-six articles published, none targeted SMEs (Dumay et al., 2016). The situation has improved over the last few years, and a few groundbreaking empirical contributions from countries as diverse as Indonesia (Muslichah et al., 2020), Italy (Del Baldo, 2017; Girella et al. 2019b) and Malaysia (Amirrudin et al., 2019) have provided food for thought on the opportunities that can arise for the SMEs that engage in <IR>.

One reason for this limited evidence is certainly the fact that only in recent years SMEs have started to turn to sustainability reporting, let alone <IR>. Eccles and Krzus in 2016 included in the Italian translation of *The Integrated Reporting Movement* a full chapter devoted to Dellas, an Italian medium-sized firm that forward-lookingly adopted <IR> and took part in the pilot group of Italian companies participating in the NIBR working group.

The lack of evidence could also be due to the absence of guidelines able to speak the language of SMEs (Del Baldo, 2017). Indeed, among the few pioneering studies observing non-financial disclosure in the context of SMEs, even fewer have investigated the factors that hinder its implementation (Del Baldo, 2015). Undoubtedly, most SMEs are not fully acquainted with management programming, control and reporting, reflecting their hallmark features, i.e. family-based corporate governance models, simplified, poorly formalized organizational structures, incremental, process-driven strategic approaches and scarce supply of managerial and financial resources. The limited diffusion of <IR> and more generally of non-financial reporting among SMEs can be linked to factors such as lack of information and skills, complexity and perceived costs: non-financial reporting is expected to require competencies and a degree of commitment that SMEs as a rule do not have (Gerwanski, 2020; Mahmood et al., 2017; Muslichah et al., 2019; Steinhöfel et al.,

2019). To make things worse, most SMEs' consultants, and chartered accountants in particular, are not knowledgeable with how to operationalize <IR> principles (Agostini et al., 2018; Del Baldo, 2017). As a result, the broader CSR agenda is perceived as too complex and focused on social aspects and "big business" frameworks, making non-financial reporting unintelligible and unrealistic for SMEs (Borga et al., 2009). On the other hand, SMEs are not facing the heterogeneous set of pressures and expectations that a large firm is expected to deal with: it is not surprising that they fail to consider non-financial reporting as a priority.

Taking these features into account, the SMEs contemplating the adoption of <IR> should assess the coherence of such framework with the entrepreneur's attitudes and purposes, the corporate culture, the limited financial and managerial resources, and the company's operating environment and rootedness (Del Baldo, 2018). There is consensus among scholars and practitioners alike that integrated thinking shall be inherently connected to the strategic management of SMEs, blending strategic and operational outlooks and implying a close connection among inputs, outputs and results. The problem rests on formalization, which requires dedicated managerial, financial and IT resources (Del Baldo, 2015, 2017): the informal approach prevailing in SMEs may hinder the capability to make integrated thinking explicit, as it often remains "trapped" in the mind of the entrepreneur due to the lack of formalized tools, procedures and management control systems. In many cases, the entrepreneur's background is not robust enough to understand and adopt the whole philosophy starting from the integrated thinking principle. Girella et al. (2019b) suggest that these companies should opt for a process-based approach to define roles, responsibilities and capabilities as clearly and consistently as possible, in the light of the paramount role that integrated thinking represents for <IR> itself.

4 Do Institutional Environments Impact <IR>?

The discussion on the rationale for companies to voluntarily adopt <IR> has recently caught the attention of researchers, and several studies have been published trying to shed light on the drivers of this decision. These studies can be grouped under the heading of contingency studies, inasmuch they all take into consideration a series of descriptive characteristics of both companies and their institutional environment to infer possible relationships with the choice of their reporting format.

By analysing similarities and differences between companies with traditional sustainability reporting and those that issue integrated reports, Jensen and Berg (2012) were the first to argue that companies implementing <IR> are based in countries benefiting from a more shareholder-friendly governance system, stronger investor and employment protection laws and a better educational system, with stronger union membership and a society more engaged towards sustainable development. Their study, which takes explicitly an institutionalist approach, suggests that by adopting <IR> companies are responding to societal pressures. These initial empirical results are confirmed by Dragu and Tiron-Tudor (2013), who find that the presence of a civil law system and per capita gross national income are positively correlated with the practice of <IR>, while surprisingly, a higher National Corporate Responsibility Index matches lower interest for reporting in an integrated manner.

Garcia-Sanchez et al. (2013) extend the analysis to include the impact of Hofstede's national cultural system (Hofstede, 1980), which is representative of the values of local stakeholders, to the list of external factors that influence disclosure. Their findings suggest that companies located in countries with a collectivist, feminist cultural system, i.e. characterized by concern for the public good and social relations, place greater emphasis on ethics, sustainability and good governance, and thus are more likely to engage in <IR> so as to provide relevant, comparable information for decision-making. Similar results are presented by Raimo et al. (2019), who explored the relationship between GLOBE dimensions of national cultures and <IR> quality and found that assertiveness, institutional collectivism, uncertainty avoidance and humane orientation are positively associated with <IR> quality, whereas performance orientation and future orientation are negatively associated with it.

Frias-Aceituno et al. (2013) analysed a sample of 750 international companies for the years from 2008 to 2010 to understand the influence of the legal system on the development of integrated reports. The results show that companies located in civil law countries, and where indices of law and order are high, are more likely to publish integrated reports, thus facilitating decision-making by their stakeholders. In a different paper, the same authors observed instead the importance of intra-sectoral competitive rivalry between companies in the development of <IR>. The evidence they collected shows that a decrease in rivalry strongly discourages companies to opt for additional communication and transparency costs. In more concentrated sectors, companies can benefit more easily from positional rents, thus avoiding the need to engage in more sophisticated relational strategies with external stakeholders or investors (Frias-Aceituno et al., 2014).

Fasan and Mio (2016) come to different conclusions concerning the role of the legal environment where companies operate. Their study focuses on the quality of the information provided by materiality matrixes, i.e. the section of integrated reports summarizing the importance for the company and for stakeholders of the key issues that can influence value creation in the short, medium and long term. The sectoral affiliation of companies and some firm-level characteristics (board size and diversity) seem to play a significant role in the determination of materiality disclosure, whereas the legal environment in which companies operate does not.

Also Gianfelici et al. (2018) fail to identify differences amenable to the nationality of the company publishing integrated reports in their study on stakeholder salience. Their analysis confirms that industry membership is likely to impact on the contents of integrated reports: they found a strong association between industry and the degree of salience acknowledged to consumers, and a partial association between industry and the salience attributed to the natural environment, but in their sample—contrary to the original hypothesis of the authors—reporting entities' nationality was not recognized as a differentiating factor. The same conclusion was reached by Dilling and Caykoylu (2019), who in their study on the features of global companies disclosing high-quality integrated reports considered the currency used in the report as a proxy of their location.

Finally, further evidence is provided by Girella et al. (2019a) with their analysis of a sample of 71 international listed companies that published integrated reports in 2016, meant to understand the influence that firm- and country-specific characteristics have on the voluntary uptake of <IR>. According to their results, large size, profitability, market-to-book ratio and board size are found to be significant variables. As for country-specific characteristics, the type of legal system resulted to be not significant; firms are more likely to engage in <IR> if they are headquartered in countries with a higher level of corruption perception and a better risk rating, and that are considered as relatively more collectivist and feminist and with a longer-term orientation.

This review of extant literature demonstrates that more empirical work is needed on the relationship between <IR> and institutional environments: different authors came so far to completely opposite conclusions in their attempt to pinpoint what reporting practices depend upon, and the research question "Do institutional environments impact <IR>?" still does not have a clear answer.

We maintain that the studies described in this paragraph share two limitations, since they all use the features of existing integrated reports as the starting point and find ingenious ways to associate them to specific countries and to the variables suitable to describe them. Firstly, the country variables used for the analysis are clearly selected because of the availability of quantitative data sets suitable for statistical elaboration, notwithstanding the fact that these data sets reflect only to a limited degree the specific features of the institutional environment likely to influence <IR>. Secondly, the approach is contaminated by survivorship bias (Brown et al., 1992), since it concentrates on the companies that did publish integrated reports, and often English-language integrated reports, while overlooking entirely those that did not, and by doing so it skews our understanding of which institutional features have an impact on <IR> practices and how.

For this reason, this volume takes a different perspective. As the first step, the institutional environments of six different European countries are described according to the same research protocol, highlighting both formal regulatory requirements in the field of corporate reporting and institutional pressures in terms of political, economic, social, cultural and technological factors that may shape <IR> development. Next, the empirical evidence on <IR> practices in each country is presented, based on a systematic mapping of the features of the integrated reports published in that country. While this approach does not allow the identification of statistical correlations, we believe it addresses effectively both the limitations described above: the institutional environment suitable to influence <IR> is described in detail, and the systematic mapping of existing integrated reports, including those only available in domestic languages, allows to understand both what has been published and what has not.

In comparison with extant studies, this volume is also innovative in that it focuses on SMEs' experience with non-financial reporting, and more specifically with <IR>. The good practices described in the following chapters refer both to medium-sized and larger firms (especially when evidence from the SME sector is missing), based on the assumption that the experience of the latter may represent a starting point for SMEs willing to embark on the <IR> journey. The final paragraph of each chapter includes evidence-based remarks and conclusions regarding the implementation of <IR> by SMEs, suitable to offer insights for the cross-country comparison featured in the final chapter.

Because of the focus of this volume, it is important to clarify the criteria we used for inclusion in our analysis. The generic definition of "small and medium enterprise" does not allow to fully grasp the elements of complexity and diversity that characterize these organizations. Indeed, this heterogeneous category includes a whole array of different entities, in terms of governance structures, business activities, organizational complexity, turnover, investment volumes and number of employees. All these elements have significant implications for <IR> practices, since they entail the presence of different stakeholders, different nature and urgency of the interests involved and, accordingly, different information that is material for reporting purposes.

To make our analysis as substantive as possible, it was deemed imperative to define our scope of work. A firm shall simultaneously meet the following requirements to qualify as a SME:

- It is small or medium in size according to the parameters established in Recommendation 2003/361/EC (EC, 2003); i.e., it employs on average at least 10 and no more than 250 people and has an annual turnover of more than 2 million and up to 50 million Euro or a balance sheet total of more than 2 million and up to 43 million Euro;
- Its shares are wholly owned by private law investors;
- It carries out industrial or commercial activities (thus excluding banking) that cannot be classified as public services.

These ceilings apply to the figures for individual firms only; a firm that is part of a larger group would need to include staff headcount, turnover or balance sheet data from that group too. Micro-enterprises have been excluded from our analysis, taking into account that they are reasonably far from having any interest in advanced forms of corporate reporting, as a consequence of their limited resources and restricted set of internal and external stakeholders. Similarly, the analysis did not include SMEs that are subject to peculiar management or supervisory conditions due to public ownership or the performance of specific activities (provision of public services) subject to the issuance of licenses, concessions or entrustments by public sector bodies.

References

Agostini, M., Costa, E., & Bagnoli, C. (2018). The role of small and medium practices in the sustainability reporting of Italian small and medium enterprises. In L. C. Carvalho & E. Truant (Eds.), *Maintaining sustainable accounting systems in small business* (pp. 1–23). Hershey, PA: IGI Global.

Amirrudin, M. S., Abdullah, M., Abdul Aris, N., & Mohammed, N. F. (2019). Are SMEs ready for integrated reporting? The Malaysian experience of accountability. *International Journal of Financial Research, 10*(5), 301–312.

Bebbington, J., Larrinaga, C., & Moneva, J. M. (2008). Corporate social reporting and reputation risk management. *Accounting, Auditing and Accountability Journal, 21*(3), 337–361.

Bernow, S., Godsall, J., Klempner, B. & Merten, C. (2019). More than values: The value-based sustainability report that investors want. *The McKinsey Quarterly*, July, 1–9.

Borga, F., et al. (2009). Sustainability report in small enterprises: Case studies in Italian furniture companies. *Business Strategy and the Environment, 18*, 162–176.

Brown, S. J., Goetzmann, W., Ibbotson, R. G., & Ross, S. A. (1992). Survivorship bias in performance studies. *The Review of Financial Studies, 5*(4), 553–580.

Campopiano, G., et al. (2012). Corporate social responsibility: A survey among SMEs in Bergamo. *Procedia - Social and Behavioral Sciences, 62*, 325–341.

Cheng, B., Ioannou, I., & Serafeim, G. (2014). Corporate social responsibility and access to finance. *Strategic Management Journal, 35*(1), 1–23.

Coppa, M., & Sriramesh, K. (2013). Corporate social responsibility among SMEs in Italy. *Public Relations Review, 39*(1), 30–39.

Dahlsrud, A. (2008). How corporate social responsibility is defined: an analysis of 37 definitions. *Corporate Social Responsibility and Environmental Management, 15*(1), 1–13.

Del Baldo, M. (2015). Is it time for integrated reporting in small and medium-sized enterprises? Reflections on an Italian experience. In S. O. Idowu, C. S. Frederiksen, A. Y. Mermod, & M. E. J. Nielsen (Eds.), *Corporate social responsibility and governance. Theory and practice* (pp. 183–209). Heidelberg: Springer International Publishing Switzerland.

Del Baldo, M. (2017). The implementation of integrating reporting <IR> in SMEs: Insights from a pioneering experience in Italy. *Meditari Accountancy Research, 25*(4), 505–532.

Del Baldo, M. (2018). Integrating reporting in SMEs. Issues and perspectives from Italy. In S. O. Idowu, C. Sitnikov, D. Simion, & C. Bocean (Eds.), *Current issues in corporate social responsibility. An international consideration* (pp. 195–215). Heidelberg: Springer.

de Villiers, C., Rinaldi, L., & Unerman, J. (2014). Integrated reporting: Insights, gaps and an agenda for future research. *Accounting, Auditing and Accountability Journal, 27*(7), 1042–1067.

Dhaliwal, D., Li, O. Z., Tsang, A., & Yang, Y. G. (2011). Voluntary nonfinancial disclosure and the cost of equity capital: The initiation of corporate social responsibility reporting. *The Accounting Review, 86*(1), 59–100.

Dilling, P. F. A., & Caykoylu, S. (2019). Determinants of companies that disclose high-quality integrated reports. *Sustainability, 11*, 3744.

Dragu, I.-M., & Tiron-Tudor, A. (2013). The integrated reporting initiative from an institutional perspective: Emergent factors. *Procedia - Social and Behavioral Sciences, 92*, 275–279.

Dumay, J., Bernardi, C., Guthrie, J., & Demartini, P. (2016). Integrated reporting: A structured literature review. *Accounting Forum, 40*(3), 166–185.

Eccles, R., & Krzus, M. P. (2010). One report. *AFP Exchange, 30*(6), 49–51.

EC. (2003). *Commission Recommendation of 6 May 2003 concerning the definition of micro, small and medium-sized enterprises*. 2003/361/EC, retrieved April 24, 2021 from https://eur-lex.europa.eu/legal-content/EN/TXT/PDF/?uri=CELEX:32003H0361&from=EN

EC. (2011). *A renewed EU strategy 2011–14 for Corporate Social Responsibility*. COM(2011) 681 final, retrieved April 24, 2021 from https://eur-lex.europa.eu/LexUriServ/LexUriServ.do?uri=COM:2011:0681:FIN:EN:PDF

EFAA. (2018). *Survey of non-financial reporting requirements for SMEs in Europe*. European Federation of Accountants and Auditors for SMEs. Retrieved April 4, 2021 from https://www.efaa.com/cms/upload/efaa_files/pdf/News/20181119_NFRbySMEsReport-FINAL.pdf

Elkington, J. (1994). Towards the sustainable corporation: win-win-win business strategies for sustainable development. *California Management Review, 36*(2), 90–100.

English, D. M., & Schooley, D. K. (2014). The evolution of sustainability reporting: utilizing the GRI's latest guidelines and looking to Integrated Reporting. *The CPA Journal, 84*(3), 26–35.

Fasan, M., & Mio, C. (2016). Fostering stakeholder engagement: The role of materiality disclosure in integrated reporting. *Business Strategy and the Environment, 26*(3), 288–305.

Frias-Aceituno, J. V., Rodriguez-Ariza, L., & Garcia-Sanchez, I. M. (2013). Is integrated reporting determined by a country's legal system? An exploratory study. *Journal of Cleaner Production, 44*, 45–55.

Frias-Aceituno, J. V., Rodriguez-Ariza, L., & Garcia-Sanchez, I. M. (2014). Explanatory factors of integrated sustainability and financial reporting. *Business Strategy and the Environment, 23*(1), 56–72.

Garcia-Sanchez, I. M., Rodriguez-Ariza, L., & Frias-Aceituno, J. V. (2013). The cultural system and integrated reporting. *International Business Review, 22*(3), 828–838.

Gerwanski, J. (2020). Managers' incentives and disincentives to engage with integrated reporting or why managers might not adopt integrated reporting: An exploratory study in a nascent setting. *Qualitative Research in Accounting & Management, 17*(4), 553–558.

Gianfelici, C., Casadei, A., & Cembali, F. (2018). The relevance of nationality and industry for stakeholder salience: An investigation through integrated reports. *Journal of Business Ethics, 150*(2), 541–558.

Gibbons, P. T., & O'Connor, T. (2005). Influences on strategic planning processes among Irish SMEs. *Journal of Small Business Management, 43*(2), 170–186.

Gibson, B., & Cassar, G. (2005). Longitudinal analysis of relationships between planning and performance in small firms. *Small Business Economics, 25*(3), 207–222.

Giovannoni, E., & Maraghini, M. P. (2013). The challenges of integrated performance measurement systems: Integrating mechanisms for integrated measures. *Accounting, Auditing and Accountability Journal, 26*(6), 978–1008.

Girella, L., Rossi, P., & Zambon, S. (2019a). Exploring the firm and country determinants of the voluntary adoption of integrated reporting. *Business Strategy and the Environment, 28*(7), 1323–1340.

Girella, L., Zambon, S., & Rossi, P. (2019b). Reporting on sustainable development: A comparison of three Italian small and medium-sized enterprises. *Corporate Social Responsibility and Environmental Management, 26*(4), 981–996.

Gnan, L., Montemerlo, D., & Huse, M. (2015). Governance systems in family SMEs: The substitution effects between family councils and corporate governance mechanisms. *Journal of Small Business Management, 53*(2), 355–381.

Hofstede, G. (1980). *Culture's consequences: International differences in work-related values*. Beverly Hills, CA: Sage.

IFAC. (2017). *IFAC creating value for SMEs through integrated thinking: The benefits of integrated reporting*. International Federation of Accountants. Retrieved April 24, 2021 from https://www.ifac.org/system/files/publications/files/Creating-Value-for-SMEs-through-Integrated-Thinking.pdf

IIRC. (2011). *Towards integrated reporting. Communicating value in the 21st century*. Retrieved November 3, 2013, from http://theiirc.org/wp content/uploads/2011/09/IR-Discussion-Paper 2011_spreads.pdf

IIRC. (2013a). *The international <IR> framework*. International Integrated Reporting Council, Retrieved January 30, 2020, from www.theiirc.org/international-ir-framework/

IIRC. (2013b). *Business model background paper for <IR>*. International Integrated Reporting Council. Retrieved April 24, 2021 from https://www.ifac.org/system/files/publications/files/Business-Model-IIRC.pdf

IIRC. (2019). *Integrated thinking and strategy: state of play report.* International Integrated Reporting Council. Retrieved April 24, 2021 from https://integratedreporting.org/wp-content/uploads/2020/01/Integrated-Thinking-and-Strategy-State-of-Play-Report_2020.pdf

IIRC. (2021). *The international <IR> framework.* International Integrated Reporting Council. Retrieved April 4, 2021 from https://integratedreporting.org/wp-content/uploads/2021/01/InternationalIntegratedReportingFramework.pdf

James, M. L. (2013a). Sustainability and integrated reporting: opportunities for small and midsize entities. *Entrepreneurial Executive, 18*, 17–28.

James, M. L. (2013b). Sustainability and Integrated Reporting: a case exploring issues, benefits and challenges. *Journal of the International Academy for Case Studies, 19*(8), 95–103.

Jensen, J. C., & Berg, N. (2012). Determinants of traditional sustainability reporting *versus* integrated reporting: An institutionalist approach. *Business Strategy and the Environment, 21* (5), 399–416.

Jeurissen, R., & Elkington, J. (2000). Cannibals with forks: The triple bottom line of 21st century business. *Journal of Business Ethics, 23*(2), 229–231.

Macias, H. A., & Farfan-Lievano, A. (2017). Integrated reporting as a strategy for firm growth: Multiple case study in Colombia. *Meditari Accountancy Research, 25*(4), 605–628.

Mahmood, Z., Kouser, R., Hassan, I., & Iqbal, Z. (2017). Why Pakistani small and medium enterprises are not reporting on sustainability practices? *Pakistan Journal of Commerce and Social Sciences, 11*(1), 389–405.

Manes-Rossi, F., Niccolò, G., & Levy Orelli, R. (2017). Reshaping risk disclosure through integrated reporting: evidence from Italian early adopters. *International Journal of Business and Management, 12*(10), 11–23.

Mio, C., Fasan, M., & Pauluzzo, R. (2016). Internal application of IR principles: Generali's internal Integrated Reporting. *Journal of Cleaner Production, 139*, 204–218.

Murillo, D., & Lozano, J. M. (2006). SMEs and CSR: An approach to CSR in their own words. *Journal of Business Ethics, 67*(3), 227–240.

Muslichah, M., Wiyarni, W., & Nursasi, E. (2019). The effect of knowledge, perceived usefulness and social norms on intention to prepare integrated reporting in SMEs. *International Journal of Business and Social Research, 9*(4), 13–25.

Muslichah, M., Wiyarni, W., & Nursasi, E. (2020). Model of the integrated reporting for SMEs. *Journal of Sustainability Science and Management, 15*(2), 146–161.

Network Italiano Business Reporting. (2018). *Integrated Reporting for SMEs: Implementation Guidance*, No Place: NIBR, https://integratedreporting.org/resource/integrated-reporting-for-smes-implementation-guidance/

Perrini, F. (2006). SMEs and CSR theory: Evidence and implications from an Italian perspective. *Journal of Business Ethics, 67*(3), 305–316.

Raimo, N., Zito, M. & Caragnano, A. (2019). Does national culture affect integrated reporting quality? A focus on GLOBE dimensions, In: Mihajlović, D. & Đorđević, B. (Eds.), *9th International Symposium on Natural Resources Management*, May 31st, 2019, Zaječar, 383–392.

Romero, S., Lin, B., Jeffers, A. E., & DeGaetano, L. A. (2014). An overview of sustainability reporting practices: Results of related research and recommendations for the future. *The CPA Journal, 84*(3), 68–71.

Starik, M., & Kanashiro, P. (2013). Toward a theory of sustainability management: Uncovering and integrating the nearly obvious. *Organization and Environment, 26*(1), 7–30.

Steinhöfel, E., Galeitzke, M., Kohl, H., & Orth, R. (2019). Sustainability reporting in German manufacturing SMEs. *Procedia Manufacturing, 33*, 610–617.

Tilley, F. (2002). Small firm environmental ethics: How deep do they go? *Business Ethics A European Review, 9*(1), 31–41.

Vázquez-Carrasco, R., & López-Pérez, M. E. (2013). Small & medium-sized enterprises and corporate social responsibility: A systematic review of the literature. *Quality and Quantity International Journal of Methodology, 47*(6), 3205–3218.

SMEs and IR: Evidence from Germany

Philipp Schorn, Anne Tempel, Ralf Bauer, and Ralf Klapdor

1 SME Sector in Germany

Small- and medium-sized enterprises (SMEs) are the backbone of the German economy. As accounting and disclosure rules are tied to legal form and size, SMEs face less strict requirements. Most SMEs are managed by their owners, and also the 'bigger' medium-sized enterprises are majority-owned by families. Therefore German SMEs are reluctant to disclose information voluntarily. This provides SMEs in Germany with less incentives to adopt integrated reporting. Limited empirical evidence on integrated reporting is available and focuses only on listed corporations. Nonetheless, integrated reporting can be beneficial for SMEs as our analysis shows. Despite the current absence of legal requirements to implement more sophisticated reporting approaches, we identify political and social factors that render more enhanced reporting systems useful as numerous stakeholders demand more extensive information on environmental, social and governance issues. Furthermore, integrated reporting enables SMEs to create integrated information systems not only for external reporting but far more to improve internal processes and internal decision making (Table 1).

The sectoral distribution of the value added of German SMEs is comparable with the EU28 average. In particular, the service sector with 44.5% and the trade sector with 21.8% stand out, followed by the manufacturing sector (20.1%) and the construction sector (10.9%) (Statistisches Bundesamt, 2018). The importance of SMEs for the German economy is illustrated by their contribution to value added, with SMEs contributing 54% compared to large companies with 46% (see Fig. 1).

P. Schorn (✉) · A. Tempel · R. Bauer · R. Klapdor
Faculty of Society and Economics, Rhine-Waal University of Applied Sciences, Kleve, Germany
e-mail: philipp.schorn@hochschule-rhein-waal.de; anne.tempel@hochschule-rhein-waal.de; ralf.bauer@hochschule-rhein-waal.de; ralf.klapdor@hochschule-rhein-waal.de

J. Dyczkowska et al. (eds.), *Development of Integrated Reporting in the SME Sector*, CSR, Sustainability, Ethics & Governance,
https://doi.org/10.1007/978-3-030-81903-3_2

Table 1 Number of companies in Germany according to legal form and headcounts in 2017

	Number of employees				
Legal form	0–9	10–49	50–249	>250	Overall
Sole proprietor	2.082.586	63.776	2.454	80	2.148.896
Private company	324.085	54.150	12.885	2.881	394.001
Corporations	520.524	149.112	41.510	9.706	720.852
Others	182.066	26.572	7.079	2.394	218.111
Overall	3.109.261	293.610	63.928	15.061	3.481.860

Source: Statistisches Bundesamt (2018)

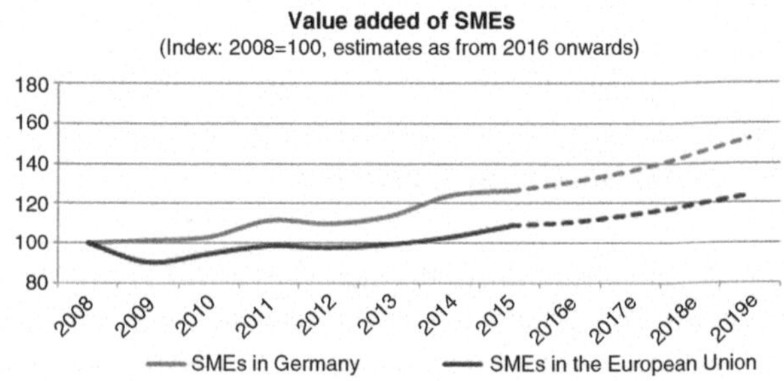

Fig. 1 Value added of SMEs in Germany compared to the EU. Source: EC (2018)

2 Overview of Reporting Regulations with Potential Impact on IR

2.1 *Financial Reporting Requirements*

Large public corporations in Germany are subject to a framework of reporting regulations, which stem primarily from European law. Corporate reporting by large public corporations in Germany is compliance-driven. In Germany, IR has been a topic pushed by auditors and consulting firms but has received a minimal uptake by large German companies. Such companies remain unconvinced of its benefits and have tended to adopt a wait-and-see mentality while devoting their attention to complying with the new European regulations on non-financial reporting. The German government and German business representatives were the fiercest opponents of the European Commission's (EC) non-financial disclosure proposals, stressing their encroachment on corporate discretion, the importance of voluntariness in this area and the feared bureaucratic burden on companies.

With the transferal of the fourth, seventh and eighth EC directives, accounting and reporting rules have been summarized and codified in the *German Commercial Code (GCC)*. The extent of rules and disclosure requirements depends on size, legal form and industry with larger companies, and companies with limited liability, facing the strictest rules (Nothelfer, 2017). Rules for all businesses are laid out in § 238 GCC–§ 263 GCC. These rules include general recognition and measurement rules. Additional rules for corporations and limited liability partnerships are laid out

Table 2 Classification criteria for corporations and limited liability

Classification criteria	Micro	Small	Medium
Total assets	<= 350.000 €	<= 6.000.000 €	<= 20.000.000 €
Revenues	<= 700.000 €	<= 12.000.000 €	<= 40.000.000 €
Average number of employees	<= 10 persons	<= 50 persons	<= 250 persons

Source: § 267 GCC and §267a GCC

in § 264 GCC to § 289f GCC. Special rules are applicable for groups (§290 GCC–§ 315e GCC), registered cooperatives, and financial institutions and insurance companies.

§ 238 GCC requires all businesses to do bookkeeping, and § 242 GCC requires all businesses to prepare a financial statement consisting of a balance sheet and a profit and loss statement. Very small businesses operating as sole proprietors with revenues not exceeding 600,000 € and profits not exceeding 60,000 € are exempted from the requirement to do bookkeeping and hence also to prepare financial statements according to § 241a GCC. General rules on recognition are laid out in § 246 CC to § 251 and measurement rules in § 252 to § 256a GCC. It is important to note that there are no general rules applicable to all businesses irrespective of their legal form and size for disclosure and auditing.

According to § 264 and § 264a–§ 264d GCC, corporations and limited liability partnerships are required to add notes, as well as a management report, to the financial statements comprising of a balance sheet and a profit and loss statement. Furthermore, § 265 GCC to § 277 GCC lay out further requirements for the structure of the balance sheet and for the profit and loss statement. Detailed rules for the structure and the contents of the notes are described in § 284 GCC–§ 289f GCC. It is important to note that only corporations and partnerships with limited liability have to disclose their financial statements according to § 325 GCC. The extent of rules to be applied by corporations and limited liability partnerships is linked to size. Size classes with references to total assets, revenues and number of employees are defined in § 267 GCC, distinguishing small, medium and large entities. Criteria for micro-entities are laid out in § 267a GCC. A corporation or limited liability partnership is classified as a micro-, a small or medium entity, if at least two of three thresholds are not exceeded for two consecutive years. Table 2 displays the quantitative thresholds.

Corporations with listed securities and those exceeding the thresholds for medium-sized entities are classified as a large entity. Large corporations face the strictest reporting and disclosure requirements. For the other size classes, considerable reliefs, e.g. longer period for preparation of financial statements, less detailed structure of balance sheet and profit and loss statement, and disclosure requirements, apply. Table 3 summarizes the key requirements for corporations.

The above-stated reliefs can be justified by the fact that smaller corporations usually have fewer addressees who are interested in their financial statements due to less dispersed ownership, less external financing and fewer stakeholders.

The GCC's disclosure rules are supplemented by the *Public Disclosure Act (PDA)*, which stipulates additional requirements, especially on sole proprietors and

Table 3 Size-related reliefs for corporations and limited liability corporations

Rule	Micro	Small	Medium	Large
Time period for preparing financial statements	Longer period of 6 month § 264 (1) S. 4 GCC		Normal period of 3 month § 264 (1) S. 3 GCC	
Audit of financial statements	Not required § 316 (1) GCC		Mandatory § 316 (1) GCC	
Structure of balance sheet	Less detailed structure § 266 (1) GCC		Normal structure § 266 (2), (3) GCC	
Structure of profit and loss statement	Less detailed structure and less information § 276 GCC		Less detailed structure § 276 GCC	Normal structure § 275 GCC
Information disclosed in notes	Usually not required § 264 (1) GCC	Relief §§ 288, 274a GCC	Relief § 288 GCC	Full requirements §§ 284, 285 GCC
Disclosure requirement	Option disclosure in Federal Gazette or filing with commercial register §326 GCC	Federal Gazette §325 GCC balance sheet and notes §326 GCC	Federal Gazette §325 GCC balance sheet, P&L and notes §327 GCC	Full requirements Federal Gazette §325 GCC

Source: Own illustration based on GCC

Table 4 Size criteria for the applicability of the Public Disclosure Act

Total assets	> 65.000.000 €
Revenues	> 130.000.000 €
Average number of employees	> 5.000 persons

Source: Own illustration based on § 1 PDA

business partnerships that exceed certain size thresholds and are not subject to disclosure according to the GCC. Two out of the three size criteria laid out in § 1 PDA have to be met for two consecutive years so that the rules from the PDA are applicable (Table 4).

Businesses that exceed the size thresholds according to § 1 PDA have to prepare financial statements (§ 5 PDA), need to have their financial statements audited (§ 6 PDA) and are subject to full disclosure requirements (§9 PDA). These requirements reflect the fact that business operations may reach significant stakeholder interest irrespective of the status of incorporation as they increase in size. Table 5 summarizes the key obligations from the GCC and the PDA that relate to legal form and size.

Considering the size thresholds for SMEs in the EU, it becomes evident that most SMEs in Germany operating in the legal form of a corporation or a limited liability partnership will qualify as a small- or medium-sized entity and hence face less strict accounting and disclosure requirements. SMEs operating as sole proprietors or as

Table 5 Summary of the key obligations from the GCC and the PDA

	Small (in terms of § 241a GCC)	Medium (exceeding threshold of § 241a GCC)	Large (exceeding threshold of § 1 PDA)
Sole proprietors	• No obligation to prepare financial statements • No obligation for audit • No obligation for disclosure	• Obligation to prepare financial statements • No obligation for audit • No obligation for disclosure	• Obligation to prepare financial statements • Obligation for audit • Obligation for disclosure
Business partnerships	• Obligation to prepare financial statements • No obligation for audit • No obligation for disclosure		
	Small/micro (in terms of §§ 267 and 267a GCC)	Medium (in § 267 GCC) terms	Large (in terms of § 267 GCC)
Corporations business partnerships	• Obligation to prepare financial statements • No obligation for audit • Partial relief from disclosure	• Obligation to prepare financial statements • Obligation for audit • Partial relief from disclosure	• Obligation to prepare financial statements • Obligation for audit • Obligation for disclosure

Source: Own illustration based on GCC and PDA

business partnerships do not meet the size criteria of § 1 PDA and hence are only obliged to prepare financial statements but not to disclose them. As many SMEs receive debt financing from banks in Germany, it is important to note that § 18 of the German Banking Act requires banks to demand financial statements for loan applications exceeding 750,000 EUR. Hence, banks are an important stakeholder that can trigger voluntary reporting for German SMEs.

2.2 *The Management Report*

The management report was the core element for the disclosure of non-financial information prior to the *Directive, 2014/95/EU of the European Parliament and of the Council of October 22, 2014*. Pursuant to § 264 (1) GCC, medium-sized and large corporations have to prepare a management report, which is not part of the financial statements. According to § 289 (1) GCC, the management report is to provide a true and fair view of the state of the company and serves as a complementary source of information to the financial statements.

It is supposed to provide an unbiased and comprehensive analysis of the development of the business in the past and the current situation of the company. Furthermore, the future developments and key risk factors and opportunities should be discussed. Based on the complexity of the business operations, financial

Table 6 Elements of the management report according to GCC

Elements	Source
• Report on development of business and current status of company • Report on risk factors and opportunities (future development)	§ 289 (1)
• Report on risks from financial transactions and on risk management • Report on research and development activities (current and planned) • Report on branches and subsidiaries	§ 289 (2) GCC

Source: Own illustration based on § 289 GCC

performance indicators are to be included and linked to the numbers of the financial statements. Required elements of the management report are depicted in Table 6.

Large corporations are to report non-financial indicators, e.g. on social or environmental issues as well to the extent that these are relevant for the understanding of the development of the business and the current situation (§ 289 (3) GCC). There is a limited overlap between the information required to be disclosed in the management report according to GCC and in an integrated report according to the IIRC framework (Barmettler, 2017; Haller & Fuhrmann, 2013).

Groups are required to prepare a management report in addition to their consolidated financial statements (§ 290 GCC). Similar rules as for the management report of a single legal entity apply to a group management report which are laid out in § 315 GCC. The rules of § 289 GCC, however, provide little practical guidance for the preparation of management reports. *The German Accounting Standards Committee*[1] has published *the German Accounting Standard 20 (GAS)* "Group Management Report" to provide practical guidance. Despite the fact that this standard is only mandatory for groups, GAS 20.2 advises to apply the standard voluntarily for the preparation of the management report of a single legal entity. The standard was adopted on 2.11.2012 and the last modifications were adopted on 4.12.2017 to account for changes in legal requirements of the GCC reflecting the implementation of Directive, 2014/95/EU into German law. According to GAS 20.3, the purpose of a management report is to provide accountability on the use of resources used within a group during the reporting period and to enable stakeholders assess the course of business, the current status and future development of a group. Hence, stakeholders receive past, current and future information, which complements the information reported in financial statements. In order to achieve this goal, GAS 20 lays out six key principles for management reports:

[1] The Accounting Standards Committee of Germany (ASCG) is an independent and not-for-profit association. It serves as the national standard setter in the area of group financial reporting in Germany and develops the German Accounting Standards. The ASCG has been acknowledged as the private standardization organization pursuant to § 342 GCC. The German Accounting Standards provide guidance and interpretation for the accounting rules codified in the German Commercial Code. According to § 342 GCC, financial statements prepared in accordance with German Accounting Standards meet all GAAP requirements. See www.drsc.de

1. *Completeness* (GAS 20.12–20.16)
    - Report must include all information a knowledgeable user requires to assess a true and fair view of the course of business, the current status and future developments.
    - Report has to be understandable on stand-alone basis.
    - Required information has to be disclosed in management report. A disclosure in other sources is not sufficient.
    - Positive and negative aspects have to be reported separately.
2. *Reliability and balance* (GAS 20.17–20.19)
    - Information reported must be correct and verifiable; facts and opinions must be clearly separated.
    - Balance presentation of positive and negative aspects.
    - Information has to be plausible, consistent and in line with information reported in financial statements.
3. *Clarity and transparency* (GAS 20.20–20.30)
    - Management report must be clearly separated from the financial statements
    - Report must have a clear structure with headings.
    - Content and structure of reporting should not change over time; any changes need to be explained.
4. *Management perspective* (GAS 20.31)
    - Report needs to present the perspective and assessments of management.
5. *Materiality* (GAS 20.32 and 20.33)
    - Focus only on material information in the management report.
6. *Complexity and degree of details of information* (GAS 20.34 and 20.35)
    - Length and degree of details of information presented in report should reflect specific condition and situation of a group, e.g. size, listing status and type of business operations.

Reflecting the requirements of § 315 GCC and § 289 GCC, GAS 20 requires a management report to consist of 10 parts:

Part 1: Information on the Group (GAS 20.36–GAS 20.52)
- Basis for the subsequent information presented in the report.
- Description on following items typically included:
    - Business model
    - Subsidiaries and branches
    - Strategies
    - Management system
    - Research and development activities

Part 2: Report on Business (GAS 20.53–GAS 20.113)

- Core of the management report including the following items:
  - Macroeconomic environment and industry condition
  - Course of business during the reporting period
  - Current status of group with respect to assets, financial situation (e.g. capital structure, liquidity and investments) and performance
  - Financial and non-financial performance indicators (quantitative information only required if reported internally to management as well)

Part 3: Report on Subsequent Events (GAS 20.114 and GAS 20.115)

- Events after the reporting period that are material and relevant for a presentation of a true and fair view have to be presented.

Part 4: Report on Future Developments (GAS 20.116–GAS 20.167)

- Forecasted development of the group must be presented as well as an analysis of opportunities and risk factors. Reported information needs to be consistent with information reported or used in financial statements.
- Presentation and assessment of risk management system of group (only applicable for groups controlled by a publicly traded entity).

Part 5: Report on Internal Control System (GAS 20.K168–GAS 20.K178)

- Presentation and assessment of internal control system and risk management system for accounting processes (only applicable for groups controlled by a publicly traded entity).

Part 6: Report on Risks from Use of Financial Instruments (GAS 20.179–GAS 20.187)

- Separate report on risks resulting from transactions with financial instruments including the following items:
  - Kind of risk exposure (price, default, liquidity risks)
  - Risk management methods and use of hedge accounting

Part 7: Report on Share Capital and Control (GAS 20.K188–GAS 20.K223)

- Groups controlled by a publicly traded entity must provide additional information on:
  - Share capital and any additional rights or limitations on rights of shareholders
  - Rights of executive board to repurchase or issue stocks

Part 8: Corporate Governance and Diversity Declaration (GAS 20.K224–GAS 20.K231d)

- Groups controlled by a publicly traded entity must prepare a declaration including:

- Confirmation of compliance with German Corporate Governance Codex
- Relevant information on management practices
- Description of structure of executive board and supervisory board and their committees
- Information on existence and implementation of diversity concept

Part 9: Non-financial Declaration (GAS 20.232–GAS 20.305)
- Guidance for disclosure of non-financial information (see next section for details)

Part 10: Assurance of Legal Representatives (GAS 20.K306–GAS.K309)
- Groups controlled by a publicly traded entity must provide assurance that management report has been prepared with best knowledge to convey a true and fair view.

2.3 *Disclosure of Non-financial Information*

Reporting of non-financial information in the management report has been and still is of limited importance for most corporations in Germany as § 289 (3) requires only large corporations to report non-financial indicators relevant for assessing the course of business and the current status of the company. This has changed with the Directive, 2014/95/EU, which was implemented into German law on 19.04.2017 (*CSR Directive Implementation Law*). Companies classified as public interest entities are required to disclose a non-financial declaration containing non-financial and diversity-related information from financial years beginning after 31.12.2016. Public interest entities include corporations with publicly traded securities issued at a regulated market and banks, financial institutions and insurance corporations. These companies need to meet the classification criteria presented in Table 7 for two consecutive years:

Special size criteria apply for the non-financial declaration of a group (§315b (1) GCC). For the preparation and disclosure of the non-financial declaration, § 289b GCC grants three options[2]:

1. Non-financial declaration included in the management report as a separate section
2. Separate non-financial declaration containing required information and disclosed together with the management reporting in the federal gazette
3. Separate non-financial declaration containing required information and published on the entity's homepage for at least 10 years

[2] § 289b (2) GCC and § 315b (2) GCC exempt public interest entities from disclosing a non-financial declaration under certain requirements, e.g. if an entity is included in a group report and a separate non-financial declaration for the group is disclosed.

Table 7 Classification criteria

Classification criteria	Corporations and limited liability partnerships (§ 289b GCC)	Banks and financial institutions (§ 340a (1a) GCC)	Insurance companies (§ 341a (1a) GCC)
Corporations or limited liability partnerships	Yes		
Publicly listed securities traded on a regulated market	Yes	Not required	Not required
Total assets	> 20.000.000 €		
Revenues	> 40.000.000 €		
Average number of employees	> 500 persons		

Source: German Commercial Code

Pursuant to § 289c GCC, the non-financial declaration needs to contain the following information:

- Description of the business model
- Information on non-financial aspects:
  - Environmental aspects
  - Employees issues
  - Social issues
  - Respect for human rights
  - Avoidance of bribery and corruption

Information on non-financial aspects needs to be reported to the extent that it is necessary and relevant not only to understand the business but also to understand the impact of the business on these aspects. For each aspect, substantial disclosures are necessary:

- Description of policies and due diligence processes (to the extent that policies exist)
- Results of policies
- Material risk factors from the business operation
- Material risk factors from business relationships, products or services
- Most important non-financial performance indicators
- References to numbers disclosed in financial statements as far as necessary for understanding

§ 289c GCC allows companies to abstain from non-financial disclosures in exceptional cases, if the disclosure leads to significant disadvantages for the company. Non-disclosure, however, is only allowed as long as the presentation of a true and fair view is still ensured. To ensure comparability of non-financial disclosures, § 289d GCC specifies that companies may use national, European or international frameworks for the preparation of disclosures. If no framework is utilized, companies have to state this and explain why. This leaves companies with a limited choice of different possible frameworks (IIRC, OECD, GRI, German Sustainability Code, etc.). Some of the information required under § 289b GCC was already required under GAS 20. With the introduction of CSR reporting in the German Commercial Code, GAS 20 was updated too and now includes limited guidance for the non-financial declaration (GAS 20.232–GAS 20.305). GAS 20 clarifies certain aspects, provides guidance on measurement issues and provides examples but cannot be seen as a surrogate for a complete framework.

3 National Factors Enabling or Constraining IR

3.1 Political Factors

Before the introduction of German legislation to comply with the EU Directive, 2014/95/EU on the disclosure of non-financial and diversity by large companies, no mandatory obligations existed in Germany for sustainability reporting or the reporting of non-financial information (apart from selected non-financial performance indicators (see GAS 20.101–20.107)) (Gamerschlag et al., 2011; Gulenko, 2018; Hoffmann et al., 2018). Germany therefore stands in contrast to many other countries in Europe that introduced legal obligations for companies to report on environmental and social issues much earlier. For example, Denmark, Norway, Sweden and the Netherlands introduced regulations during the 1990s obliging companies to report annually on environmental performance (Hoffmann et al., 2018). France and the UK brought in laws requiring firms to disclose their environmental and social impact in 2001 and 2005, respectively (Hess, 2007).

Both the German government and German business organizations showed very strong opposition to the European Commission's non-financial disclosure proposals and Germany attempted to water down the directive. In fact, Germany was the strongest opponent to the European Commission's proposals and was categorically opposed to the directive throughout the negotiations. The positions of the German government and German business organizations were virtually identical (Kindermann, 2020). In particular, business organizations regarded the proposals as encroaching massively on corporate discretion and going against the position that CSR and reporting about it should remain voluntary (e.g. BDA, BDI, DIHK and ZDH, 2011). Moreover, both German politicians and business representatives argued that the bureaucratic burden, in terms of adjustment costs incurred by companies, would outweigh benefits, particularly for small- and medium-sized companies.

In line with the emphasis on voluntary disclosure, the *German Sustainability Code*, a voluntary transparency standard of corporate responsibility, was created in 2010. The *German Council for Sustainable Development* (Nachhaltigkeitsrat) developed the code. The German government set up the council in 2001 as its advisory body and the German chancellor nominate its members. The council's mandate is to advise the German government on its sustainable development policy and to foster social dialogue on issues of sustainability.

Moreover, the international standard *ISO 26000 Guidance on Social Responsibility* has been introduced into Germany in the form of a DIN (Deutsche Institut für Normierung) standard. The goal of the IS0 26000 standard is to encourage organizations to practice social responsibility in order to improve their impacts on their workers, their natural environments and their communities. However, it is a voluntary standard without certification. The German government recognized it as part of its Corporate Social Responsibility Action Plan. However, along with German business associations, it has stressed the non-certifiability of the standard (BMU, 2014).

Although there has until recently been an absence in Germany of mandatory regulations on non-financial reporting, this absence does not reflect a reluctance by German companies to report on environmental and social issues, or a disinterest of German governments in these areas. Studies have shown that German companies engaged earlier and at a much higher level in reporting on environmental and employee issues compared to companies of other countries of origin (Adams et al., 1998; Chen & Bouvain, 2009; Cormier et al., 2005; Gulenko, 2018). The emphasis among German companies of reporting on environmental and employee issues has been attributed in particular to political pressures and legislation in these areas (Adams et al., 1998; Gulenko, 2018).

Although a relative latecomer in international comparison in environmental policy, Germany is now seen as a pioneer in climate and energy policy, particularly in the area of renewable energy (Lehr & Lutz, 2016; Weidner, 2020). It was also the first large industrial country to establish plans to phase out nuclear energy, plans that were accelerated after the Fukushima accident in 2011. It has also set ambitious targets for climate protection, in particular the reduction in greenhouse gas emissions (BMUB, 2016).

At the heart of these policies is the German energy transition (Energiewende), an integrated policy framework that covers all types of energy and sectors of the economy. It represents a series of federal laws that build on each other, in particular to stimulate the shift towards renewable energy and high-energy efficiency (Rammer et al., 2017). Key elements of this include the national support scheme for renewable energies, the Renewable Energy Act introduced in 2002, and due to be amended in 2021 (Tagesschau, 2020), and the ecological tax reform first introduced in 1999. Other important policies concern schemes that provide incentives for energy-efficient building refurbishment, for both private households and companies (Rosenow, 2013) and the funding of research and development programmes to encourage the development of energy-saving technologies (Rammer et al., 2017).

In the area of employee issues, Germany has a long tradition of strong employment law. A key element of German employment law and a key feature of the German business system are employee representation on supervisory boards at company level and through works councils at workplace level.

In contrast to the prevalence of reporting by German companies on environmental and employee issues, studies show that German companies tend to be weak in reporting on supply chain sustainability (Habisch et al., 2011) and human rights and bribery issues (IÖW, 2018). However, this may be set to change as the German government has agreed on the introduction of a law to force large companies to respect human rights and environmental issues in their supply chains (Beck-aktuell, 2021). The German government sees voluntary self-regulation by firms as having failed in this area. It initially focused on voluntary measures of compliance with UN guiding principles on business and human rights. However, estimates show that only about one fifth of companies in Germany showed compliance (Spiegel, 2021). Moreover, the German government has decided to introduce a national law on this issue rather than to wait for EU-wide regulation (IKB, 2020). The law, which business associations feared would put additional economic and administrative burdens on companies, particularly medium-sized ones (IKB, 2020; Spiegel, 2021), is set to apply to companies with more than 2000 employees from 2023. It will extend to companies with more than 1000 employees from 2024. Although it only directly applies to larger companies, it is likely to have an indirect effect on SMEs as large companies need to comply with the legislation through their supply chain.

3.2 Economic Factors

In Germany, SMEs are the backbone and success model of the German economy. Of the approximately 3.5 million businesses, over 99% are SMEs (Statistisches Bundesamt, 2018). Therefore, all questions relating to the future viability of German SMEs deserve much attention in the political and economic spheres.

The shortage of skilled labour is an important economic challenge that affects German SMEs. If companies do not find qualified professionals, this can result in companies or entire economic sectors growing less. In a study by Ernst and Young from January 2020, 1500 SMEs in Germany indicated that they currently see the greatest danger for their own company in the shortage of skilled labour (EY, 2020). To counteract this, companies must remain interesting for existing and potential employees. Thus, SMEs should know the social and ecological expectations of these stakeholders and to a certain extent consider them in their decision-making process.

In an increasingly complex economic world, stakeholders have elevated information needs and require transparency in reporting, which should also include ecological and social aspects in addition to the economic perspective. If you take the example of banks as stakeholders, they rely on detailed information from companies to provide important information for example in addition to the annual financial statements, for instance, to get to the market environment, business model, opportunities and risks. The financial and economic crisis from 2008 has shown that the banks' rating system is insufficient to determine qualitative corporate characteristics. While analysts have so far perceived qualitative information subjectively and have not always passed it on in the lending decision process, the industry's demand for non-financial information disclosure by companies is growing. The use of IR would therefore have a direct impact on the capital base, on the liquidity strength and consequently on the overall economic situation of a company.

In summary, the satisfaction of stakeholder requires a holistic view of companies based on IR and will have a positive long-term impact on the profitability of the reporting company and the entire economy.

3.3 *Social Factors*

Parallel to political interest in environmental and social issues, companies in Germany are subject to social pressures from interest groups and the general public in these areas. For example, Germany has a strong green movement and powerful environmental pressure groups (Adams et al., 1998; Cormier et al., 2005). Moreover, surveys have shown that environmental and climate protection and social justice are regarded by the German public as among the top societal challenges (Umweltbundesamt, 2020a). The climate crisis in particular has become the focus of environmental consciousness in Germany in recent years (Umweltbundesamt, 2020b). Sustainability labels and certifications also play an important role in Germany and are widely used by companies to communicate their sustainability information to their customers (Barbe et al., 2013). The concept of the eco-label was initiated in Germany, when the first eco-label, the Blue Angel, was created in 1977 (Kirchhoff, 2000). Therefore, companies in Germany, both large corporations and SMEs, face social pressures to demonstrate and communicate their sustainability efforts and their effects on natural capital and human capital in particular.

3.4 *Cultural Factors*

Traditionally, most of the 3.6 million German SMEs are owner-managed. Further, nearly 3000 medium-sized enterprises that employ more than 250 employees are run by families, who own the majority of the enterprises (Eckert, 2018). In 2018, their main sources of investment financing were equity (ca. 45%) and bank loans (34%) (Statistisches Bundesamt, 2020). The capital market (e.g. bond market) does not play an important role for financing. In 2010, Börse Stuttgart (local stock exchange) tried to establish a new market segment "Mittelstandsanleihen" (fixed income bonds issued by medium-sized companies), but in 2014 the insolvency rate of all issuers of bonds was 17% (Zinnecker, 2014). Consequently, Börse Stuttgart announced the closure of this trading segment after the last maturity (Zinnecker, 2014). While exchange-traded shares do not exist for SMEs, there is one traded preferred share ("Genussschein") on Exchanges Hamburg-Hannover, which was issued by Stadtwerke Hannover AG, a publicly owned company (Börsen Hamburg-Hannover, 2020).

The main characteristic of many German SMEs is the identity of ownership and management so that the manager is also a major owner and therefore works for his own risk and benefit (BDI, 2019). Normally, it is not necessary to inform external shareholders or other stakeholders about the company's situation. The main sources of financing are retained earnings (equity financing) or bank loans but not extruded financial instruments (e.g. bonds). Therefore, there is no need to report figures and data externally. German SMEs are not very transparent, trying to hide rather than to disclose information as from their view any published information may be used, e.g. by a competitor. Generally, the financing banks are the only stakeholders to receive additional information and reports (e.g. budgets and forecasts) by German SMEs as they are required to analyse the economic situation and to rate their debtors before granting loans.

3.5 Technological Factors

The discussion in Germany about the influence of technical developments on IR is—as in most other countries—driven by digitalization. A good overview is given by Krause and Pellens (2018), stating that digital technologies have a high synergetic potential for IR. They see digitalization as an important enabler for IR by helping to overcome the complexities like connectivity, future orientation and stakeholder inclusion. Giving the possibility to analyse a large quantity of data, digital technologies offer an effective base for integrated thinking in management.

An influence of technology on accounting can be seen by the "*Principles for Duly Maintaining, Keeping and Storing Books, Records and Documents in Electronic Form and for Data Access*" of the German tax authorities (Grundsätze zur ordnungsmäßigen Führung und Aufbewahrung von Büchern, Aufzeichnungen und Unterlagen in elektronischer Form sowie zum Datenzugriff, GoBD). With these principles, in 2015 the tax authorities implemented rules for electronic bookkeeping and access to this electronic data by the German tax auditor (Goldshteyn & Thelen, 2016; Kling, 2018). In Germany, tax accounting is an extremely important part of accounting of SMEs, for SMEs with higher equity ratio (and therefore limited need of bank loans) the most important one. Therefore, the need to adjust the accounting system to these principles and the need to integrate more and more information for tax compliance (Pielke, 2018) might be an additional reason for SMEs to rethink accounting and to integrate new elements in reporting systems.

4 Empirical Evidence on IR in Germany

4.1 Existing Studies on IR in Germany

Recent practitioner studies have analysed DAX 160 companies' reporting behaviour since the implementation of the Directive, 2014/95/EU into German law (Kirchhoff, 2018, 2019; PWC, 2018). The most recent study, which analyses the reporting year 2018 (Kirchhoff, 2019), shows that of the 92 companies analysed, 75% of the companies published a separate sustainability report and 25% chose some form of a combined report. 88% of the analysed companies used the GRI framework. Two companies also used the IIRC framework—BASF and SAP.

For the reporting period 2013 and 2014, PWC conducted benchmark surveys of the reporting behaviour of DAX 30 companies. It analysed the reporting behaviour of the companies against the content elements of the IIRC framework. For the reporting period 2013, PWC concluded that DAX 30 companies were increasingly moving towards IR. This assessment was based on the increase in the number of companies publishing combined reports and the increase in IIRC-relevant information being included in annual reports (PWC, 2014). Three companies (BASF, Bayer and SAP) published integrated reports, of which BASF and SAP referred to the IIRC framework. A further four companies published combined reports and the remaining companies, a suite of multiple reports. However, some of the changes in reporting behaviour, in terms of IIRC-relevant information being included in reports, were brought about by changes in German law (German Accounting Standards GAS 20). For the reporting period 2014, PWC's survey highlighted a decrease in the pace with which DAX 30 companies were moving towards IR, with reporting remaining primarily "compliance-driven" at most of the DAX30 companies (PWC, 2016).

Two recent scientific studies have sought to analyse the reasons for the limited uptake of IR in Germany (Günther et al., 2017; Hahn et al., 2018). Both studies are based on expert interviews with companies, auditors and academics. The studies argue that IR in Germany is being pushed by consultancies and auditors, while companies are adopting a wait-and-see mentality, so long as the integration of financial and non-financial information in one report is not mandatory—the law implementing the Directive, 2014/95/EU did not stipulate IR (Hahn et al., 2018). The IIRC framework was regarded by experts as not being coherent or concrete enough (Günther et al., 2017), thus creating uncertainty among companies as to how exactly to implement it. It was therefore seen as providing only an addition to existing frameworks, which are already globally recognized rather than being innovative and a new standard setter (Günther et al., 2017). Moreover, the benefits of IR were not seen by companies as being clear enough for them to adopt the practice. Integrating financial and non-financial information in one report was also regarded as being too complex to win the interests of specific stakeholders or broader target groups. Companies also feared that they had more to lose than to gain by integrating sustainability storytelling into the logic of financial company reports (Hahn et al., 2018). Finally, both studies highlighted the barriers which experts saw in adopting IR because of the significant internal changes necessary to organizational and communication processes within companies and the high costs associated with integrated thinking and IR, particularly for SMEs.

The EU requirement to disclose non-financial information has triggered several studies on reporting behaviour in general. Hoffmann et al. (2018) analyse the sustainability reports of German stock corporations for the years 2014 and 2015 to identify key trends and shortcomings prior to the introduction of a mandatory reporting requirement. Their findings reveal that a growing number of companies are using either national or international standards to draft either a separate or an integrated report. Despite making reference to some standards, not all information required by the new law is being presented and reporting quality can be enhanced. Graßmann et al. (2018) analyse a sample of 27 stock-listed German companies issuing a mandatory CSR report for the first time. The authors limit their content analysis to the reporting of information on environmental issues. As the current rules on disclosure of non-financial information provide only limited guidance, the study reveals a great heterogeneity with regard to the amount and quality of information disclosed as well as the standards used for reporting. Kajüter and Wirth (2018) follow a more general approach and analyse the mandatory non-financial reports of a sample of large German stock-listed corporations. Their findings confirm the great variation in reporting behaviour due to lacking guidance in the respective law and the significant options granted for the disclosure of non-financial information. Most companies limit their disclosures to items explicitly required by law and opt to disclose a separate report on non-financial information. These results are confirmed by Lenger et al. (2019) for a sample of companies listed in the MDAX (mid-sized stock corporations). Cikanek and Landis (2019) analyse the development of the content sustainability reports of a sample of 33 German full-service banks for the time period 2014 till 2017. The findings indicate that the number of banks disclosing a sustainability report increased during the sample period, whereas the average number of the pages of the reports declined significantly from 75 in 2014 to 60 in 2017. During the sample period, the number of banks using a relevant standard for drafting their report (e.g. GRI) increased despite the fact that most banks only comply with minimum requirements.

4.2 Current Corporate Reporting Status DAX 30

Our analysis of the reporting behaviour of the DAX 30 companies in the reporting years 2018 and 2019 shows that two DAX 30 companies published what they called "integrated reports": BASF and SAP. Both of these companies refer to the IIRC and its framework in their 2018 and 2019 reports, and both are also members of the IIRC pilot group in Germany. SAP has taken the IIRC framework into consideration since 2012. It referred to the IIRC framework in its integrated report for the first time in 2016. BASF first published what it refers to as a report integrating financial and non-financial information in 2008. It first mentioned the IIRC framework in its integrated report in 2014. The company states that it served as a pilot enterprise in the IIRC from 2012 to 2014 and continued its activities in the IIRC after 2014.

In 2018, a further 4 DAX30 companies published combined reports (Adidas, Bayer, Deutsche Börse, Fresenius Medical Care), but did not refer to the IIRC in their reports. None of these four companies published a separate sustainability report in 2018. In 2019, Adidas and Bayer chose to publish separate sustainability reports.

In 2018 and 2019, the remaining 24 companies published an annual report and a separate sustainability, corporate responsibility or non-financial report. To comply with the CSR Directive Implementation Law, 12 of these companies chose to include their non-financial report in their annual reports, eight as part of their sustainability reports and three as separate non-financial reports. None of them mentioned the IIRC framework in their reports in 2018 or 2019. The final company, Linde Plc., has different reporting patterns as its headquarters are in the UK.

So, even the other DAX30 companies, Deutsche Bank and Deutsche Börse, which were listed members of the IIRC pilot group (https://integratedreporting.org/wp-content/uploads/2013/11/IIRC-Pilot-Programme-Business-Network-backgrounder-October-2013.pdf), did not refer to the IIRC framework in their 2018 and 2019 reports, although Deutsche Börse states on its website that it supports initiatives on sustainability reporting such as the GRI and IIRC.

All of the DAX30 companies include key content elements outlined in the IIRC framework in their reports, such as business model, risks and opportunities, and governance. However, as outlined in the section on corporate reporting regulations in Germany, these elements are required of them. Therefore, the inclusion of these elements in the reporting behaviour of the DAX companies is not evidence that large German companies are moving towards the implementation of IR, but rather their compliance with German regulations.

Two other companies, which are not part of the DAX30 group, but which are part of the IIRC pilot group—*EnBW* and *Munich Airport*—were also included in this current reporting status analysis of large companies. *EnBW* has been publishing integrated reports based on the IIRC framework since 2014 and refers to itself as an "active supporter of integrated reporting and the IIRC from the very beginning" (EnBW Integrated Report 2018). *EnBW* is listed on the CDAX, but as a regional energy provider, is subject to particular regulations. *Munich Airport* has been publishing integrated reports since 2009 and refers both to the IIRC framework and integrated thinking in its 2018 and 2019 integrated reports. *Munich Airport* is not currently listed on a stock exchange.

In summary, there are currently four large companies in Germany that can be considered to publish an integrated report according to the classification of the Corporate Register (referring to IIRC and its framework and referring to at least two capitals): *BASF*, *SAP*, *EnBW*, and *Munich Airport*.

4.3 Current Reporting Status of SMEs

An analysis of SMEs, which according to the Amadeus database were in operation in 2018 and had more than 50 and up to 150 employees, revealed no evidence of IR or sustainability reporting. This is not surprising due to the compliance-based culture of reporting in Germany, and as sustainability reporting for SMEs in Germany is voluntary. We found anecdotal evidence of three SMEs, for whom sustainability is at the core of their strategy, which publish sustainability reports.

4.4 Examples of German Best Practices in IR

Connectivity of Information

EnBW Integrated Report 2018: Connectivity of information is depicted in the form of the interdependencies between key financial and non-financial performance indicators using the concrete examples of the construction of HVDC connections and digitalization. These are visualized for the areas of customers/society, finance, employees and environment. (See the link, p. 54–55).

Materiality

Munich Airport Integrated Report 2018: Materiality is depicted in a materiality matrix, which identifies and integrates key issues for internal and external stakeholders along with the six capitals (see the Integrated Report 2018, p. 39).

Business Model

BASF Integrated Report 2018. "*How we create value—an overview of BASF's business based on the IIRC framework*". Inputs and outputs in the business model are clearly delineated along with the six capitals, which are adapted by BASF to financial: innovation, environment, operations, employees and partnerships (see the link, p. 22).

5 Conclusion and Remarks

Our review of the current reporting regulations, as well as our empirical analysis, reveals that reporting behaviour of German companies is compliance-driven. Currently, only four public corporations prepare integrated reports in Germany applying the IIRC framework. We were not able to identify any SME currently preparing and disclosing integrated reports. This finding is attributable to the fact that publicly traded corporations are obliged to disclose a non-financial information declaration, which they can prepare using the IIRC framework or other frameworks such as GRI. The four analysed reports do not necessarily reflect an adoption of integrated thinking either. This is due to the fact that the financial statements were included as a separate element in most integrated reports and a consistent integration and cross-referencing were not always recognizable. According to Section 1.15 of the IIRC framework, an integrated report can either be issued as a stand-alone report or be a part of another report. This can limit the integrated report to being just another report, an additional section in an existing report and adds to the clutter of reports (Flower, 2015). In this case, producing an integrated report increases the costs of the reportable entities and limits its benefits.

German SMEs are characterized by limited dispersion in ownership and a high share of debt financing obtained in form of bank loans. This renders strict disclosure requirements unnecessary as costs of disclosure are likely to exceed the benefits from disclosure. Furthermore, owners are reluctant to disclose information voluntarily. As discussed earlier, SMEs face only very limited disclosure requirements and are not required to disclose a non-financial declaration. As a consequence of the small amount of information available, other forms of information production, e.g. strong lending relationships (Boot, 2000; Elsas & Krahnen, 1998), have evolved. This reluctance to disclose information voluntarily is supported by the fact that we were able to find only a very small number of SMEs currently disclosing a sustainability report. These companies chose to disclose these reports as they obviously served their business purposes and enhanced the reputation of the company with its suppliers and customers.

These findings highlight the necessity that SMEs voluntarily adopting IR need to understand the costs and specifically the benefits of doing so. Both require that the relevant stakeholders and their informational needs have to be identified (Haller, 2015). A changing economic, social and technological environment has to be considered in this process. The benefits of integrated reports increase as more suppliers, customers and investors demand sustainability-related information. The costs of IR can be significantly reduced by the current digitalization of business by using big data, employing data analytics and communicating directly with stakeholders on social media platforms (Krause & Pellens, 2018). Furthermore, regulatory developments may push IR as well. Germany has reached a high standard in environmental-related regulation in the past few years. Further developments may call for additional requirements and disclosure for all companies in the future.

For corporations, only limited evidence on positive impact of IR on the capital market perception of corporations is available (Zhou et al., 2017). Integrating non-financial information into the financial report of an entity also positively affects professional investors' evaluations of an entity's sustainability performance as experimental evidence shows (Reimsbach et al., 2018).

In conclusion, we argue that it is important that IR is framed for SMEs not in the sense of representing additional reporting requirements, but rather as a management tool. SMEs need to grasp the concept of integrated thinking and understand that IR is not just a tool for reporting information to outside stakeholders but also, and more importantly, a management tool that they can use internally to structure their businesses and gain a comprehensive view of their value creation. This understanding allows SMEs to capture benefits from IR more comprehensively. Such an approach would bring the concept of integrated thinking more into centre stage.

References

Adams, C., Hill, W.-Y., & Roberts, C. (1998). Corporate social reporting practices in Western Europe: Legitimating corporate behaviour? *British Accounting Review, 30*(1), 1–21.

Barbe, F., Gonzalez-Triay, M., & Hensel, A. (2013). Eco-labels in Germany. *Journal of Customer Behaviour, 12*(4), 341–359.

Barmettler, P. (2017). Chancen und Risiken des integrated reporting. In W. Funk & J. Rossmanith (Eds.), *Internationale Rechnungslegung und internationales controlling*. Wiesbaden: Springer Gabler.

BDA, BDI, DIHK and ZDH. (2011). *Position on the European Commission's CSR communication. A renewed EU strategy 2011–2014 for Corporate Social Responsibility (COM(2011) 681)*. Berlin. 13 Dec.

BDI (Bundesverband der deutschen Industrie e.V.), (2019, June 14). *Familienunternehmen. Wer sie sind und was sie ausmach*t. Retrieved February 17, 2020 from https://bdi.eu/artikel/news/familienunternehmen-wer-sie-sind-und-was-sie-ausmacht/

Beck-aktuell. (2021) *Referentenentwurf für Lieferkettengesetz vorgestellt*. Retrieved February 2, 2021 from https://rsw.beck.de/aktuell/daily/meldung/detail/referentenentwurf-fuer-lieferkettengesetz-vorgestellt

BMU (Federal Ministry of Environment, Nature Conservation and Nuclear Satefty). (2014). *Gesellschaftliche Verantwortung von Unternehmen: Eine Orientierungshilfe für Kernthemen und Handlungsfelder des Leitfadens DIN ISO 26000*. Retrieved February 18, 2021 from https://www.bmu.de/fileadmin/Daten_BMU/Pools/Broschueren/csr_iso26000_broschuere_bf.pdf

BMUB (Federal Ministry of the Environment Nature Conservation and Nuclear Safety). (2016). *Climate Action Plan* 2050*: Principles and goals of the German government's climate policy 2016*. Retrieved February 18, 2021 https://www.bmu.de/ileadmin/Daten_BMU/Pools/Broschueren/klimaschutzplan_2050_en_bf.pdf

Boot, A. W. A. (2000). Relationship banking: What do we know? *Journal of Financial Intermediation, 9*(1), 7–25.

Börsen Hamburg-Hannover. (2020). Retrieved February 17, 2020 from https://www.boersenag.de/Anleihen/DE0007255358/Stadtwerke%20Hannover%20AG

Chen, S., & Bouvain, P. (2009). Is corporate responsibility converging? A comparison of corporate responsibility reporting in the USA, UK, Australia and Germany. *Journal of Business Ethics, 87*, 299–317.

Cikanek, S., & Landis, C. (2019). Nachhaltigkeitsberichterstattung im Bankensektor: Eine Analyse der Berichtspraxis deuther Universalbanken im Lichte des CSR-Richtlinie-Umsetzungsgesetzes. *Betriebswirtschaftliche Forschung und Praxis, 4*, 411–443.

Cormier, D., Magnan, M., & Van Velthoven, B. (2005). Environmental disclosure in large German Companies. Economic incentives, public pressures or institutional conditions. *European Accounting Review, 14*(1), 3–39.

Directive 2014/95/EU of the European Parliament and of the Council of 22 October 2014 amending Directive 2013/34/EU as regards disclosure of non-financial and diversity information by certain large undertakings and groups. Retrieved March 20, 2021, from https://eur-lex.europa.eu/legal-content/EN/TXT/?uri=CELEX%3A32014L0095

Eckert, D. (2018). *Die EU lähmt dem deutschen Mittelstand, Die Welt* [Online, February 26, 2018] Retrieved February 17, 2020 from https://www.welt.de/wirtschaft/article173842543/Dem-deutschen-Mittelstand-droht-die-Luft-auszugehen.html

EC. (2018). *2018 SBA Fact Sheet Germany*. European Commission: Belgium.

Elsas, R., & Krahnen, J. P. (1998). Is relationship lending special? Evidence from credit-file data in Germany. *Journal of Banking and Finance, 22*(10), 1283–1316.

EnBW (2018). Integrated Annual Report 2018. https://www.enbw.com/enbw_com/bericht/bericht_2018/downloads/integrated-annual-report-2018.pdf

EY. (2020). *Mittelstandsbarometer. Befragungsergebnisse 2020*. Retrieved February 17, 2020 from https://assets.ey.com/content/dam/ey-sites/ey-com/de_de/news/2020/01/ey-mittelstandsbarometer-januar-2020.pdf

Flower, J. (2015). The integrated reporting council: A story of failure. *Critical Perspectives on Accounting, 27*, 1–15.

Gamerschlag, R., Möller, K., & Verbeeten, F. (2011). Determinants of voluntary CSR disclosure: Empirical evidence from Germany. *Review of Management Science, 5*, 233–262.

Goldshteyn, M. & Thelen, S. (2016). *Praxishandbuch digitale Betriebsprüfung*, Stuttgart.

Graßmann, M., Krannich, T., Günther, T., & Günther, E. (2018). Die nichtfinanziellen Erklärungen der DAX30-Unternehmen – Eine empirische Analyse der Berichterstattung über die Umweltbelange nach § 289c Abs.2 Nr. 1 HGB. *Zeitschrifüt für internationale und kapitalmarktorientierte Rechnungslegung., 18*(10), 431–441.

Gulenko, M. (2018). Mandatory CSR Reporting - Literature review and future developments in Germany. *Sustainability Management Forum, 26*, 3–17.

Günther, E., Herrmann, J., & Lange, A. (2017). Hemmnisse der integrierten Berichterstattung: Warum entscheiden sich Unternehmen gegen die Umsetzung? *Zeitschrift für Corporate Governance, 12*(3), 131–136.

Habisch, A., Patelli, L., Pedrini, M., & Schwartz, C. (2011). Different talks with different folks: A comparative survey of stakeholder dialog in Germany, Italy, and the U.S. *Journal of Business Ethics, 100*, 381–404.

Hahn, R., Endenich, C., Reimsbach, D. & Wickert, C. (2018). What explains the "dormant" stage of management ideas: The case of integrated reporting. *Academy of Management Proceedings*.

Haller, A. (2015). Integrierte Berichterstattung im Mittelstand. In G. Fahrenschon, A. Kirchhoff, & D. Simmert (Eds.), *Mittelstand - Motor und Zukunft der deutschen Wirtschaft*. Wiesbaden: Springer Gabler.

Haller, A., & Fuhrmann, C. (2013). Die Lageberichterstattung deutscher Unternehmen im Lichte des "Integrated Reporting" – Erste empirische Erkenntnisse. *Zeitschrift für internationale und kapitalmarktorientierte Rechnungslegung., 13*(5), 243–251.

Hess, D. (2007). Social reporting and new governance regulation: The prospects of achieving corporate accountability through transparency. *Business Ethics Quarterly, 17*(3), 453–476.

Hoffmann, E., Dietsche, C., & Hobelsberger, C. (2018). Between mandatory and voluntary: Non-financial reporting by German companies. *Sustainability Management Forum, 26*, 47–63.

IKB (Deutsche Mittelstandsbank). (2020). *Lieferkettengesetz: Gefahr für den Mittelstand?*. Retrieved February 12, 2021 from https://www.ikb-blog.de/lieferkettengesetz-gefahr-fuer-den-mittelstand/

IÖW—Institut für ökologische Wirtschaftsforschung. (2018). *Deutsche Unternehmen vor der CSR-Berichtspflicht: Monitoring zur nichtfinanziellen Berichterstattung*. Retrieved February 14, 2021 from http://www.rankingnachhaltigkeitsberichte.de/data/ranking/user_upload/2015/Ranking_Nachhaltigkeitsberichte_2015_Ergebnisbericht.pdf

Kajüter, P., & Wirth, M. (2018). Praxis der nichtfinanziellen Berichterstattung nach dem CSR-RUG – Empirische Befunde für die DAX-Unternehmen. *Der Betrieb, 27–28*, 1605–1612.

Kindermann, D. (2020). The challenges of upward regulatory harmonization: The case of sustainability reporting in the European Union. *Regulation and Governance, 14*, 674–697.

Kirchhoff, S. (2000). Green business and blue angels. *Environmental and Resource Economics., 15*, 403–420.
Kirchhoff Consult. (2018). *Nachhaltig gut berichten. Studie zur aktuellen Nachhaltigkeitsberichtserstattung der 160 DAX-Unternehmen*. Retrieved January 4, 2020 from https://www.kirchhoff.de/fileadmin/20_Download/Studien/2018_KC-BDO_DAX-160-Studie_CSR-Reporting.pdf
Kirchhoff Consult. (2019). *Nachhaltig gut berichten! Verdrängt die CSR-Berichtspflicht die bisherige Nachhaltigkeitsberichtserstattung?* Retrieved January 4, 2020 from https://www.kirchhoff.de/fileadmin/2019_KC_BDO_DAX160-Studie_CSR-Reporting.pdf
Kling, P. (2018). GoBD und Archivierung aus IT-Sicht, *Düsseldorf*.
Krause, S. & Pellens, B. (Eds.) (2018). *Betriebswirtschaftliche Implikationen der digitalen Transformation*, Wiesbaden.
Lehr, U. & Lutz, C. (2016). German Energiewende - quo vadis? In R. Bardazzi, M.G. Pazienza & A. Tonini (Eds.), *European energy and climate security*. Lecture notes in energy, 31. Cham, Heidelberg: Springer International Publishing.
Lenger, S., Maniora, J., & Pott, C. (2019). Implikationen des CSR-Richtlinien-Umsetzungsgesetzes für den Mittelstand – Empirische Analyse der MDAX-Unternehmen. *WPg - Die Wirtschaftsprüfung, 14*, 779–789.
Nothelfer, R. (2017). *Financial accounting – Introduction to German GAAP with exercises*. Berlin: De Gruyter Oldenbourg.
Pielke, W. (2018). *Tax Compliance, Effektive Organisation der Einhaltung steuerlicher*. Wiesbaden: Pflichten.
PWC. (2014). *Integrated Reporting in Germany. The DAX 30 Benchmark Survey 2014*. Retrieved January 3, 2020 from https://www.pwc.de/de/rechnungslegung/assets/pwc-studie_integrated-reporting-bei-den-dax-30-unternehmen-langsam-aber-sicher-kommt-der-integrierte-bericht.pdf
PWC. (2016). *Integrated Reporting in Germany. The DAX 30 Benchmark Survey 2015*. Retrieved January 3, 2020 from https://www.pwc.de/de/rechnungslegung/assets/studie-integrated-reporting-2015.pdf
PWC. (2018). *Erstanwendung des CSR-Richtlinie-Umsetzungsgesetzes. Studie zur praktischen Umsetzung im DAX-160*. Retrieved January 3, 2020 from https://www.pwc.de/de/nachhaltigkeit/pwc-studie-csr-berichterstattung-2018.pdf
Rammer, C., Gottschalk, S., Peneder, M., Woerter, M., Stucki, T., & Arvanitis, S. (2017). Does energy policy hurt international competitiveness of firms? A comparative study for Germany. *Switzerland and Austria. Energy Policy, 109*, 154–180.
Reimsbach, D., Hahn, R., & Gürtürk, A. (2018). Integrated reporting and the assurance of sustainable information: An experimental study on professional investors' information processing. *European Accounting Review, 27*(3), 559–581.
Rosenow, J. (2013). The politics of the German CO_2-Building Rehabilitation Programme. *Energy Efficiency, 6*, 219–238.
Spiegel. (2021). *Große Koalition einigt sich auf Lieferkettengesetz*. Retrieved February 12, 2021 from https://www.spiegel.de/wirtschaft/unternehmen/koalition-einigt-sich-auf-lieferkettengesetz-a-4312009c-0875-4d74-90ca-f26a51711916
Statistisches Bundesamt. (2018). *Anzahl der Unternehmen in Deutschland nach Rechtsform und Anzahl der Beschäftigten im Jahr 2017*. Retrieved February 21, 2020 from https://de.statista.com/statistik/daten/studie/237346/umfrage/unternehmen-in-deutschland-nach-rechtsform-und-anzahl-der-beschaeftigten/
Statistisches Bundesamt. (2020). *Investitionsfinanzierung. Verteilung der Finanzierungsquellen von mittelständischen Unternehmen in Deutschland von 2006 bis* 2018. Retrieved February 17, 2020 from https://de.statista.com/statistik/daten/studie/261431/umfrage/finanzierungsquellen-von-mittelstaendischen-unternehmen-in-deutschland/
Tagesschau. (2020). *Novelle des EEG: Deutschland, Land der aufgehenden Sonne*. Retrieved February 12, 2021 from https://www.tagesschau.de/wirtschaft/technologie/eeg-solarenergie-101.html

Umweltbundesamt. (2020a). *Umweltbewusstsein und Umweltverhalten*. Retrieved February 18, 2020 from https://www.umweltbundesamt.de/daten/private-haushalte-konsum/umweltbewusstsein-umweltverhalten#stellenwert-des-umwelt-und-klimaschutzes.

Umweltbundesamt. (2020b). *Umwelteinstellungen in Deutschland von 1971 bis 2019. Zeitreihenanalyse anhand externer Datenquellen*. Retrieved February 18, 2021 from https://www.umweltbundesamt.de/sites/default/files/medien/479/publikationen/texte_103-2020_umwelteinstellungen_in_deutschland_von_1971_bis_2019_0.pdf

Weidner, H. (2020). Ups and downs in environmental policy: Japan and Germany in comparison. In L. Mez, L. Okamura, & H. Weidner (Eds.), *The ecological modernization capacity of Japan and Germany. Energiepolitik und Klimaschutz. Energy policy and climate protection* (pp. 25–40). Wiesbaden: Springer.

Zhou, S., Simnett, R., & Green, W. (2017). Does integrated reporting matter to the capital market? *Abacus, 53*(1), 94–132.

Zinnecker, S. (2014). *Mittelstandsanleihen: Börse Stuttgart beerdigtden den Mittelstandsmarkt*. Handelsblatt [Online, December 11, 2014]. Retrieved February 17, 2020 from https://www.handelsblatt.com/finanzen/maerkte/anleihen/mittelstandsanleihen-boerse-stuttgart-beerdigt-den-mittelstandsmarkt/11109590.html?ticket=ST-5823427- XdYkisBxw54faubJAeK6-ap1

SMEs and IR: Evidence from Hungary

Andrea Madarasi-Szirmai, Miklós Losoncz, Zsuzsanna Győri, Judit Sági, and Szilárd Hegedűs

1 The SME Sector in Hungary

Hungary defines SMEs using the standard criteria provided by the European Union. The definition is stipulated in Law No. XXXIV of 2004 on the SMEs and on the support of their development. An SME is an enterprise with fewer than 250 employees and an annual turnover not exceeding EUR 50 million or the balance sheet EUR 43 million. The capital or voting rights share the state or any local government holds, either directly or indirectly and either solely or jointly, is not more than 25%. In terms of employment, entities with no more than 49 employees qualify as small enterprises. Within this category, micro-enterprises employ less than ten persons, whereas medium-sized ones have 50–249 employees.

In 2018, SMEs generated 54.1% of Hungary's GDP (slightly less than the EU average according to Table 1) and accounted for 68.3% of employment (somewhat more than the EU average).

Labour productivity of Hungarian SMEs reached more than 50% of the level of large companies. There are considerable differences in the productivity levels of domestic firms and companies with foreign participation. Hungarian-owned firms, particularly SMEs, have not benefited too much until recently from the inflow of foreign direct investments and the domestic activity of foreign firms in terms of higher sales, employment or productivity. The promotion of productivity growth by the government has to address the gap between the two company segments.

Regarding international comparisons, based on EUROSTAT figures, labour productivity of Hungarian enterprises defined as the ratio of value added at factor

A. Madarasi-Szirmai (✉) · M. Losoncz · Z. Győri · J. Sági · S. Hegedűs
Faculty of Finance and Accountancy, Budapest Business School, University of Applied Sciences, Budapest, Hungary
e-mail: szirmai.andrea@uni-bge.hu; losoncz.miklos@uni-bge.hu; Gyori.Zsuzsanna@uni-bge.hu; Sagi.Judit@uni-bge.hu; hegedus.szilard@uni-bge.hu

J. Dyczkowska et al. (eds.), *Development of Integrated Reporting in the SME Sector*, CSR, Sustainability, Ethics & Governance,
https://doi.org/10.1007/978-3-030-81903-3_3

Table 1 Basic figures on Hungary's corporate sector according to size in comparison with the EU average in 2018

	Number of enterprises			Number of persons employed			Value added		
	Hungary		EU	Hungary		EU	Hungary		EU
Class size	Number	Share	Share	Number	Share	Share	Billion €	Share	Share
Micro	548,744	94.1%	93.0%	908,108	32.6%	29.7%	13.0	18.7%	20.8%
Small	28,514	4.9%	5.9%	532,675	19.1%	20.1%	11.9	17.2%	17.6%
Medium-sized	4669	0.8%	0.9%	459,153	16.5%	16.8%	12.7	18.3%	18.0%
SMEs	**581,927**	**99.8%**	**99.8%**	**1899.936**	**68.3%**	**66.6%**	**37.7**	**54.1%**	**56.4%**
Large	990	0.2%	0.2%	882,138	31.7%	33.4%	31.9	45.9%	43.6%
Total	582,917	100.0%	100.0%	2782.074	100.0%	100.0%	69.6	100.0%	100.0%

These are estimates for 2018 produced by DIV Econ, based on 2008–2016 figures from the Structural Business Statistics Database (EUROSTAT). The data cover the "non-financial business economy", which includes industry, construction, trade and services (NACE Rev. 2 sections B to J, L, M and N), but not enterprises in agriculture, forestry, fisheries and the largely non-market service sectors such as education and health. The following size-class definitions are applied: micro-firms (0–9 persons employed), small firms (10–49 persons employed), medium-sized firms (50–249 persons employed), and large firms (250+ persons employed). The advantage of using EUROSTAT data is that statistics are harmonized and comparable across countries. The disadvantage is that for some countries the data may be different from those published by national authorities

Source: EC (2019, p. 2)

costs in euro and the number of employed amounted to 41.6% of German companies in 2019. Since 2015, labour productivity growth has been well below real wage growth, resulting in higher unit labour costs. Nevertheless, the gradual depreciation of the Hungarian currency counterweighted somewhat the loss in international competitiveness caused by rapid wage increases. Furthermore, companies with foreign stake calculating their costs in euro benefit from the depreciation of the Hungarian forint.

In 2019, the share of high-tech manufacturing and knowledge-intensive services of SMEs in value added at factor costs was 29% in Hungary, lower than the 34% German figure. No data are available on the ownership breakdown of SMEs. It can be assumed without exaggeration that SMEs with foreign participation are the flagships of high-tech manufacturing and knowledge-intensive services in Hungary (EC, 2019).

The general state of affairs in the SME sector is highlighted by the SBA Fact Sheets of the European Commission. According to the implementation of the Small Business Act (SBA) for Europe, Hungary's performance in the reference period ranging from 2017 to the first quarter of 2018 was evident in the fields of state aid and public procurement, access to finance and the single market. Nevertheless, it was "below the EU average for entrepreneurship and 'responsive administration' and significantly below the EU average for skills & innovation, internationalisation, environment, and 'second chance'" (EC, 2018). In the subsequent reference period between 2018 and the first quarter of 2019, Hungary's performance relative to the EU average did not change significantly except for minor improvements in entrepreneurship and a small decline in state aid and public procurement and for the single market in spite of the fact that the government addressed eight out of the ten policy areas under the Small Business Act (EC, 2019).

In the 2019 European Innovation Scoreboard, Hungary is a moderate innovator. The share of SMEs accomplishing innovation is half the EU average. Regarding innovative firms, small-scale innovation is still dominant. The major challenge for Hungarian SMEs is to introduce more innovative products and services in the market. This will certainly contribute to the increasing supply of higher value added products and services and the improvement of productivity. The Hungarian supplier programme responded to this challenge, but it is still in the initial phase.

Although Hungary meets the major SBA principles in SME internationalization, it is still behind the EU average. The major reason for this is the shortage of exporting capacities and the lack of foreign language knowledge of the staff.

The Non-Financial Reporting Directive (NFRD) of the EU created the appropriate legal environment for sustainability, CSR and GRI reports. However, the scope of the SBA overview does not cover accounting and business reports. Nevertheless, with measures undertaken to lower the administrative burden for SMEs (3.3 "Responsive administration" in the SBA Fact Sheets), the possibilities of preparing <IR> have become more favourable. The implementation of the SBA, too, requires a broader context in the operation and development of SMEs that are in line with the latter and the spirit of <IR>.

2 Overview of Reporting Regulations with Potential Impact on IR

In Hungary, accounting and bookkeeping are regulated by Act C of 2000 on Accounting and some additional explanatory legal rules issued by the Ministry of Finance. Act C of 2000 shall apply to all economic entities. However, as exceptions it shall not apply to:

- private entrepreneurs (sole proprietors),
- civil law associations,
- building groups,
- the Hungarian commercial representation offices of foreign-registered companies.

"Economic entity" in the law denotes undertakings, government agencies, other organizations, the National Bank of Hungary and healthcare, social and educational institutions created by the prior or by natural persons.

"Company" denotes in the law all economic entities that are engaged in regular business operations—whether production or service—for consideration, in their own name and at their own risk for the purpose of acquiring profits or accumulating assets. The term "Company" includes credit institutions, financial enterprises, investment firms and insurance companies as well as non-profit business associations, professional associations, social cooperatives, school cooperatives, European Economic Interest Groupings, European public limited liability companies, European cooperative societies, water management associations, forest management organizations and Hungarian branches of foreign-registered companies, other than government agencies and other organizations.[1]

Types of Financial Statements

1. IFRS for consolidation and individual FS,
2. Consolidated FS,
3. Annual financial statements,
4. Simplified annual financial statements,
5. Simplified financial statements for micro-entities.

2.1 The Use of IFRS

As a member of the EU, Hungary's law is in accordance with European Commission (EC) Regulation No. 1606/2002, which requires the application of IFRS in the

[1] In this report, synonyms of company include enterprise, undertaking and firm without implying any value judgement.

preparation of consolidated financial statements of listed companies. Companies must annually produce a balance sheet, a profit and loss account and an appendix.

Hungarian Accounting Standards are supplemented by government decrees based on special requirements for banks, insurance companies, stockbrokers, investment funds, pension funds and various non-profit institutions.

From 2016 on, companies whose shares are traded in a regulated market of any European Economic Area member state shall prepare their individual financial statements in accordance with IFRS. In Hungary, the number of the listed entities that shall apply this rule totals appr. 50.

As of 1 January 2018, credit institutions and other financial enterprises subject to prudential regulations equivalent to those applicable to credit institutions shall prepare their individual financial statements under IFRS. The number of financial institutions that shall apply this provision is appr. 50 entities. Some of the financial institutions are listed entities as well.

The following entities may prepare their individual financial statements in accordance with IFRS (Paragraph 9/A of Act C of 2000 on Accounting):

1. whose direct or indirect parent company prepares its consolidated financial statements in accordance with IFRS,
2. insurance companies,
3. where the company is obliged for statutory audit that is if the entity's net sales revenue is higher than HUF300 million or the number of employees exceeds 50 in two consecutive years before the actual business year,
4. financial enterprises, payment institutions, electronic money issuers, investment enterprises, the central securities depository, the central counterparty, the stock exchange, employer pension schemes, financial market intermediaries and insurance intermediaries included in the consolidated financial statements prepared in accordance with IFRS based on the parent company's decision and funds and fund managers subject to the Act on Collective Investment Trusts and their Managers and on the Amendment of Certain Financial Regulations operating under the supervision of the National Bank of Hungary acting in its capacity as the supervisor of the financial intermediary system,
5. Hungarian branches of enterprises registered abroad.

Until the end of 2019, 254 companies were registered to prepare their individual financial statements under IFRS.

2.2 Local Consolidated Financial Statements

A consolidated annual report and a consolidated business report are required by any business that qualifies as a parent company in its association with one or more businesses, except if any of two values of the following three limits are not exceeded in two consecutive years on the balance sheet date prior to the business year:

- balance sheet total: HUF 6 thousand million,
- annual net revenue: HUF 12 thousand million,
- the average number of employees during the business year: 250.

(Paragraph 117 of Act C of 2000 on Accounting)

Hungarian accounting regulations include several exemptions from the preparation of consolidated financial statements. Furthermore, IFRS serves both individual and consolidated financial reporting purposes. Consequently, consolidation according to the Hungarian Act C of 2000 on Accounting is not widely applied.

2.3 Local Annual and Simplified Annual Financial Statements

The annual financial statements consist of the balance sheet, the income statement and the supplementary notes. A business report must also be prepared simultaneously with the financial statements, but it shall not be published together with the other elements of the financial statements.

A company using double-entry bookkeeping may prepare a simplified annual report if any of two values of the following three limits are not exceeded in two consecutive years on the balance sheet date:

- balance sheet total: HUF 1200 million,
- annual net revenue: HUF 2400 million,
- the average number of employees during the business year: 50.

(Paragraph 9 (1–5) of Act C of 2000 on Accounting)

The structure of the simplified annual report's balance sheet, the income statement and the supplementary notes is not required to be too detailed. The balance sheet and the income statement present the main categories of these documents and do not provide information on the lines and items within the main categories. The details should be included in the supplementary notes. Nevertheless, according to our research, the quality and usefulness of notes are rather low in terms of detailedness, accuracy and transparency. This type of annual report—according to the regulations—does not contain cash flow statement and business report.

2.4 Local Simplified Financial Statements for Micro-entities

This type of financial statement can be an option for a company if it is not obliged for statutory audit and meets two of the following three criteria on the balance sheet day in two consecutive business years:

Table 2 Size-related accounting regulations and requirements

	Micro	Small	Medium	Large
Time period for preparing financial statements—date of publishing FS	5 months from the balance sheet date for individual FS 6 months from the consolidated balance sheet date for consolidated FS (Paragraph153 (1–2) of Act C of 2000 on Accounting)			
Audit of financial statements	Statutory audit is not obligatory if the following two criteria meet based on the previous two years' data: • net sales revenue is less than HUF 300 million (appr. EUR 900,000) • the number of employees is less than 50 Audit is obligatory independently of the size in the case of: • any of other act requires the audit • public interest companies • savings cooperatives • companies involved in consolidation • foreign companies' branch offices (Paragraph 155 (1) of Act C of 2000 on Accounting)			
Structure of balance sheet and income statement	Simplified financial statements for micro-entities: not detailed	Simplified financial statements: less detailed		Annual financial statements: detailed
Information disclosed in notes	Not required	Relief		Full requirements
Publishing, disclosure requirement	Upload on e-Company information the full financial statement and the audit report (if the company was audited), and the owners' decision on the acceptance of the financial statement and dividend payment.			

Source: Compilation of the authors based on relevant Hungarian legal rules

- Total assets may not exceed HUF 100 million,
- Annual net sales may not exceed HUF 200 million,
- The average number of employees in the business year may not exceed 10.

(Paragraph 9 (6–10) of Act C of 2000 on Accounting)

In this type of report, there are more simplifications in terms of presentation and valuation compared to the simplified annual report. No supplementary notes and business reports are required to present to this type of financial statement. It means that published data mainly meet requirements of taxation with only very basic accounting and financial information on the company. It is not suitable for conducting deeper analysis, understanding the business and getting an overall view on the company.

Since 94.1% of SMEs are micro-entities, the major part of Hungarian SMEs could prepare this type of report. It is an astonishing fact that according to the statistical data of the Hungarian Court of Registration, 95–97% of Hungarian companies publish either simplified annual financial statements or financial statements for micro-entities. Consequently, published figures of these companies are available, but explanations, information and other relevant data about their business conditions, strengths, risks, etc., are not (Table 2).

2.5 Non-financial Information in Financial Statements

EU law requires large companies to disclose certain information on the ways they operate and manage social and environmental challenges even if they do not issue proper non-financial reports outlined above. The provision of such information is meant to help stakeholders to evaluate the non-financial performance of large companies and encourage these enterprises to develop a responsible approach to business. Based on the principles of <IR>, the European Commission's guidelines on the implementation of Directive, 2014/95/EU encourage businesses to adapt their existing reporting to this directive in order to reflect the broader, long-term vision of their company and to give an account of both the resources they are using and their relationships (Eurosif, 2018).

According to the data of the Hungarian Central Statistical Office (HCSO), the share of companies other than SMEs (in other words large corporations) amounted to 0.87% of the total in 2019. In the light of this number and the Hungarian accounting regulation on different reporting formats, it can be concluded that a very small fraction of Hungarian companies disclose annual reports. The overwhelming part of firms publishes simplified annual reports or micro-financial statements.

Thus, non-financial information released by Hungarian firms covers only a tiny segment of the relevant corporate sector. The share of companies preparing annual financial statements (reports) is about 5% of the total. From the perspective of published non-financial information, the above-mentioned 5% represent even fewer firms since according to Act C of 2000 on Accounting, companies with public interest shall submit non-financial information in their financial statements.

Paragraph 95/C of Act 2000 C on Accounting whose modification was passed by Hungary's Parliament at the end of 2016 defines—in compliance with Directive, 2014/95/EU on the disclosure of non-financial and diversity information by certain large undertakings and groups—the criteria of the categorization of public interest entities based on their total assets, net sales revenues, and average number of employees. If such economic entities reach the relevant threshold criteria in their annual business reports, they have to publish non-financial statements containing as extensive information as necessary for understanding the company's development, performance and the position and the impact of its activity relating to environmental, social and employee issues, respect for human rights, and anti-corruption and bribery matters as a minimum requirement (while concurrently respecting business and trade secrets).

There are other legal rules that regulate the classification of public interest entities. Accordingly, public interest entities are classified as any of the following: entities trading their securities on a regulated market of any Member State of the European Economic Area, credit and insurance institutions, investment firms and the investment management companies of issuers of investment units (Table 3).

The financial statements of these companies are audited by external auditors; thus, the information and data contained therein are verified.

Table 3 Number of public interest entities companies in Hungary in 2017

Public interest entities	Number
Credit/financial institutions	51
Investment firms	16
Insurance companies	22
Listed entities	43
Total	132

Source: Hungarian Ministry of National Economy (MNE, 2018)

Such non-financial statements of public interest companies shall minimally contain the following:

- A brief description of the company's business model.
- A description of the policies and the outcomes of the policies pursued by the company in relation to environmental, social and employee matters, respect for human rights, anti-corruption and bribery matters, including implemented due diligence processes.
- A description of the principal risks related to the company's operations and the management of these risks including its business relationships, products or services in relation to environmental, social and employee matters.
- Non-financial key performance indicators relevant to the particular business.

This reporting scheme is compulsory for defined companies. It may have implications for other undertakings by offering a list of topics that could be discussed in non-financial and other reports.

Although non-financial statements/disclosures are not equal to non-financial reports (in terms of their quality or quantity of data), the EU—with the help of the directive—again expressed the significance of non-financial performance and sustainability impacts characterizing business life. "There has been strong growth in CR reporting across a number of EU countries. While the full effect of the EU Non-Financial Reporting Directive is not expected to be felt for another two years or so, it is possible that awareness of the Directive has helped to boost reporting rates in some EU countries. In line with the Directive, companies that do not disclose their social, environmental and Board diversity policies can be named publicly. This risk of reputational damage may already have convinced some non-reporters to start reporting with more expected to follow suit" (KPMG, 2017, p. 16).

Voluntary Corporate Reporting Regulations in Hungary that May Affect IR

In Hungary, voluntary corporate reporting is associated mostly with corporate social responsibility (CSR). Based on his quantitative and qualitative studies, Bank (2017) indicates that multinationals and large state-owned companies are the most active entities as far as explicit CSR is concerned, and they also play an important role in creating patterns for Hungarian CSR. In the case of local affiliates of large multinationals, initiatives come very often from the parent companies. However, even multinationals do not generally have dedicated budgets or strategies for CSR in Hungary. CSR can be part of the basic strategy of the parent company, but in practice it is often not a serious issue at Hungarian subsidiaries. CSR activities still tend to be ad hoc, depending on the situation, and are often shaped by the leader of the company. HPRA (2017) also indicates that only 40% of large companies and 20% of SMEs have developed CSR strategies. Among others, personal values and leaders' level of altruism can have fundamental influence on corporations' CSR activities (Benedek, 2017).

Besides the expectations of the parent companies, other foreign actors, such as competitors, international organizations with their voluntary regulations (UN, GRI, ISO, CSR Europe, WBCSD) and potential or existing investors, have been the main motivators for CSR initiatives. Nevertheless, the role of the government is significant as well: the Hungarian government published its National CSR Action Plan according to the EU requirements in 2015.

The provision of non-financial information of various foci can be presented in several diverse ways. Companies can produce non-financial reports under different names (e.g. environmental report, HSE report, sustainability report and CSR report). These names indicate the widening of the concept of non-financial performance and CSR. When companies first started to publish stand-alone non-financial reports more than twenty years ago, such reports focused on environmental (emission and discharge, waste management) and on health and safety (injuries, fatalities) issues. As the concept of sustainable development gained ground, the content of these reports also changed in reflection to this (Corporate Register, 2013). Since 1997, when the Global Reporting Initiative (GRI) was established, more efforts have been made for the improvement of the accountability and the harmonization of content in non-financial reports. Today, there is a larger credibility of GRI reports in Hungary as well.

Based on the 2017 report of BCSDH, environmental responsibility and sustainability remain the most important focus areas in Hungary (81% of the companies claimed to be engaged in such issues), followed by the strategic approach. Connected to environmental focus, 71% of the companies operate environmental management systems (30% of them has ISO 50001), 63% have carbon reduction strategies, but only 21% cooperate with suppliers on sustainability initiatives. Summarizing Hungarian CSR research in the last decade, Géring (2015) points out that, next to environmental directives, issues connected to employees and employer branding are also significant. Other studies also indicate that gender initiatives and family-friendly practices are the most frequent internal initiatives (HPRA, 2017), which are sometimes coupled with employment programmes for people with disabilities (Csillag et al., 2018). In addition, Csutora et al. (2014) note that diversity issues less frequently appear in CSR practice in Hungary than in the international sample used for their research.

Companies operating in Hungary claim that the government has an important role in encouraging CSR activities, especially by providing economic incentives (HPRA, 2017). 52% of Hungarian companies believe that the government and legal regulations have the strongest influence on corporate operation (the global figure is 15%), while other stakeholders (such as consumers, clients, employees and competitors) exert much weaker influence. At the same time, 70% of Hungarian companies believe that balancing between the interests of different stakeholders is the mission of companies (BCSDH, 2016). Bank (2017) concludes that NGOs' presence and influence are much weaker in Hungary than in Western Europe and that their role in society is marginal, so they cannot contribute to the spread of CSR. For instance, the Hungarian Association of Conscious Consumers has been aiming to support and strengthen sustainable and responsible consumption and corporate operations since 2002, but consumers' decisions are still driven by price, quality and other factors of self-interest (Braun and Partners, 2011). Companies claimed that the main reason why they do not prepare non-financial reporting is that nobody requests such documents (BCSDH, 2016). Csutora et al. (2014) also conclude that society does not have much influence on CSR because community involvement and participative methods in sustainability management do not have a long tradition in Hungary. The paternalistic legacy of the previous socio-political regime still has an impact on current attitudes towards stakeholder involvement (Bodorkós & Pataki, 2009).

Based on her quantitative research, Rátz-Putzer (2015) claims that the majority of companies still consider CSR only a communication tool and use it merely for positioning themselves in a more favourable light. Csutora et al. (2014) maintain the view that in Hungary external communication on environmental and social activities (e.g. sustainability reporting) and on environmental and social-oriented cost management (e.g. using cost-effective recycling products) lags behind external communication in other countries. Pataki et al. (2015) examined the online CSR communication of ten large companies and pointed out credibility problems especially in retail trade, telecommunications and construction.

3 National Factors Enabling or Constraining IR

3.1 Political Factors

HBLF (2012) results indicate that in Hungary—similarly to other transitional economies—the codes of ethics and ethical institutions are underdeveloped. The main purpose of the existing codes is to provide guidelines for employees, declare ethical commitment and develop corporate cultures. Emphasis is usually laid on protecting the interests of companies. Other factors, such as meeting the expectations of stakeholders and improving the competitive positions of the company play insignificant role (contrary to the findings of Géring (2015)), also suggest that the formalization of CSR practices is uneven. Furthermore, HPRA (2017) indicates that objectives and key performance indicators (KPIs) connected to CSR are not part of the performance evaluation systems.

Small companies are not required to prepare management reports based on Article 19 of the NFRD. There is no obligation for medium-sized companies to prepare management reports either, but on their own initiative, they may do so. Medium-sized companies are exempted from attaching non-financial performance information to their management reports if they compile such documents at all (for further details, see European Federation of Accountants and Auditors for SMEs 2018).

Small-sized and particularly medium-sized companies may typically feel like preparing CSR and sustainability reports if they are involved in global value chains or simple supplying relations of TNCs (transnational corporations) or large companies with foreign participation. Nevertheless, for the time being this practice is rather scarce in Hungary. Large corporations request from their SME partners various certificates that prove their relevant competencies, abilities to perform and quality, ecological and social standards. Although their objectives are different, some of these certificates may be considered a certain kind of substitutes for CSR and sustainability reports. In fact, few companies are involved in <IR> and produce GRI documents.

Concerning a shift towards <IR>, the Hungarian regulatory environment is neither supportive nor restrictive. The most adequate qualification could be it is permissive. The possibilities are open, i.e. it is up to the companies to make use of existing opportunities. Regulators might have assumed that companies act on their own interests, and therefore did not consider explicit legal enforcement essential or necessary. This assumption does not consider the fact that, first, many SMEs are not aware of the importance of integrated thinking and, second, the switch to <IR> would impose additional burden on them. The latter factor may have been exaggerated. Nevertheless, along with the efforts of the government to promote the internationalization of SMEs, sooner or later the necessity will arise for them to be involved in <IR>. The lack of the complex approach of <IR> will certainly limit the development possibilities of SMEs, particularly if <IR> becomes organic element in the operation of businesses. According to our knowledge, for the time being, no profound changes are on the horizon in relevant Hungarian legislation and policies. In addition, the principle-based approach of <IR> is hardly compatible with the rule-based preferences of the Hungarian government. The application of rules can be enforced more easily by legal means than that of principles. Companies, too, are much more prone to abide legal rules than to apply principles.

3.2 Economic Factors

As a small country integrated deeply into the world economy, Hungary's exposure and dependency on global economic and political development trends are outstandingly high. For the time being, Hungary is facing several short- and medium-term external and internal challenges. The general external environment of the Hungarian economy is becoming gloomier than before with negative implications for economic growth.

In the short term, external challenges associated with global trends in general and the spread of the COVID-19 pandemic in particular. The lockdowns introduced to contain the pandemic triggered severe recession in 2020 in almost all countries of the world including Hungary, and due to its recent third wave, the pace of the recovery in 2021 is uncertain, despite the pickup of vaccination. Financial sources of the Next Generation EU (NGEU) fund allocated for Hungary may ease the aftermath of the recession caused by the pandemic in the second half of 2021 the earliest.

The pandemic has weighed heavily on business and consumer expectations. In Hungary, car manufacturing and the tourist industry are most exposed to the deterioration of the external environment in general and the consequences of the COVID-19 pandemic in particular.

In the medium term, one of the major challenges Hungary is facing is the structural transformation of the global motor industry with the diffusion of electric cars in both production and consumption. Hungarian car manufacturing based on assembly work commissioned by foreign companies with local affiliates accounts for about one third of industrial output and is only partially prepared for meeting the challenge of global transformation. This concerns not only foreign manufacturers, but also their local suppliers with the inclusion of SMEs as well.

Internal challenges are not negligible either. As a consequence of the strong domestic cyclical recovery since 2017 and the growing outflow of skilled workforce to find jobs in more developed EU countries, labour shortage has appeared and became acute in the domestic economy constraining investments and limiting the possibilities of firms in general and SMEs in particular to raise output. The shortage of qualified labour force has been particularly pressing. In spite of the anti-immigration rhetoric of the government, the employment of foreign workers (mostly from Ukraine) has been easing the labour shortage to some extent, mainly in construction. With the COVID-19 pandemic, unemployment increased particularly in the service sector (tourism, restaurants, entertainment, etc.), but structural unemployment has not disappeared.

In addition, cyclical recovery and labour shortage have generated significant wage increases. Hungarian SMEs were particularly hard handicapped by labour shortage and first of all by surging wages. Due to their limited financial resources and reserves as well as lower productivity level, they cannot raise wages as dynamically as large companies. Large firms syphon off their employees, thereby exacerbating their difficulties. The combination of skilled labour shortage and high wages is the most pronounced challenge SMEs are facing in Hungary. To remain more competitive, many SMEs may opt for paying wages and salaries with the avoidance of the tax system. This practice goes against government efforts to whiten the economy. In the macroeconomic context, labour shortage and wage increases are eroding Hungary's comparative advantages for foreign companies based on low labour costs. The introduction of <IR> may improve the position of SMEs in terms of attracting skilled labour and foreign investors. Nevertheless, consequences of the pandemic such as rising unemployment and part-time employment eased the wage pressure temporarily.

Another internal challenge is related to the next Multiannual Financial Framework (MFF) of the EU. From 2021 to 2027, transfers from the common budget of the EU are expected to total about 4% of Hungary's GDP. In the medium term, disbursements of EU funds to beneficiary countries are tied to the predominance of the rule of law. With Hungary's bad performance in corruption, conditioned disbursements would imply significant risks in obtaining the previously allocated funds. SMEs could benefit much from any reduction in the corruption level.

Nevertheless, both the NGEU scheme and the MFF with their priorities focused on combatting climate change and achieving sustainability may open new chances to SMEs to absorb additional funds for investments.

3.3 Social Factors

Sustainability and climate awareness have been rather low in Hungary's public. With the gradual upgrading of these issues, the state of the art tends to undergo significant changes. We expect that sustainability and climate, including the environment consciousness of households and shifts in consumer behaviour towards the manufacture of environment-friendly goods, will get more attention in the future with positive implications for corporate reporting in general and reporting of SMEs in particular. This focus, together with the meeting of ESG (environmental, social and governance) criteria, will be underpinned by the funds of the NGEU and the MFF. The general public mood associated with sustainability and climate reinforced by adequate government policies may induce undertakings to adapt <IR> in their business models in order to demonstrate that they are ready to meet relevant expectations. The spread of this kind of attitude does not need strict legal regulations, and it can take place on the basis of general principles.

3.4 Cultural Factors

Hungarian SMEs in general and family business in particular are rather non-transparent. Their general approach is to disclose as few information to external stakeholders as possible. They fear not so much of their competitors, but of government institutions in general, and the National Tax and Customs Authority (NTCA) in particular. Until recently, the majority of Hungarian SMEs counterweighted the tax preferences enjoyed by large corporations through the involvement in the unobserved economy (disbursing wages in the "pocket" by avoiding the payment of taxes and social contributions on employees and value added tax, etc.).

In addition, Hungarian SMEs, including family businesses, are not interested in corporate growth in general and crossing corporate size thresholds in particular. It is not attractive to change corporate size, i.e. turning small undertakings into more transparent medium-sized firms in terms of taxation and employment. Managing a medium-sized company requires the employment of professional managers. Owners of family businesses are reluctant to transfer certain key competencies to "outsiders", and to pay them high salaries even if these costs will come back in the long term. For medium-sized enterprises, it is much more difficult to avoid taxation and to be involved in the shadow or grey or unobserved economy. With the change in corporate size, the costs of employment rise disproportionally compared to small entities. Medium-sized companies are facing more stringent operational rules in terms of quality, reporting, etc., than small or micro-firms.

The latest government measures, such as the connection of cash registers to the NTCA and the continuous control of road transport by electronic means and other trust-enhancing measures, are considered successful steps to limit the size of the unobserved economy and establish a more open regulatory environment. With reduced possibilities to operate in a non-transparent way combined with changed public attitudes, SMEs could be more inclined to accept openness in reporting.

Progress in organizational culture can contribute to the development of SMEs. One of the best practices initiated by the government concerns the Hungarian National Tax and Customs Authority. The aim of its mentoring programme is to educate SMEs. The NTCA first warns SMEs, rather than punish them, if they make mistakes in their tax declarations. This is very helpful to prevent SMEs from making similar mistakes in the future.

The objective of the national entrepreneurship programme is to provide personal and professional mentoring services for SMEs and improve their financial and entrepreneurial attitude. The mentoring programme embraces all the broad target group categories of SMEs, such as female and young entrepreneurs, firms close to generation change and SMEs aiming at internationalization and becoming suppliers.

3.5 Technological Factors

The supplier development programme of the Hungarian government aims to raise the competitiveness of SMEs by promoting their cooperation with large corporations in Hungary and abroad. Involvement in the programme enables SMEs to become integrated into the supply chains of TNCs. With the help of this programme, Hungarian SMEs become familiar with the technical, technological and quality requirements (including Industry 4.0 and its applications) of TNCs posted to potential and actual SME suppliers.

In 2018, Hungary ranked 23rd out of the 28 EU member states in the 2018 Digital Economy and Society Index (DESI) ranking. Most of the Hungarian SMEs have not yet recognized the business potential involved in digitization. To help them, government measures must address the mindset of the management and thereby promote to understand the importance of digitization. The Hungarian government launched two programmes to reach about 7000–8000 SMEs in cohesion regions and encourage them to develop a more advanced use of ICTs. The Digital Welfare Program introduced at the end of 2015 and its upgraded 2.0 version inaugurated in 2017 envisaged funds to digitize SMEs and thereby to improve their competitiveness in the value of HUF 7.5 billion. One company may request HUF10 million—HUF 500 million for digitization, depending on size.

Although the submission of company reports takes place electronically, further digitization may create more favourable conditions for SMEs to turn to <IR>. More extensive information sources and more appropriate analytical means will be available to them to support the application of <IR>.

4 Empirical Evidence on <IR> in Hungary

The first Hungarian non-financial report was issued in 1996 by MOL Hungarian Oil and Gas Company and that very company was also the one to issue the first integrated report in 2008. Nonetheless, the IIRC framework was not applied. The term “integrated report” referred to the fact that the financial and non-financial reports of the company were published in one document. Genuine integrated reports combine the financial and non-financial disclosures indicating a higher level of sustainability engagement on the part of the company in question.

After the international financial and economic crisis of 2008–2009, a significant decrease took place in the number of non-financial reports issued in Hungary. The explanation for this could be decreasing stakeholder demand and budgetary cuts. The proportion of externally audited reports fell as well, but there was an overall improvement in the use of GRI (sustainability.hu, 2019). In 2014, 39 companies prepared some kind of sustainability report, and in 2017, the same figure was 28 (the peek number was 71 in 2009).

However, according to a KPMG study, Hungary is one of the countries where the CSR reporting rate is higher than the global average (89% versus 72%). Although in 2015 84% of the companies under the scope of the Directive, 2014/95/EU on disclosure of non-financial and diversity information published CSR reports, in 2017 their share fell to as low as 77% (KPMG, 2017).

In 2017, 2014 GRI reports were published in Europe: out of this 28 by Hungarian companies. From the 28 published reports, 8 was prepared by transnational corporations, 14 by large entities and 6 by SMEs. Sectors that published the majority of such reports include financial services (four reports), public agencies (three reports), energy and water utilities (three reports), telecommunications (two reports), food and beverage (two reports) and energy (two reports).[2]

In 2017, 2014 GRI reports were published in Europe: out of this 28 by Hungarian companies versions of their social responsibility policies or social and environmental reports. Although their Hungarian subsidiaries usually provide their parent companies with data for their global reports, there are few documents with relevant Hungarian topics and figures.

[2]GRI database: http://database.globalreporting.org/search/, 2019 Owing to the development of the website and the review of the database, the search function for the years 2018, 2019 and 2020 has been disabled since December 2020 until further notification.

An increasing number of organizations support IR all over the world including Europe. In Hungary, there is no official database on companies publishing integrated reports. Some of the companies, mainly TNCs and large corporations such as MOL Group (Hungarian Oil and Gas Company), Hungarian Telekom and public interest entities such as MVM Group (Hungarian Electric Utilities) prepare such reports.

4.1 Best Practices from Hungary in Integrated Reporting

In the first stage of our research aimed at identifying the pool of companies (large-, small- and medium-sized alike) preparing <IR>, we made a search in the IIRC database.[3] We limited the search to Europe and included all the three large items (guiding principles, fundamental concepts and content elements) of <IR> simultaneously. As a result, 36 reports of large companies came out of the database. Some companies published their reports more than one year before. After the adjustment for this, 33 corporations were left. Out of them, five TNCs (*British American Tobacco, Aegon, Generali, ING* and *Vodafone*) have affiliates in Hungary.

The parent companies of these TNCs do not allow their affiliated companies or subsidiaries to operate in Hungary as independent entities. These national entities may not present their operations, resources, etc., independently of their mother companies. The overall picture and the integrated thinking are relevant only at consolidated group level.

In the second stage of the research, we scrutinized the companies whose shares are listed in the *Budapest Stock Exchange* (BSE). Our first obvious finding was that no medium-sized companies are introduced in the BSE. Hungarian medium-sized undertakings are rather small to meet the introductory requirements. Consequently, they are also small by international standards. In addition, for reasons described in the above chapters, they are not interested in the transparency required by the BSE. Our second finding was that out of the 39 listed companies only two (*MOL Hungarian Oil and Gas Public Limited Company* and *OTP Bank*) published non-financial reports. MOL produced integrated reports and OTP Bank sustainability reports.

In the third stage, we turned to Moody's Amadeus database. This database contains non-financial companies with double-entry bookkeeping. Firms not included in this database are irrelevant for our research because they are too small to be interested in. We defined characteristics for medium-sized for-profit undertakings corresponding to the requirements of the project. From among the provisions of Act XXXIV of 2004 on small and medium enterprises, their support for development ("SME Law"), we considered those relating to employment (50–249 persons). The latest complete year of the database was 2017.

[3] http://examples.integratedreporting.org/leading_practices

Based on the factors described above, we received a sample of 3729 organizations. According to figures originating in the NTCA, they corresponded to 77.4% of the medium-sized companies that were active in Hungary in 2017.

Following this step, the companies of the obtained sample were allocated among the ten members of the Hungarian project team. Each member of the team selected five enterprises to scrutinize. The selection was based on the following factors:

- number of employees (50–249);
- industry and activity of the company with relevance to <IR>;
- the ownership structure of the company.

This way we received 50 medium-sized companies to survey. Finally, 43 firms were included in the overview. The members of the research group analysed the content of the annual reports of the selected companies including the balance sheet, the profit and loss account and the notes. They evaluated the compliance of the reports to <IR>. In addition, they looked at the web pages of the respective companies as well. The team members wrote short profiles on the individual companies. From among the sample consisting of 43 medium-sized firms, only one company (*Dunacell*) disclosed sustainability report.

In addition to medium-sized firms, we surveyed the documents of banks operating in Hungary. We found five banks with relevant non-financial reports. *CIB Bank, OTP Bank* and *K&H Bank* published sustainability reports, UniCredit Bank integrated report and *MagNet Bank* community report. *CIB, K&H* and *UniCredit* are in foreign ownership, and *MagNet Bank* is in 100% Hungarian private ownership. OTP Bank is a listed company with a high rate of free float (74%).

We identified four large companies with reports close to our criteria. *Alteo Plc.* (energy) produced integrated report, and *Borsodi Brewery* (food industry) and *Csaba Metal* (metal processing), sustainability reports. The annual report of *Richter Gedeon* (pharmaceuticals) includes both financial information and non-financial information.

We have to state at the very beginning of this part that we could identify only one medium-sized company with GRI report (*Dunacell Ltd.*). In addition, we found only listed companies, financial institutions and large companies publishing non-financial information in different approaches.

4.2 Strategic Focus and Future Orientation

Dunacell Ltd. (Medium-sized Company)

From among the surveyed medium-sized enterprises, *Dunacell* belonging to the *JRS Group* is one of the few Hungarian medium-sized companies that produced its own sustainability report based on GRI. Integrated thinking is enshrined in its core strategy. “In case of planning new investments or developments, we consider environmental as well as occupational safety aspects to the extent possible. We apply the precautionary principle to prevent emergencies" (Dunacell, 2018, p. 8).

The *JRS Group* issued its Group Policy in March 2016, covering employee rights, occupational health and safety issues and energy management. The main objective of the policy is to minimize negative and maximize positive impacts on the environment and society. "*Dunacell's* management strictly obliges to the principles and goals of this policy in every area of its operation" (Dunacell, 2018, p. 8).

We found some relevant hints in the reports of companies involved in other businesses such as the manufacture of food and real estate. Since regulation and supervision are strict in case of food producers, transparency of operations is a legitimate claim of major stakeholders (consumers, related authorities). Corporations of the industry should report on the source of purchased and used ingredients, the number of produced meals, the qualification of employees, certificates, etc.

Since there is significant information asymmetry in the real estate business, consumers (both sellers and buyers) are major stakeholders. Therefore, transparency of business model and regular reporting on market situation and outlook are highly recommended, and it should be clarified in <IR>.

4.3 Connectivity of Information

Richter Gedeon Plc. (Listed Company)

In terms of reporting, the case of *Richter Gedeon* is very interesting because it was one of the few companies in Hungary that had issued sustainability reports on a regular basis (from 2001 to 2013, based on GRI). After the international financial and economic crisis of 2008 and 2009, this reporting practice was finished, but the Annual Report of 2018 issued in 2019 contained a great number of non-financial data. The report included topics such as finances, economic performance, innovation (especially within women's health care), quality management and CSR (and as a part of it: environmental protection, employee, health and safety and other related themes and community involvement). The choice of topics seemed arbitrary, at least we did not receive any information on whether a materiality analysis had been carried out. Nonetheless, this annual report was a great step towards <IR> connecting different types of information (Richter Gedeon Nyrt, 2018, 2020).

4.4 Stakeholder Relationships

Borsodi Brewery Ltd. (Large Company)

In line with the Molson Coors global targets, *Borsodi Brewery* launched in 2017 its sustainability strategy going until 2025. As a part of the strategy, they issued their first sustainability report in 2019. The most important stakeholders are consumers, natural environment and employees, that is why the sustainability strategy is based on them and the relationships with them. That is why the three main goals of the sustainability strategy cover the following: responsibly refreshing (product safety and consumer health, responsible marketing, corporate governance, anti-corruption), sustainably brewing (supplier chain, usage of natural environment, waste management) and collectively crafted (employees' engagement, working environment, diversity and equal opportunity, career development).

The sustainability report is not based on any reporting guidelines but follows the triple bottom line approach: reports on economic performance and the use of natural resources and social issues (mainly on employees, but it mentions community relations and volunteering as well) (Borsodi, 2019, 2020).

4.5 Materiality

None of the medium-sized companies surveyed by our team presented materiality matrix or any information on materiality.

UniCredit has periodically carried out materiality analyses since 2010. This is a thorough approach that identifies critical economic, environmental and social aspects that could have a significant impact on the company's business performance, and therefore on long-term value creation.

The materiality matrix represents the upper-right quadrant of the overall matrix and results from the ranking of a number of topics based on their relevance (medium or high) expressed by the bank's stakeholders as the outcome of an intense process of dialogue, as well as UniCredit approach to the same topics, measured in terms of managerial focus and investments (advanced or highly advanced) (UniCredit, 2020, p. 36).

In this process, current and emerging issues are assessed from the perspective of different stakeholders and based on the bank's strategy. Datamaran's E-Revalue data analytics platform is used in addition to other sources (e.g. sustainability rating agencies, research on global risks and opportunities). The Datamaran sources employed to complete and consolidate the opinion of stakeholders include the following items:

- Benchmarking analysis on reports published by their peers: sustainability, integrated and financial reports.
- Regulatory analysis to identify the main laws and directives that affect the financial sector in the regions where the bank operates (both mandatory and voluntary regulations).
- Assessment of the latest news related to topics relevant to the financial sector in the press and social media.

As a result, it was possible to rank relevant issues for various stakeholders. This was done according to the level of importance of the items, with considering the frequency with which the topic comes up and its percentage of use in the included sources.

4.6 Organizational Overview and External Environment

Alteo Energy Provider Plc. (Listed Company)

Alteo is one of the few (exactly four) companies in Hungary that have ever issued an integrated report with financial and non-financial performance information. "In addition to presenting consolidated financial data, this report also proves our commitment to sustainability and transparency, with the added purpose of also presenting the company's annual activities, financial and non-financial results and plans to all stakeholders" (Alteo, 2020, p. 9). The report is based on the GRI standards (in accordance core), including the materiality matrix. The content of the integrated report was based on the results of the materiality assessment carried out in January 2016. The main stakeholders are employees, suppliers, customers, local communities and the natural environment. The topic of the external environment is attached to the organizational overview. The environmental part—as it is strongly related to the core business—got a separated part in the report. In the social performance chapter, the value chain (both customers and suppliers), employees and local communities are highlighted (Alteo, 2019, 2020).

4.7 Governance

MOL Hungarian Oil and Gas Public Limited Company is one of the few enterprises that issue integrated reports in Hungary (*MOL's* report is not based on IIRC, but integrated the financial and non-financial data). *MOL* has always been committed to implementing the highest standards of corporate governance structures and practices. Among other things, the voluntary approval of the Budapest Stock Exchange Corporate Governance Recommendations by the Annual General Meeting in 2006, before the official deadline, served as an evidence of the Company's commitment to corporate governance. *MOL's* Corporate Governance Code that contains the main corporate governance principles was adopted in 2006 for the first time, and its last update was accomplished in 2015. This code summarizes the shareholders' rights, the main governing bodies and remuneration and ethical issues. The Corporate Governance Code is available on the website of the Company (MOL Group, 2018).

4.8 Performance

MVM Group—also having issued integrated report—is a key energy group in Hungary and supplies energy to its customers according to their needs by generating, transmitting, distributing and trading energy and by improving its activities through R&D and innovation projects.

The company reports its performance in integrated thinking: after introducing the group, they use the three pillars of sustainability (according to GRI) to present their performance: business operation, environmental protection and society (employees and social relations). For ensuring the reliability and accuracy of data, the report has two independent endorsements: one from Deloitte Auditing and Consulting Ltd. for the financial part and one from KÖVET Association for Sustainable Economies for the environmental and social part (MVM, 2019).

5 Conclusion and Remarks

In Hungary, Act C of 2000 on Accounting and other auxiliary and specific legal rules regulate corporate reporting. They are complied with international standards and harmonized with the relevant EU law. They contain the most essential compulsory requirements in terms of structure and content. Among other things, various compulsory rules apply to different types of companies and corporate sizes. The two poles include IFRS for consolidation and individual financial statements on the one hand and simplified annual financial statements for micro-entities with some other forms in-between on the other hand. Most medium-sized companies are requested to compile simplified annual reports. Again, in line with international standards, more stringent reporting and disclosure rules apply to companies listed in regulated stock markets. The general conclusion drawn from the above-mentioned facts is that there is interrelationship between corporate size and reporting requirements: on the one hand, size has implications for reporting and, on the other hand, reporting for corporate size.

The Non-Financial Reporting Directive (NFRD) of the EU created the appropriate legal environment for sustainability, CSR and GRI reports and <IR>. Act C of 2000 on Accounting is based on this directive. It defines the set of non-financial information that has to be included in annual company reports. With the definition of certain thresholds, the target groups of the relevant provisions of this law are basically large and public interest companies. Elements of voluntary corporate reporting include CS, CSR, GRI and various sustainability reports as well as <IR>.

According to empirical evidence, in Hungary, these reports are generally prepared by large companies or their local affiliates with foreign ownership stake, and they play a pivotal role in this respect. Some of their indigenous counterparts follow suit. Nevertheless, best practices are scarce in Hungary. Most medium-sized firms with a very few exception have not pursued the examples of the few large firms involved in voluntary non-financial corporate reporting. The gap between large companies and SMEs is present not only in terms of productivity levels, efficiency, volume of output, etc., but also in terms of the nature of business reports as well. Nevertheless, some medium-sized undertakings that have established cooperative relations with large foreign companies (supplying, contract work, etc.) integrate some elements of non-financial reports in their various certificates, etc., rather than in formal reports.

In the SME sector, pressure on the spread of <IR> may come directly from legislation and government policies and indirectly from changes in the external and internal corporate environment that could be shaped by government measures as well. As far as direct stimuli or implications in terms of legislation are concerned, Hungarian regulation is based on rules rather than principles. This may have been associated with the official deep-rooted perception that the implementation of compulsory rules can be enforced more straightforward by legal means than that of principles. This could be a limiting factor in bolstering the switch of SMEs to principle-based <IR>. Companies, too, are much more prone to abide legal rules than to apply voluntarily accepted principles. For the time being, the attitude of the Hungarian government does not seem to change on this issue, and its neutral stance is expected to remain.

As far as indirect stimuli or implications are concerned, Hungarian SMEs in general and medium-sized undertakings are facing severe external and internal (domestic) challenges. The growing pressure on further internationalization, the need to raise productivity and enhance competitiveness, rising labour costs, tightening financial conditions, etc., drive medium-sized companies to reconsider their current operation and future strategies. Their stakeholders have to realize that changes in the general approach to business have implications for reporting. <IR> could be an adequate response to the growing complexity of the general environment in which businesses operate. This has not been realized by representatives of the corporate sectors and the government. Ongoing government programmes, such as the promotion of digitization, the national entrepreneurship programme and the supplier development programme, create favourable technical and technological conditions for the introduction and/or the adoption of <IR>.

Under the conditions of fierce competition in the market, impetus to establish and apply <IR> is likely to come from external stakeholders. According to our survey, this holds true primarily for food producers due to stringent safety regulations, the real estate business due to information asymmetry. To put it more generally: the relevance of <IR> is particularly pronounced in industries where transparency is of outstanding importance for the operation of the firms. Further research is needed to identify the implications of the COVID-19 pandemic for <IR>.

References

Bank, D. (2017). The double-dependent market economy and corporate social responsibility in Hungary. *Corvinus Journal of Sociology and Social Policy, 8*, 25–47.

BCSDH. (2016). *Transparency: Obstacle or benefit to companies in Hungary?* Budapest.

Benedek, A. (2017). A stratégiai CSR személyiségi gyökerei (Personality roots of strategic CSR). In: *Vállalkozásfejlesztés eszközei a XXI.* században.

Bodorkós, B., & Pataki, G. (2009). Local communities empowered to plan? Applying PAR to establish democratic communicative spaces for sustainable rural development. *Action Research, 7*(3), 313–334.

Braun and Partners. (2011). Erősödő stratégiai felelősségvállalás - Good CSR kutatás (Increasing Strategic Responsibility - Good CSR Research), *CSR Newsletter*, May.

Corporate Register. (2013). *CR Perspectives 2013 - Global CR Reporting Trends and Stakeholder Views*. London.

Csillag, S., Gyori, Z. S., & Matolay, R. (2018). Two worlds apart? Corporate social responsibility and employment of people with disabilities. In: *The Critical State of Corporate Social Responsibility in Europe* (pp. 57–81).

Csutora, M., Kerekes, S., & Tabi, A. (2014). Sustainability management in Hungary. In S. Schaltegger, S. E. Windolph, D. Harms, & J. Hörisch (Eds.), *Corporate sustainability in international comparison state of practice, opportunities and challenges*. Springer.

Directive 2014/95/EU of the European Parliament and of the Council of 22 October 2014 amending Directive 2013/34/EU as regards disclosure of non-financial and diversity information by certain large undertakings and groups. Retrieved March 20, 2021, from https://eur-lex.europa.eu/legal-content/EN/TXT/?uri=CELEX%3A32014L0095

EC. (2018). *2018 SBA Fact Sheet United Kingdom*. Belgium: European Commission.

EC. (2019). *2019 SBA Fact Sheet Hungary*. Belgium: European Commission.

Eurosif. (2018). *European SRI Study 2018*. Retrieved 31.01.2020 from http://www.eurosif.org/wp-content/uploads/2018/11/European-SRI-2018-Study.pdf

Géring, Zs. (2015). *A társadalmi felelősségvállalás online diskurzusa (Online discourse on social responsibility)*. PhD dissertation, Corvinus University of Budapest, Hungary.

HBLF (Hungarian Business Leaders Forum). (2012). *Etikai kódexek Magyarországon (Ethical codes in Hungary)*, Budapest.

HPRA (Hungarian Public Relations Association). (2017). *Kutatás a hazai vállalatok társadalmi felelősségvállalásáról (Research on CSR activities of domestic companies)*, Inspira Visionary Research, Budapest.

KPMG. (2017). *The road ahead. The KPMG Survey of Corporate Responsibility Reporting 2017*, Geneva https://assets.kpmg/content/dam/kpmg/xx/pdf/2017/10/kpmg-survey-of-corporate-responsibility-reporting-2017.pdf

MNE. (2018). *Beszámoló a Könyvvizsgálói Közfelügyeleti Hatóság 2017.* évi tevékenységéről (Ministry of Finance: Report on the activities of the Accounting Monitoring Agency - 2017). Nemzetgazdasági Minisztérium, Budapest. http://ngmszakmaiteruletek.kormany.hu/download/9/4e/12000/KKH%20Éves%20beszámoló%202017_FINAL.pdf

Pataki, G, Szántó, R. & Matolay, R. (2015). CSR online and in real terms: A critical analysis of controversial sectors in Hungary. In: *Corporate Social Responsibility in the Digital Age* (Developments in Corporate Governance and Responsibility, Volume 7) (pp. 241–264). Emerald Group Publishing Limited.

Integrated Reports

Alteo. (2020). *Integrated report 2019*. Retrieved March 20, 2020, from https://alteo.hu/fenntarthatosag/fenntarthatosagi-jelentesek/

Alteo. (2019). *Integrated report 2018*. Retrieved March 20, 2020, from https://alteo.hu/fenntarthatosag/fenntarthatosagi-jelentesek/

Borsodi. (2019). *Sustainability report 2018*. Retrieved March 20, 2020, from http://www.borsodisorgyar.hu/-/media/global-sites/molson-coors-corporate/hungarian/privacy-and-terms/borsodi_fenntarthatosagi_jelentes_2018_hu.ashx?la=hu-hu

Borsodi. (2020). *Sustainability report 2019*. Retrieved March 20, 2020, from http://borsodisorgyar.hu/-/media/global-sites/molson-coors-corporate/hungarian/privacy-and-terms/20200805_borsodi_fenntarthatosagi-jelentes-mod20201012-01-online.ashx?la=hu-hu

Dunacell. (2018). *Sustainability report 2015–2017*. Retrieved March 20, 2020, from http://dunacell.com/letoltheto/Dunacell_Fenntarthatosagi_jelentes_2015_2017%20vegleges.pdf

MOL Group. (2018). *Integrated annual report 2018*. Retrieved March 20, 2020, from https://molgroup.info/storage/documents/publications/annual_reports/2018/mol_group_integrated_annual_report_2018.pdf

MVM. (2019). *Integrated report 2019*. Retrieved March 20, 2020, from http://mvm.hu/download/Integralt-jelentes-2019_V10_2.pdf

Rátz-Putzer, E. P. (2015). A CSR lehetséges jövájének vizsgálata külöönös tekintettel a hazai gyakorlatra (Examining the possible future of CSR with particular regard to domestic practice). PhD dissertation, University of Pecs

Richter Gedeon Nyrt. (2018). *Sustainability report 2016–2017*. Retrieved March 20, 2020, from https://www.richter.hu/hu-HU/felelossegvallalas/Documents/Richterfenntarthatosagijelentes20162017.pdf

Richter Gedeon Nyrt. (2020). *Sustainability report 2018–2019*. Retrieved March 20, 2020, from https://www.richter.hu/hu-HU/felelossegvallalas/Documents/Richter_Fenntarthatosagijelentes_20182019.pdf

Unicredit. (2020). *Integrated report 2019*. Retrieved March 20, 2020, from https://www.unicreditgroup.eu/content/dam/unicreditgroup-eu/documents/en/sustainability/sustainability-reports/2019/IR_ENG2019.pdf

SMEs and <IR>: Evidence from Italy

Luca Brusati, Caterina Fuso, and Andrea Garlatti

1 The SME Sector in Italy

The role of MSMEs is relevant across the European Union, but it is even more important in the case of Italy. Indeed, the numbers featured in Table 1 speak for themselves. MSMEs generate 66.9% of overall value added in the Italian non-financial business economy, which includes industry, construction, trade and services (NACE Rev. 2 sections B to J, L, M and N), but not enterprises in agriculture, forestry, fisheries and the largely non-market service sectors such as education and health, thus exceeding the EU average of 56.4%.

The share of employment that Italian MSMEs generate is even larger, at 78.1%, compared to the EU average of 66.6%. Whereas the role of SMEs in Italy is broadly in line with average EU figures, micro-firms are particularly important, providing 44.9% of employment compared to the EU average of 29.7%. As a consequence, on average Italian MSMEs employ 3.1 people, slightly fewer than the EU average of 3.9 (EC, 2019).

The overall value added generated by Italian MSMEs rose by 12.4% from 2014 to 2018; in contrast, employment rose by only 4.7%, still 9.3% below its 2008 pre-crisis level, and lagging behind the 10.7% employment growth of large firms. If we focus on the latest available data, from 2017 to 2018 employment grew by only 1.1%, whereas value added increased by 1.8% (EC, 2019).

L. Brusati (✉) · A. Garlatti
Udine University, Udine, Italy
e-mail: luca.brusati@uniud.it; andrea.garlatti@uniud.it

C. Fuso
Deloitte Tax & Consulting, Luxembourg, Luxembourg
e-mail: cfuso@deloitte.lu

J. Dyczkowska et al. (eds.), *Development of Integrated Reporting in the SME Sector*,
CSR, Sustainability, Ethics & Governance,
https://doi.org/10.1007/978-3-030-81903-3_4

Table 1 Overview of the SME landscape in Italy and Europe

Class size	Number of enterprises			Number of persons employed			Value added		
	Italy		EU-28	Italy		EU-28	Italy		EU-28
	Number	Share	Share	Number	Share	Share	Billion €	Share	Share
Micro	3,599,695	94.9%	93.0%	6,719,319	44.9%	29.7%	208.1	28.4%	20.8%
Small	172,324	4.5%	5.9%	3,088,490	20.7%	20.1%	151.8	20.7%	17.6%
Medium-sized	19,226	0.5%	0.9%	1,873,898	12.5%	16.8%	131.0	17.9%	18.0%
SMEs	**3,791,245**	**99.9%**	**99.8%**	**11,681,707**	**78.1%**	**66.6%**	**490.9**	**66.9%**	**56.4%**
Large	3380	0.1%	0.2%	3,270,222	21.9%	33.4%	242.5	33.1%	43.6%
Total	3,794,625	100.0%	100.0%	14,951,929	100.0%	100.0%	733.3	100.0%	100.0

Estimates for 2018 produced by DIW Econ, based on 2008–2016 figures from the Structural Business Statistics Database (EUROSTAT). The data cover the non-financial business economy, which includes industry, construction, trade and services, but excludes enterprises in agriculture, forestry, fisheries and the largely non-market service sectors such as education and health

Source: EC (2019)

The role of Italian medium-sized enterprises is very similar to the EU average, with 18% of overall value added, but a lower share of employment (12.5% vs. 16.8%), thus suggesting a higher productivity; actually, between 2014 and 2018 medium-sized firms generated the highest value added growth, with a rise of 16.4%. The large role played by micro- and small firms is balanced by a more limited role of large firms, accounting for only 21.9% of the total number of persons employed in Italy, compared to the EU average of 33.4%, and for 33.1% of overall value added, compared to the EU average of 43.6% (EC, 2019). In aggregate terms, the socio-economic impacts of Italian SMEs are far from being marginal and they deserve to be adequately and timely addressed.

2 Overview of Reporting Regulations with Potential Impact on IR

Italian Legislative Decree No. 139/2015 has introduced significant amendments to the provisions on annual financial statements in order to transpose Directive 2013/34/EU of the European Parliament and the Council of 26 June 2013. Among the amendments made to the Italian Civil Code, it is worth mentioning two main lines of reporting innovations:

- improving the comparability of the financial statements of Italian companies by approximating the rules for preparing the financial statements of Italian GAAP companies to IAS/IFRS international accounting standards (Capodaglio et al., 2016; Cortesi et al., 2017; Quagli, 2018; Santesso & Sostero, 2016);
- minimizing the administrative burden for small companies, in keeping with the "think small first" principle enshrined in the Small Business Act for Europe, the EU's flagship policy initiative to support SMEs (Sorrentino & Smarra, 2014).

Legislative Decree No. 139/2015 thus tries to balance two diverging goals, i.e. to ensure more comprehensive and more comparable information on the financial performance of Italian firms, while avoiding additional requirements and costs for smaller entities, which in many cases are already struggling in this respect.

The latter goal has been achieved by introducing the status of "micro" enterprises, which are exonerated from many disclosure requirements, including the inclusion from cash flow statements and the application of amortized cost of receivables, other than being granted the option of providing financial statements in a simplified form (basically, without any addendum to it).

It is worth remembering that Directive 2013/34/EU envisaged four size classes: "micro", "small", "medium" and "large" enterprises. The choice of the Italian legislator has been to establish only three size classes, bundling medium enterprises with large ones. This means that, from 2016 onwards, the Italian legal system foresees micro enterprises, small enterprises that are allowed to draft financial statements in a simplified format and medium-to-large enterprises that are required

Table 2 Financial reporting requirements per class size based on Italian Legislative Decree No. 139/2015

Class size	Total assets	Net Revenues	Average number of employees	Mandatory elements of annual financial statements
Micro (Art. 2435-ter Civil Code)	Up to € 175,000	Up to € 350,000	Up to 5	• Statement of assets and liabilities • Income statement
Small (Art. 2435-bis Civil Code)	Up to € 4,400,000	Up to € 8,800,000	Up to 50	• Statement of assets and liabilities • Income statement • Notes to the financial statement
Large (Art. 2423 Civil Code)	Over € 4,400,000	Over € 8,800,000	Over 50	• Statement of assets and liabilities • Income statement • Cash flow statement • Notes to the financial statement

In order to qualify as a "micro" or "small" enterprise, two of the specified limits must not be exceeded in the first financial year or, subsequently, for two financial years
Source: Italian Legislative Decree No. 139/2015

to provide cash flow statements on a compulsory basis. It follows that, for statutory purposes, there are three different annual mandatory financial statement frameworks, naturally linked to the three different classes of enterprises (Table 2):

- Financial statements for micro enterprises, referred to in Article 2435-ter of the Italian Civil Code;
- Financial statements in "abridged" form for small companies;
- Financial statements in "ordinary" form for medium and large companies.

Obviously the different types of financial statements provide different levels of detail on financial performance. The "ordinary" form is complete with all the information and documents required by the Italian Civil Code, i.e. the "extended" balance sheet, the "extended" income statement, the full notes to the financial statements and the cash flow statement, whereas the financial statements in "abridged" form are simplified, as the name itself implies.

In the opinion of many experts and practitioners, Legislative Decree No. 139/2015 has certainly helped micro-enterprises by providing for a significant reduction in their administrative burden; bundling medium companies together with large firms, though, may not always be a proportionate nor adequate provision. As a matter of fact, companies that comply with the above parameters do not always qualify as medium–large, and often do not have the organizational capacity to report in full compliance with the obligations of the new financial statement discipline, which envisages, among other requirements, mandatory cash flow statements and the estimation of durable losses ("impairment test") based on the assessment of expected cash flows, excluding the application of the simplified approach based on depreciation (Provasi & Sottoriva, 2015; Sottoriva, 2015).

2.1 Financial Statement Mandatory Information and Evaluation Criteria

Bearing in mind the target companies, i.e. SMEs, thus excluding micro and large ones, and the new categories identified by the Italian legal system for accounting purposes, it is deemed appropriate to understand the mandatory requirements foreseen for financial reporting by small companies.

The simplifications granted in the drafting of financial statements have remained largely unchanged. The only change is that accumulated depreciation and amortization and write-downs of tangible and intangible assets, as is already the case for non-small companies, are no longer deducted directly from the statement. Information on these values can anyway be found in the notes to the financial statements (Article 2427, paragraph 1, no. 2, Civil Code).

It is worth pointing out that even small companies are required to account for derivative financial instruments, in accordance with the provisions of Article 2426, paragraph 1, no. 11-bis, of the Italian Civil Code. In the income statement, the revaluations of equity investments, financial fixed assets and securities in current assets other than equity investments may also be aggregated with the revaluations of derivative financial instruments (new sub-item d18(d)). The same applies to the write-downs of the above items, which can be summed up with the decreases in value of derivatives (new sub-item d19(d)).

For small companies, as it is the case with medium and large companies, memorandum accounts (conti d'ordine) are no longer envisaged.

Small companies are exempted from the requirement to provide a cash flow statement (Article 2423-ter, Civil Code), which is required instead by Legislative Decree No. 139/2015 as a compulsory component of the statutory financial statements of medium and large companies. Indeed, the above requirement could not be envisaged for small companies, considering that the introduction of any financial statement documents additional to those provided for by the directive can only be required of medium and large companies, as the accompanying report to the Decree (Relazione illustrativa al Decreto) explicitly points out.

Prior to the enactment of Legislative Decree No. 139/2015, simplifications were confined to the fields of disclosure and information. The Decree also introduces simplifications in terms of evaluation criteria. Even though the Italian Civil Code introduced the criterion of amortized cost for investment securities, receivables and payables, the traditional evaluation criteria have been left unchanged for small businesses, i.e. purchase cost for investment securities, estimated realizable value for receivables and nominal value for payables. The exemption is an option granted by the legislator with a view to simplification. If a small company opts to adopt amortized cost, it follows the new provisions of the Civil Code (Article 2426, paragraphs 1, 8 and 12). In this case, the transitional rules allow all companies to adopt amortized cost prospectively, i.e. continuing to account for the items concerned recorded in the financial statements before 1 January 2016 using the old criteria.

2.2 Notes to the Financial Statement and Report on Operations

A number of simplifications concerning the content of the notes to the financial statement are granted to small companies. The new provisions list explicitly which information should be featured in the notes, in line with the "maximum harmonization" approach of Directive 2013/34/EU, whereas the old provisions indicated what companies may not include. The distinction is important: the new Article 2427 of the Italian Civil Code spells out what to insert, whereas the old Article 2427 provided an option not to insert. All in all, information is certainly more limited than in the past. The intention of the European Union legislator is to keep the information deemed useful for readers of the financial statements of small companies: in essence, it is assumed that less information would not coincide with worse information. Doubts remain in this regard.

The new version of Article 2427 reminds that the notes to the financial statements of small companies should contain information concerning:

- any additional information required to obtain a true and fair representation (Article 2423, paragraph 3);
- criteria illustrating how the principle of materiality has been implemented (Article 2423, paragraph 4); this provision is the only additional disclosure requirement compared to the past;
- the reason that led to the derogation of the adoption of the provisions of the Italian Civil Code, as well as an indication of the impact that its application has on the balance sheet, the financial position and the economic result (Article 2423, paragraph 5);
- a separate presentation of the items that are grouped together, when this has been done to improve clarity of the financial statements (Article 2423-ter, paragraph 2);
- reporting and commenting on the non-comparability and the adjustment of the amount of the corresponding item of the previous year, or the impossibility to do so (Article 2423-ter, paragraph 5);
- if an asset or liability item falls under several items of the scheme, the annotation that it also belongs to items other than the one in which it is recorded, where necessary for the understanding of the financial statements (Article 2424, paragraph 1);
- the reason why, on initial recognition of a subsidiary or associated company using the equity method, the excess of the purchase cost over the corresponding value

of the shareholders' equity resulting from the last financial statements of the investee company is recorded in the financial statements (Article 2426, paragraph 1, no. 4);
- an explanation of the period over which goodwill is written off (Article 2426, paragraph 1, no. 6).

It is no longer explicitly required to record changes in the depreciation criteria and the coefficients applied (Article 2426, paragraph 1, no. 2) in the notes to the financial statements of small businesses. Similarly, it is no longer required to spell out why an investment in a subsidiary or associate is recorded at a value higher than that resulting from the application of the equity method or, if there is no obligation to prepare consolidated financial statements, at the value corresponding to the portion of shareholders' equity resulting from the last financial statements of the investee company (Article 2426, paragraph 1, no. 3).

Finally, the provisions of Article 2427-bis, paragraph 1, no. 1, have been integrated in keeping with the new disclosure requirements concerning derivative financial instruments. As a consequence, for each category of derivative financial instruments the notes to the financial statements of small businesses must feature:

- their fair value;
- information on their size and nature, including significant terms and conditions that may affect the amount, timing and certainty of future cash flows;
- the assumptions on which the valuation models and techniques are based, if the fair value has not been determined on the basis of market evidence;
- the changes in value recorded directly in the income statement, as well as those charged to equity reserves;
- a table showing the changes in fair value reserves in the year.

The provision is also maintained that small companies may not prepare the report on operations if they provide the information referred to in Article 2428, nos. 3 and 4 of the Italian Civil Code, i.e. the number and nominal value of shares held, purchased and sold, in the notes to the financial statements.

2.3 *Non-financial Reporting Requirements Provided by Legislative Decree No. 254/2016*

Substantive Requirements

In order to transpose Directive 2014/95/EU, Italian Legislative Decree No. 254/2016 regulated the minimum content of the non-financial report to be issued by large public interest companies with over 500 employees. Non-financial reports shall necessarily disclose information about:

- environmental performance, including in particular information on the use of energy and water resources, greenhouse gas emissions and the present and

foreseeable impact of environmental and health risk factors that characterize corporate activities;
- social policies;
- HR management practices, including in particular information on the actions taken to ensure gender equality, the measures planned to implement the relevant conventions of international and supranational organizations and the way in which dialogue with social partners is established;
- information concerning human rights protection, including at least the provisions in place to prevent human rights violations and those to hinder discriminatory conduct;
- information on the fight against active and passive corruption, identifying the policies chosen and adopted to this end.

The above-mentioned information should not only fulfil the requirement of materiality, assessed in relation to the activity and features of the company, but also provide a description of at least:

- the company's management, internal organization and control model;
- policies, results achieved and key non-financial performance indicators;
- the main risks generated or incurred in, related to the issues covered by the Decree.

The disclosure requirement may be waived if the company concerned does not pursue any policy in one or more of the aforementioned areas. In this case, however, it must clearly and articulately state in the report the reasons why it has opted not to provide any information on these matters.

Disclosure of information on forthcoming developments and transactions not yet finalized may be omitted only where their disclosure would seriously affect the firm's trading position, provided that such entity expressly refers to Article 3, paragraph 8 in its report and that it intends to make use of this option. However, the omission of such information shall in any case not be permitted if it jeopardizes the correct and balanced understanding of the undertaking's performance and the effects generated by its activity on the aspects covered by the declaration.

Formal Requirements

Non-financial reports must be prepared in accordance with a recognized national or international reporting standard. In this regard, Article 1 of Directive 2014/95/EU provides that "In requiring the disclosure of the information referred to in the first subparagraph, Member States shall provide that undertakings may rely on national, Union-based or international frameworks, and if they do so, undertakings shall specify which frameworks they have relied upon". Legislative Decree No. 254/2016 goes one step further than the Directive and, in Article 3, paragraph 3, provides that "The information referred to in paragraphs 1 and 2 is provided with a comparison with that provided in previous years, according to the methodologies and principles provided by the reporting standards[1] used as a reference or by the independent reporting methodology[2] used for the preparation of the statement". Should an independent reporting methodology be adopted, the report shall include a clear and detailed description of the methodology, along with a justification for its selection.

When an enterprise decides which reporting standards to adopt, it must bear in mind that these have a direct impact on the set of indicators it employs to monitor and evaluate its performance, as these must be necessarily those identified by the chosen reporting standard, meaningful and specific for each area reported, as well as consistent with the business core operations and their outcomes.

As for communication means, Legislative Decree No. 254/2016 allows enterprises to choose among three options. Indeed, the non-financial report may be included in the mandatory annual report referred to in Article 2428 of the Italian Civil Code, in a specific section marked as such. Non-financial information may be otherwise disclosed as a stand-alone report, without prejudice to the obligation to mark it with a similar wording; in this case, the specific section of the annual report referred to in the previous point must indicate that an ad hoc non-financial report has been published, providing the information required by law. Lastly, should it come as an integral part of the management report, the specific section in which non-financial information is disclosed may indicate any additional chapter of said report (or any other file) in which the non-financial report is included. Whether or not issued as a stand-alone document, non-financial disclosure shall be considered as an annex to the annual financial statement.

Audit

Pursuant to Italian provisions, the management body shall approve the non-financial report and submit it to the supervisory board and to any other party in charge of auditing the issuance "of the declaration of compliance (of the information provided) with respect to the principles, methodologies and reporting standards required by the decree [...] within the same time limits as those provided for the presentation of the draft financial statements, and it shall be published in the business registry, by the

[1] Reporting standards are defined as "those standards and guidelines issued by authoritative supranational, international or national bodies, of public or private nature, instrumental, in whole or in part, in fulfilling the non-financial reporting obligations provided for by this Legislative Decree and by Directive 2014/95/EU" (Legislative Decree No. 254/2016, Article 1, paragraph 1, letter f).

[2] An independent reporting methodology is defined as "the composite set, consisting of one or more reporting standards, as defined in point f), and the additional principles, criteria and performance indicators, independently identified and complementary to those provided for by the adopted reporting standards, which is functional to meet the non-financial reporting requirements of this Legislative Decree and Directive 2014/95/EU" (Legislative Decree No. 254/2016, Article 1, paragraph 1, letter g).

directors themselves, together with the management report" (Legislative Decree No. 254/2016, Article 5, paragraph 1).

Legislative Decree No. 254/2016 provides three different types of audit of non-financial reports, concerning both substantive and formal requirements (the latter sanctioned by the issuance of the above-mentioned "declaration of compliance" with the provisions of the Decree), and overall compliance with the provisions established by the law. In order to make these provisions as prescriptive and pragmatic as possible, the Italian National Foundation of Chartered Accountants (Fondazione Nazionale dei Commercialisti) has identified three potential professional subjects in charge of auditing, namely:

- the statutory auditor of the company (revisore legale dei conti, formerly known as revisore contabile), carrying out the statutory audit of financial statements;
- a third party responsible of certifying the compliance of the non-financial report to the requirements of the Decree, different from the statutory auditor, but who must be a certified auditor as well;
- a supervisory body entrusted with the control of legality.

Even though they are responsible for carrying out two independent auditing activities, the first two subjects may coincide. In this respect, it should be pointed out that, according to Legislative Decree No. 139/2005, Italian statutory auditors are expected to have the "technical skills required to (...) prepare and (...) audit environmental, social and sustainability reports for enterprises as well as public and private bodies" (Article 1, paragraph 3, letter o).

Italian Legislative Decree No. 254/2016 features an explicit provision applicable to organizations with less than 500 employees that choose to issue a non-financial report: "Subjects other than those included in the scope of application [...] that voluntarily develop and publish individual or consolidated non-financial reports and that comply with the Legislative Decree, may include a declaration of compliance with the Decree" (Legislative Decree No. 254/2016, Article 8, paragraph 3).

3 National Factors Enabling or Constraining <IR>

3.1 *Political Factors*

The broader regulatory environment in Italy is supportive to the development of <IR>, even though primarily as a way to secure the disclosure of non-financial performance for the purpose of backward-looking external accountability, rather than as a way to promote forward-looking integrated value creation. Both the central government (in particular the Ministry of Labour and Social Affairs and the Ministry of Economic Development) and the regional governments over the years have expressed a sustained interest for corporate social responsibility, seen explicitly as an opportunity to complement governmental welfare, and supported by dedicated initiatives and provisions (e.g. "2012–2014 National Action Plan on CSR", regional laws, support for corporate benefit programmes, targeted financial contributions, especially in the framework of EU-funded programmes). As mentioned in the previous paragraph, already in 2005 a Legislative Decree pointed out that statutory auditors are expected to have the "technical skills required to (. . .) prepare and (. . .) audit environmental, social and sustainability reports for enterprises as well as public and private bodies" (Legislative Decree No. 139/2005, Article 1, paragraph 3, letter o). As a consequence of this political support, it is not surprising to notice that Legislative Decree No. 254/2016 broadens, at least in some respects, the provisions of Directive 2014/95/EU (Aureli et al., 2018).

3.2 *Economic Factors*

Italian firms have a mixed track record in addressing effectively the challenges of increased competition and globalized markets. Whereas in some industries they established themselves as global leaders, in others they are definitely lagging behind, partly due to the fact that small and very small firm size makes it difficult both to harness scale and scope economies and to provide value added services. The situation is widely diversified not only across industries, but also across regions. All in all, though, Italian firms must address multiple challenges to their long-term viability, basically in all areas of performance. Notwithstanding some improvements over the last few years, Italian SMEs perform below the EU average in eight out of the nine SBA principles monitored by the "SBA Fact Sheets", including "Access to finance", "Skills and innovation" and "Environment" (EC, 2019). The systematic adoption of the "six capitals" reporting framework would help SME managers track challenges and improvements in terms of financial capital, manufactured capital, human capital, intellectual capital, social and relationship capital and natural capital, and contribute to the diffusion of more advanced, forward-looking, "integrated" value creation models.

3.3 *Social Factors*

According to Edelman (2020: 66), 61% of Italians agree with the statement "Capitalism as it exists today does more harm than good in the world". Italian society shows widespread concern about the fact that private entrepreneurs tend to pocket profits but to rely on governmental contributions in case of losses. Privatizing governmental services and opening up markets to competition are seen as threats much more than opportunities, in particular as a possible cause of job losses. Profits are not necessarily considered positively. This is especially true for large, international companies; family-owned SMEs tend to score better (Edelman, 2020: 50). Public opinion demonstrates major expectations towards the social responsibility of private firms, in different areas, including labour conditions, support for local communities and environmental impact, often with limited understanding of the trade-offs they face; as a consequence, it shows appreciation for entrepreneurs who take a proactive approach in these areas. In principle, this backdrop creates favourable conditions for the adoption of <IR> as a way to help companies demonstrate the value they created across multiple dimensions of performance. On the other hand, deep-seated suspicion and mistrust towards the claims of private firms should be taken into account, together with the limited ability by "single-issue" stakeholders to appreciate multidimensional performance reporting.

3.4 Cultural Factors

Italy, as the country that prides itself with the invention of accounting, has long attached prestige and visibility to sound reporting practices, as testified by the popularity of the "Balance Sheet Oscar", in its 57th edition in 2021, which includes an award for integrated reports. Non-financial reporting is well established in Italy, thanks to a long-standing academic tradition in management studies that, at least from the late Seventies, emphasized the social performance of private firms and their ability to engage multiple stakeholders (Coda, 1984; Ianniello & Fedele, 2011; Signori & Rusconi, 2009). Long before it was made compulsory by Legislative Decree No. 254/2016, voluntary sustainability reporting has been common practice for many firms, as well as public sector bodies and NGOs (Contraffatto, 2014; Rusconi, 2021; Rusconi & Dorigatti, 2004). As a consequence, a variety of domestic sustainability reporting standards has evolved over the years, the most widespread being the "GBS model" (GBS, 2005, 2007, 2013) issued by the Italian Group for Studies on Social Reporting, established in 1998. Recently, both the academic and professional literature emphasized the merits of <IR>, albeit primarily for the purpose of external accountability, rather than as a way to promote integrated value creation (reflecting the fact that "formalized" performance measurement is an accounting issue rather than a managerial issue). Taking into account the role of SMEs in the Italian economy, at least two <IR> standards specifically targeted to SMEs have been developed:

- "Integrated Reporting for SMEs" (Commissione Bilancio Integrato, 2016), issued by the Integrated Reporting Committee of Milan Board of Certified Accountants (Ordine dei Dottori Commercialisti);
- "Integrated Reporting for SMEs: Implementation Guidance" (Panizza et al., 2018), issued by Organismo Italiano Business Reporting (formerly Network Italiano Business Reporting), based on IIRC standards.

3.5 Technological Factors

The Digital Economy and Society Index (DESI) 2019 Country Report 2019 points out that Italy as a whole has a long way to go to fully exploit the benefits of digitalization: Italy ranks 24th out of the 28 EU Member States in the European Commission Digital Economy and Society Index (DESI, 2019: 3). Italian SMEs are adjusting slowly to digital technologies; accounting and finance, though, are usually the most advanced organizational function in this respect, also thanks to the fact that paperless invoicing was made compulsory by law as of 1 January 2019. In a survey among 57 SMEs of the Friuli Venezia Giulia region performed in January 2020, 47.4% reported the adoption of IT-enabled enterprise resource planning (ERP) systems, integrating accounting and non-accounting information and allowing automated data monitoring and exchange among organizational functions. The availability of an ERP system is a major enabling factor for <IR>, because it signals the availability of electronic data repositories and sensitivity to the interconnected nature of organizational functions.

4 Empirical Evidence on <IR> in Italy

4.1 <IR> By Italian Large Firms

Thanks to a long-standing tradition of non-financial reporting, the provisions of Legislative Decree No. 254/2016 did not face significant implementation obstacles, and there is a wealth of literature tracking developments in this field (Caputo et al., 2020; De Luca, 2020; Mion & Loza Adaui, 2020; Venturelli et al., 2017). A fully fledged "National observatory on non-financial reporting" has been established and published its first report in October 2018, covering 194 reports for 2017 (Amelio et al., 2018), followed by updates in January 2020, covering 211 reports for 2018 (Osservatorio Dichiarazioni Non Finanziarie, 2020), and March 2021, covering 202 reports for 2019 (Amelio et al., 2021). On top of this, a recent article mapped sustainability reporting practices among Italian companies (Gazzola et al., 2020), at least three studies tracked systematically the adoption of <IR> (Gesuele & Pozzoli, 2017; Paolucci & Cerioni, 2017; Rubino & Garzoni, 2018), and many more analyzed individual companies' experience with <IR> in a longitudinal pespective (e.g., Bocchi & Venier, 2019; Mio et al., 2016).

Many Italian large firms subject to the provisions of Legislative Decree No. 254/2016 in terms of non-financial reporting publish sustainability reports separately from financial accounts, usually based on Global Reporting Initiative (GRI)'s sustainability reporting standards (e.g. Ansaldo, Cattolica Assicurazioni, Edipower, ENAV, ENEL, FCA, Ferrovie dello Stato, Leonardo, Maire Tecnimont, Mondadori, Monte dei Paschi di Siena, SNAM, Terna). International Integrated Reporting Council (IIRC) standards are mentioned by all the corporate reports included in the sample. Some companies (e.g. ENI) structure their reports along the list of items featured in Legislative Decree No. 254/2016. A growing number of large firms are starting to report their non-financial performance referring explicitly to the United Nations' Sustainable Development Goals (e.g. A2A, Barilla, Luxottica).

A relatively small number of larger companies have opted instead for a fully fledged <IR>. Most tend to adopt explicitly the "six-capital" model (e.g. DESPAR, Fideuram, GTS, UNICREDIT), with exceptions based anyway on International Integrated Reporting Council (IIRC) standards (e.g. Atlantia and Generali Group do not refer anywhere in their documents to intellectual capital). Other companies (e.g. A2A, Poste Italiane) published sustainability reports for many years, but have more recently switched to <IR>. A peculiar case is represented by UnipolSAI, which publishes both an integrated report and a sustainability report, on top of dedicated information focusing on climate change, ethics and advancements towards its commitments vis-à-vis the United Nations Global Compact.

There are also examples of firms that stopped the issuance of sustainability reports (e.g. Landi Renzo) and of integrated reports (e.g. Bombardier Transportation Italy).

Interestingly, not only firms but also the Italian Football League have adopted <IR> as early as 2013, and the Municipality of Sasso Marconi was the very first in Italy to adopt <IR> in 2019. Other companies (e.g. A2A) published for a few years a sustainability report, but have more recently switched to <IR>.

In terms of <IR> guiding principles, the picture emerging from our analysis shows both strengths and weaknesses. The strengths usually include the aspects directly associated with faithful compliance with reporting standards, such as connectivity of information, materiality, completeness, consistency and comparability.

The weaknesses are instead related to the strategic dimension, i.e. the guiding principles of an integrated report that cannot rely exclusively on compliance with the reporting standards:

- Strategic focus and future orientation—this is usually the weakest aspect: integrated reports tend to emphasize backward-looking external accountability rather than forward-looking integrated thinking; in particular, no report clarifies whether and to what extent intended medium-term objectives have been reached;
- Stakeholder relationships—this section is also unconvincing: in many cases, only market stakeholders are referred to;
- Conciseness—probably in order to demonstrate transparency, or as a way to address the concerns of "single-issue" stakeholders, details abound, at the expenses of an integrated understanding of corporate performance;
- Reliability—the information featured in the reports tends to paint an ideal picture of the company, which seems to deliver on all possible aspects of performance; a critical assessment of the KPIs featured in the reports raises the suspicion that they have been selected in order to glorify the performance of the company. As an example, Atlantia fails altogether to report the fact that Italian highways are the most expensive in Europe, with very negative consequences on both Italian families and the economy as a whole—let alone the systematic underinvestment in maintenance that led among others to the collapse of the "Morandi" Bridge in Genoa.

Our analysis shows both strengths and weaknesses also in terms of <IR> content elements. One more time, the strengths are associated with the most descriptive aspects of <IR>, which include past performance, especially important for accountability purposes:

- organizational overview and external environment;
- governance;
- performance.

The weaknesses concern instead the content elements directly associated with the strategic dimension of <IR> such as:

- business model—usually unclear and rarely associated with an integrated perspective on value creation, which is expected to be the hallmark of <IR>;
- strategy and resource allocation—same as above;
- risks and opportunities—unconvincing, especially as far as risks are concerned;
- outlook: weak.

Having said this, examples of good practices in <IR> by Italian large companies can be identified as a consequence of the well-established practice of developing non-financial reports. An excellent example in terms of strategic focus and future orientation among larger firms is the integrated report issued by A2A, which outlines explicitly its sustainability policy and plan, including the objectives it aims to achieve in the medium term, in both qualitative and quantitative terms, distinguished in four clusters: "circular economy", "decarbonization", "smartness in networks and services" and "people innovation". Again in terms of content, the integrated report issued by A2A is an excellent example also in terms of business model: a graphical representation of its value chain outlines effectively the company's *modus operandi*. DESPAR is also very effective in this respect: the overall strategic goal of a 3% increase in market share (ambitious in the very competitive food retail business) is articulated into five objectives, and a detailed connectivity matrix outlines the relationship among these objectives, the SDGs and the six capitals.

DESPAR provides also an interesting example in its analysis of stakeholder relationships; whereas many companies focus primarily on market stakeholders and only include generic players such as "institutions", DESPAR stands out by featuring explicitly, among its stakeholders, banks, competitors, industry associations, universities, local governments and local communities. For each stakeholder, both engagement patterns and relevant KPIs are spelled out. Fideuram also offers an interesting synthesis in this respect, by including a table that connects effectively capitals, material topics, stakeholders and SDGs.

Materiality matrixes in many cases are not especially insightful, but two insurance groups, Generali and UNIPOL, stand out in this respect: both cluster effectively topics in terms of their strategic significance and connect them with SDGs.

The integrated report issued by DESPAR is instead extremely effective in outlining risks and opportunities. They are clustered in four groups (compliance risks, financial risks, operational risks, market risks), and each risk is connected to a specific stakeholder, spelling out briefly what interventions are envisaged to mitigate that risk and what metrics are used to monitor the situation. A summary matrix presents the likelihood and potential impact associated by the company to that risk.

DESPAR stands out one more time by being the only company that touches explicitly and reports on the trade-offs among the six capitals.

4.2 *<IR> By Italian SMEs*

The relative popularity of non-financial reporting in Italy means that different medium enterprises and even a few small enterprises have experienced over the years with these documents, albeit in many cases on the basis of "ad-hoc" reporting methodologies. A search performed on the Global Reporting Initivative (GRI) database at the end of 2019 identified 157 reports issued by European SMEs; out of them, 20 were from Italy (Ortiz-Martinez & Marin-Hernandez, 2020). Italian SMEs have started to approach <IR> only recently, as this innovative reporting model was initially hampered by the negative opinion of SMEs themselves. This mistrust stemmed from the actual and perceived burden of considerable management and structural costs. Indeed, should a company decide to adopt <IR>, it must inevitably rethink and redesign its reporting procedures, which are probably inadequate to handle non-financial information. Significant investments in technology are also to be sustained to develop information systems suitable for detecting, measuring and guaranteeing the quality of KPIs linked to environmental and social performance, and make them as valid as those for collecting and managing financial data. Further costs may also arise to ensure coordination between departments—called upon to collect and integrate the information disseminated between the different business units—and to implement adequate procedures for controlling the data transmitted to the public, because if sustainability data is integrated into the annual report, investors and other stakeholders will expect the data to have the same level of quality as the financial ones.

Our analysis identified three medium-sized Italian joint-stock companies that have been publishing integrated reports:

- *Monnalisa jsc* (2009 to date), based on the GBS model and the AccountAbility 1000 framework: "six capitals" as of 2018;
- *Dellas jsc* (2014 to date), based on GRI's sustainability reporting standards: "six capitals" as of 2017;
- *Stafer jsc* (2016 and 2017 only), based on IIRC standards and the "six capitals".

Although a considerable improvement in the overall quality and applicability of <IR> can be observed, none of these examples can be defined as an undisputed best practice. In this still infant phase, no company has yet developed an integrated report that outshines in all respects. As Deloitte (2015) attests, "a company may excel in stakeholder engagement, while another one may be best in class in communicating the sustainability impacts along the supply chain". Nevertheless, the experience with <IR> of these three medium-sized companies was analysed in depth along the same protocol to understand the challenges that they faced when they introduced this innovation and the levers that allowed them to succeed. Empirical evidence was collected by triangulating the results of three data collection strategies, i.e. documental analysis, focusing in particular on available integrated reports, a review of the studies already published on these companies (Del Baldo, 2019; Eccles & Krzus, 2016; Giovannoni & Maraghini, 2013; Girella et al., 2019; Maraghini & Tommasiello, 2008), and semi-structured interviews to the people who were or are directly in charge for <IR>.

Three more firms are often or can be included in this sample. Two of them are actually well above the threshold identifying SMEs, but the former has a large majority of seasonal employees, so the "core" functions can be assimilated to an SME, whereas the latter used to be a medium-sized enterprise when it embarked on its journey to <IR>:

- *Costa Edutainment jsc* (2014 to date), based on IIRC standards and the "six capitals" (on average 504 employees);
- *GUNA jsc* (2012 to date), no reporting standard (currently 300 employees).

One more firm can be squarely included among small firms based on its headcount, but it is a financial intermediary specialized in sustainable investments, so its peculiar business model makes it difficult to compare with the other firms in the sample:

- *Etica Fund Management* (2013 to date), loosely based on IIRC standards (bank).

4.3 *Monnalisa jsc*

Monnalisa is a family business born in Arezzo in 1969 from the idea of Mr. Piero Iacomoni, today president of the company's Board of Directors, operating in the field of clothing and accessories for young girls. In 2013, *Monnalisa's* governance underwent some major structural changes, as the Board of Directors was redefined, introducing members from outside the Iacomoni family. Today, the company is among world leaders in the high-end market, selling its products in more than sixty countries through four types of distribution models: wholesale, wholesale retail, corporate retail and e-business retail, of which retail accounts for 25% of the company's total turnover. In addition, *Monnalisa* sells its clothing products also through the "shop in shop" model, which entails brand corners inside department stores such as *La Rinascente*, *Harrods* and the *Galeries Lafayette*. *Monnalisa's* mission can be summarized by the following three pillars:

- "To excel in innovation, creativity and functionality with a view to succeed in new markets";
- "To promote an encompassing managerial approach within the company to successfully address the challenges of small and medium-sized family businesses";

- "To expand globally both at a production and commercial level, without ever operating at the expense of its values and identity fostering a culture of social responsibility".

The company's increase in size and complexity occurred in the last two decades, both from an operational and organizational point of view, did not jeopardise core features such as the human dimension and participatory management, which have always been crucial to *Monnalisa*'s success. Moreover, the transition from management control to strategic control has been gradual with a continuous refinement of measurement and reporting techniques. In order to ensure dynamic control, the company has extended its operating scope by analysing data also in relation to future development, and by creating synergies with its strategy and between strategic goals and indicators.

As for the commitment of the company to CSR, this has been officially formalized in 2001 with the implementation of a dedicated CSR system, certified by the SA8000 standard. Furthermore, *Monnalisa* has extended its evaluation and control process to include the social sphere, which encompasses customers, suppliers and employees. Such a reform of CSR management has been undertaken to achieve two objectives, namely completing the quality certification of the company and rationalizing its commitment towards stakeholders. The milestones of this CSR journey are the following:

- In 2001, *Monnalisa* developed a code of corporate social responsibility and a document outlining its values, other than an "ethical label" describing the ethical commitment of the product from manufacturing to the final consumer.
- Since 2002, the company has been implementing a sustainability report to meet the expectations of the local region, build social capital based on trust, communicate the processes of value creation to its stakeholders and enhance its identity and corporate culture, with the aim of encouraging values disclosure, commitment and sense of belonging.
- In 2003, *Monnalisa* has embarked on a path of stakeholder inclusion and dialogue through the involvement of employees, "trend setters", customers and the local community. For this reason, the company has been selected by the European Commission as a best practice in the field of stakeholder engagement.
- To crown the above initiatives, in 2005, *Monnalisa* has adopted <IR> to offer its stakeholders an overarching vision of the company, integrating financial and socio-environmental reporting. This has provided for a significant consolidation between the two forms of reporting, namely financial reporting according to community provisions and socio-environmental reporting along content (GBS 255) and process (GRI) methodologies, providing evidence that economic performance relies on non-financial performance and intangible capitals as well.

Table 3 summarizes the insights collected through a semi-structured interview on the challenges Monnalisa faced during the introduction and refinement of <IR> and the factors that allowed to meet these challenges effectively.

Table 3 A summary of the challenges faced by *Monnalisa* in the implementation of <IR>

	Issue/challenge	Observations collected in the interview
✓	Senior management support	Family imprinting: the founding family has always been very committed to the themes related to CSR. It can be said that "it is in the DNA of the company". The CEO, although not a member of the Iacomoni family, is also a person who is particularly sensitive to these issues. The result is a "very lucky marriage".
✗	Size of the report	It has been argued that Monnalisa's integrated report is too lengthy. To address this criticism, the working group decided to structure the report along the different capitals analysed, so that readers can decide what to read and find the information that interests them more easily. A future investment will be to develop an online solution allowing users to customize fruition. Best practices would much help implementers in doing so.
n/a	Time pressure and data gathering	No remarks.
✓	Skills development and corporate governance	Monnalisa's HR policies foresee periodic trainings on both technical and soft skills, along other initiatives aiming at the empowerment of its employees.
✗	Primacy of shareholders' interests	A real challenge is to leverage all the efforts made by SMEs to valorize non-financial (intangible) capitals towards Italian capital providers—and banks, especially—which, to date, base their lending assessments almost exclusively on financial measurements and see non-financial disclosure as an "ornamental accessory".
✓	Lack of understanding of the role of and need for <IR>	Within the company, thanks to integrated thinking, a significant improvement in terms of disclosure has been observed, so, in general, the report has never been seen negatively. Indeed, the informative purpose of this tool is oriented towards external stakeholders, but also—and above all—towards the company's employees, as it creates a sense of enhancement of human resources. It is also a valid support to understand "where you stand after a reporting period".
✓	High upfront financial investments	*Monnalisa's* integrated report is the result of a journey lasting about two decades, when the company started to draw up a sustainability report along mandatory financial statements. It follows that financial investments were not made all at once, but gradually along the journey of valorization of intangibles. Furthermore, the CSR culture has always been

(continued)

Table 3 (continued)

	Issue/challenge	Observations collected in the interview
		instilled in the company's core values, so that no additional investments were deemed necessary when the decision of implementing IR was made.
✗	Lack of prescriptive reporting standards and guidance on specific data to be included	It would be useful to have guidelines that allow comparisons, especially by sector. As for the possible mandatory requirement to implement a non-financial reporting system, it is true that it creates significant work within the company, but in 2020 it really is imperative to report fully on its governance. "It is a chance to understand yourself better and remain competitive in the market".
✓	Lack of "connectedness"	For the same reasons highlighted in "Lack of understanding of the role of and need for <IR>" and for the innate propensity for CSR of the company, spreading the notion of integrated thinking across different departments was not a challenge for the promoters.
✗	Challenges of non-financial information	Non-financial information can entail some problems: self-referentiality, issues in finding homogeneous standards and performance indicators, challenges in making comparisons with the results of previous years and with competing companies, confinement of non-financial disclosure to an accessory role.

Source: Personal interview with Ms. Sara Tommasiello, Finance & Control, Human Resources and CSR Manager of *Monnalisa*

4.4 *Dellas jsc*

In its forty years of activity, *Dellas*, a medium-sized company from the Verona area, has achieved a leading position in the international market for the manufacture and distribution of diamond tools for working marble, granite and agglomerate. It is led by the second generation of the Ferrari family, together with the company's Board of Directors. Founded in Desenzano del Garda in 1973, the company moved to Lugo di Valpantena in 1982, an industrial district specialized in cutting marble and granite of local, national and international origin. This relocation has therefore allowed *Dellas* to be strategically closer to the beating heart of stone working, to test its products and to have immediate feedback on their performance.

Dellas has established itself as a company with a marked propensity for research and development, dynamism and the innovation of products and processes, to the extent that over the years many companies operating in the surrounding area have become the "extended laboratory" of its tools. Its excellence comes from human, entrepreneurial and managerial resources.

As part of its internationalization strategy, focused on controlling new markets through investments and partnerships in various non-EU countries, *Dellas* has chosen to develop and implement an <IR> system as the core of its risk management model, with the aim of highlighting and measuring those intangible assets that are strategic for the evolution and sustainability of its business activities. Embarking in the <IR> journey has been a major step forward in recognizing that organizational resources depend not only on financial and production capital, but also increasingly on human, intellectual, social and relational capitals—i.e. intangibles. Indeed, over the years, *Dellas* has observed that the impact of its operations on environmental and natural resources—as inputs, outputs and outcomes—consistently affects its business activities, financial returns and overall sustainability of value.

Thanks to this reporting practice, *Dellas* has witnessed:

- An improvement of its brand image and reputation;
- A better positioning at supply chain level;
- An increase in the quality of its recruitment process and talent development;
- A better and easier access to the credit market due to greater trust from financial capital providers.

The first step, which made it possible to overcome the limits of the financial report, was the issuance of a sustainability report, thanks to which the *Dellas Group* ensured an effective reporting of environmental, social and governance (ESG) aspects of its performance. This report, however, was only the starting point, preparatory to the implementation of <IR>, which shifted the focus to the illustration of medium–long-term value creation. The adoption of GRI international reporting standards was therefore not an end in itself, but aimed at measuring natural, social and relational capital more effectively within the broader IIRC framework, which also describes intellectual, human, financial and productive capital in an integrated manner. Table 4 summarizes the insights collected through a semi-structured interview on the challenges the Dellas Group faced during the introduction and refinement of <IR> and the factors that allowed to meet these challenges effectively.

4.5 *Stafer jsc*

Founded in 1960 in Faenza, *Stafer* manufactures and markets systems, solutions and accessories for the movement of roller shutters and awnings. More specifically, its operations revolve around the production of all the components and tools that allow the support, opening and closing of roller shutters, with both manual and automated modes, up to fully automatic mechanisms for some systems. Located in the Emilia-Romagna industrial district of mechanics, this B2B company, despite being an SME with about sixty employees, operates on both domestic and international markets, selling its products through a diversified network of international distributors.

Table 4 A summary of the challenges faced by *Dellas* in the implementation of <IR>

	Issue/challenge	Observations collected in the interview
✓	Senior management support	The <IR> initiative, promoted by the finance department through its CFO, has been immediately supported by the top management. The engagement of senior management—and of the CEO in particular—proved decisive when faced with the challenge of involving other departments, which initially were unwilling to cooperate.
✓	Size of the report	The length of the report does not represent a particular issue for SMEs. It is more a problem concerning larger companies. Observation at SME systemic level, which, however, does not refer specifically to *Dellas*: generally, SMEs do the "bare minimum" (e.g. they fill in a couple of pages dedicated to CSR in the notes to the financial statement), so the effort should be to delve deeper.
n/a	Time pressure and data gathering	No remarks.
✗	Skills development and corporate governance	Apart from the initiative's promoters and "CSR insiders", no one within the company was familiar with the topics of non-financial reporting and of <IR> in particular. Therefore, when the intra-departmental working team was first set-up, investments in training and skills development were required.
✓	Primacy of shareholders' interests	The integrated report is particularly well perceived by the company's (large) suppliers. The CFO organizes an annual meeting with financial institutes and other capital providers to present *Dellas'* financial statements and integrated report, whose non-financial performance indicators are regarded with interest and appreciation each year more.
✗	Lack of understanding of the role of and need for <IR>	Getting the whole company to embrace the culture of IR has certainly not been an easy task, despite the fact that *Dellas'* path to non-financial reporting has been a gradual process that has been diluted over the years.
✓	High upfront financial investments	Financial investments were not made all at once, but gradually. The result is that costs have been spread over time. In order to set up and train the implementation team, funding from Regione Veneto was employed. Certainly, a lot of time was invested, but unfortunately it was not measured. The effects of the investments in <IR> on the reputation capital are very positive.

(continued)

Table 4 (continued)

	Issue/challenge	Observations collected in the interview
✗	Lack of prescriptive reporting standards and guidance on specific data to be included	The principles issued by the IIRC must be very broad and comprehensive in nature in order to be applicable by companies of different size classes operating in different countries and different sectors. In other words, <IR> principles must be necessarily universal. To overcome this problem, Mr. Pasquotti developed a set of KPIs and other metrics, but he did not do it completely from scratch: in fact, he used standards prescribed by GRI and WICI framework, in order to be compliant with them. Guidelines that are more specific should be defined at national level, targeting SMEs and different productive sectors. These guidelines should be SME-friendly, i.e. leaner and not financially burdening. Thanks to their more agile structure, SMEs are faster than larger firms to put in place an <IR> system. For the moment, the only option that companies have is to "take cues" from <IR> principles, but these cues, of course, are not structured. This implies that it is not possible to compare integrated reports of different companies operating, for example, in the same sector and region. Assurance on <IR> should also be foreseen, since as of today, it is not possible to audit the information provided in integrated reports. Therefore, the value, correctness and adherence to the KPIs used are entirely discretionary.
✗	Lack of "connectedness"	In order for the report to reflect the company's modus operandi and processes, thus achieving an authentic integrated narrative of corporate identity and global value created, the promoting parties had to face the difficult challenge of directly involving the different departments of the company, namely the managing director (CEO) and sales director (CSO), the chief financial officer (CFO), the chief operations officer (COO), the director of human resources (CHRO) and the R&D manager. Indeed, when <IR> was first implemented, the key leaders had to explain to the whole organization that IR "was not a waste of time", but "a brand-new mindset to be rooted in the company strategy". The role of the CFO has been to facilitate and encourage the working group to approach this tool, explaining how they were not simply working for the finance department in the preparation of an evolved financial report, but that the result of the whole integrated journey

(continued)

Table 4 (continued)

	Issue/challenge	Observations collected in the interview
		would serve each business function to better design their KPIs and, for investors, to understand in depth the strategies and added value of the key processes of each business area. Initially, the greatest resistance towards <IR> was that of the R&D department, as reporting and disclosing on projects of this nature may sometimes be a rather sensitive issue. So, there were some debate and negotiation about what could be shared externally and what could not, but with due coordination, an agreement was eventually found.
✗	Challenges of non-financial information	The path towards non-financial reporting has taken place gradually, in an incremental logic of continuous analysis, monitoring and improvement. For monitoring purposes, the working group has devised a measurement system to assess improvement on an annual basis. Specifically, it has developed a stakeholder diagram that provides numerical performance indicators for each stakeholder group. Thus, for every year, a certain target is set, and progress is tracked along KPIs. The challenge lies in connecting the numerical value of KPIs with the equivalent monetary value.

Source: Interview with Mr. Marco Pasquotti, Chief Financial Officer of Dellas and member of the Board of Directors of Organismo Italiano di Business Reporting (OIBR)

Stafer's governance model provides a functional structure involving various bodies. It is administered by a Board of Directors, which, within the scope of its powers, has delegated powers to two of its members, while its general manager is Ms. Sara Cirone. The company's governance structure and internal organization are structured to allow continuous improvement and stakeholder management is carried out through periodic activities and is fuelled by the objective of enhancing the synergistic relationship between the company and its territory, with a view to overall economic, social and environmental sustainability.

It follows that the "human dimension" of business—both internally and externally—represents the key element of its strategic and operational positioning. Indeed, in the very introduction to the company's 2017 integrated report, Ms. Cirone states that "Constant investments in the improvement of internal dynamics, the use of new technologies, new means of communication and the enhancement of human resources allow our organization to adapt to continuous external changes and to offer a personalized service to customers' needs. For this reason, the design, technical assistance, quality control, wide range and experience in different international markets give added value to our products. We look to the future by investing our energies in the development of sustainable thinking in full respect of the environment, its natural processes and the well-being of people".

Stafer's path towards <IR> began in 2016 and continued in 2017. This approach is also evident in the way "strategy" and "business model" were defined in the process leading to the first integrated report. A peculiar support tool is the "strategic map", which the firm was already using, and which has been adapted to the <IR> international framework through the inclusion of the six capitals. In this way, the links between the different perspectives, indicators and the multi-capital approach to <IR> were identified. In 2018, *Stafer* won the Special Award in the "Integrated Reporting" category of the "Balance Sheet Oscar" for the best integrated report by an Italian company.

As a means of promoting a culture of accountability, disclosure and sustainability, in addition to the UNI EN ISO 14001 environmental certification obtained in 2005 and the validation of the EMAS Regulation, *Stafer* has implemented a number of CSR initiatives:

- Since 2009 it has been measuring and monitoring its environmental and social performance through the adoption of the balanced scorecard (BSC);
- It supports a number of different social and sport initiatives, linked to local junior teams;
- It had developed projects for the participation and involvement of employees in company activities, such as training events related to arts and culture;
- It has deployed a communication strategy to promote CSR principles, both inside and outside the organization, through its corporate value charter and the sustainability section on its website. To the same end, the company partners with different associations aimed at promoting the culture of sustainability and value creation, as well as the development of the local territory and its enterprises.
- In 2017, a corporate benefit programme—the "Wellness Path"—was designed along the United Nations' Sustainable Development Goals (SDGs): this cross-cutting project embraced SDG issues and had the objective of informing people at all organizational levels about the most pressing sustainability issues, as well as making a positive contribution to the environment and society.

Table 5 summarizes the insights collected through two semi-structured interviews on the challenges Stafer faced during the introduction and refinement of and the factors that allowed to meet these challenges effectively.

The three companies analysed in depth score differently in their adherence to the spirit, if not to the letter, of <IR>. As already mentioned, *Stafer* reported only for two years, probably also as a consequence of challenging market conditions. *Dellas* has been preparing an integrated report since 2016, but its annual report included explicitly elements of non-financial reporting since 2013; its chief financial officer is very active in Organismo Italiano di Business Reporting, the network of professionals and academics promoting <IR> in Italy, and compliance to the requirements of sound <IR> are a constant feature of the reports produced by *Dellas*. *Monnalisa* stands out, in terms of both process and contents, even though the path towards the adherence to formal <IR> standards has been less linear (the "six-capital" approach

Table 5 A summary of the challenges faced by *Stafer* in the implementation of <IR>

	Issue/challenge	Observations collected in the interview
✓	Senior management support	The input towards <IR> was provided by Ms. Sara Cirone, hired first as a consultant and then as managing director.
✗	Size of the report	It can be quite tricky to summarize information of different nature coming from different departments in a single document. Nevertheless, only if synthetic and reader-friendly, the final report can give the company a concrete opportunity to tell its story comprehensively and become an added value (and not only a financial burden).
n/a	Time pressure and data gathering	No remarks.
✗	Skills development and corporate governance	The ability of SMEs to attract and retain talents is much lower than that of larger companies, especially in Italy. This is the greatest challenge SMEs face, and it involves very high costs. For this reason, HR management in SMEs plays a crucial role and should be dealt with by senior management accordingly. Observation at SME systemic level, which does not refer specifically to *Stafer*: many Italian SMEs are not yet familiar with the concept of corporate governance. This implies, for example, that these companies do not have a formally defined organization chart nor an appropriate contractual framework and operate with little "structural" clarity in general. A prerequisite for <IR> is the corporate structure, which obviously must be clearly defined in the first place.
n/a	Primacy of shareholders' interests	No remarks.
✓	Lack of understanding of the role of and need for <IR>	*Stafer* chose to adopt the framework because the company had already undertaken an evolutionary process in terms of HR management, strategy development, and was addressing many of its efforts towards in the field of intangibles. For this reason, when <IR> was first published, *Stafer* had already a thorough understanding of the rationale behind integrated thinking and many of the necessary information/systems to implement it. Thus, it took advantage of this opportunity to further formalize and disclose the process through which it creates sustainable value.
✓	High upfront financial investments	In 2008, *Stafer* decided to undertake a process of intangibles enhancement, focusing especially on HR management and investing in professional training, skills and process development, technology updating (shift to data

(continued)

Table 5 (continued)

	Issue/challenge	Observations collected in the interview
		storing and sharing on cloud), etc. The <IR> project, launched eight years later in 2016, was the crowning achievement of this process. Therefore, at the level of upfront financial investments, these were done upstream, and not so much for <IR> per se. These investments in intangible capitals yielded considerable economic returns and, due to the liquidity generated, acted as a safety net during the 2008 crisis.
n/a	Lack of prescriptive reporting standards and guidance on specific data to be included	No remarks.
✗	Lack of "connectedness"	Being able to give a holistic and integrated representation of how the company operates and what it generates on different levels (e.g. products/services sold, added value created) is a challenge for SMEs. An overview of the entire system allows all citizens to live in connection with one another. "Having an overview of the global system allows all citizens to live in connection with one another. In *Stafer's* corporate system, this element represents the main point on which the entire organization is based". The above issue depends particularly on people's tendency to focus only on their own tasks and the department to which they belong, although often and willingly it is necessary to cooperate and liaise with colleagues from other business areas. Overall, this "silo mentality" has an impact on business operations and on the morale and quality of employees, on the working environment, and if not addressed, can lead to the detriment of the company.
✗	Challenges of non-financial information	The ability to innovate of Italian SMEs, especially at corporate governance and strategic level, is traditionally much lower than that of large business groups. It follows that implementing a new reporting system, which takes into account "non-traditional" figures and measures, is often beyond the capacity of such companies.

Source: Interview with Ms. Sara Cirone, Managing Director of *Stafer* and member of the Steering Committee of Organismo Italiano di Business Reporting (OIBR) and Mr. Andrea Ragazzini, former chief value officer and member of the Management Board of Organismo Italiano di Business Reporting (OIBR)

was explicitly included only in 2018, and the document bears the name of "annual" report). As an example, the latest integrated report issued by *Dellas* features only two pages dedicated to natural capital, focusing on energy savings, water consumption and production waste, and no details are provided about future performance targets in this area. In its report for 2019 *Monnalisa* instead included eight pages devoted to natural capital, providing information on:

- People mobility;
- Logistics of goods;
- Consumption of fuel, water, electricity and raw materials (cardboard packaging, paper packaging, textiles, paper and printer cartridges);
- Direct and indirect emissions;
- Mechanisms for the accountability of suppliers.

The final point is especially interesting, as GRI Standard No. 308 envisages the provision of this piece of information, but *Monnalisa* is unique in the sample we analysed in actually providing it, and actually including this aspect among its own performance targets. Two more pages in the report outline:

- the performance targets set in the previous Integrated Report for 2019 and whether they have been achieved (which is not always the case!);
- the performance targets set for 2020, with two targets out of four concerning the accountability of suppliers.

The interviews with the representatives of the Italian SMEs that experimented the adoption on <IR> yield a clear signal: the willingness to pay attention to non-financial reporting and to understand corporate performance in a holistic perspective should come primarily from the top. A similar message comes also from our interviews with the representatives of Italian SMEs that engaged in sustainability reporting.

Some players, including both associations of experts and individual practitioners, are very active in "pushing" aggressively <IR>. The presence of a "push" instead of a "pull" factor seems to translate into inconsistent <IR>: some of the firms involved do issue integrated reports for a while (as little as two years in the examples we analysed) and then stop.

An important factor, though, is likely to be at work triggering more demand for <IR> in the future: larger companies are more and more often required to report on the social and environmental performance of their entire supply chain and, as a consequence, are likely to request relevant information from their suppliers in this respect. The changes that the EU Non-Financial Reporting Directive (2014/95/EU) seems poised to undergo as a consequence of the European Green Deal are likely to increase pressure in this direction. As it happened in the past with quality certifications, the SMEs unable to present detailed information about their non-financial performance may be barred from supplying larger firms: in other words, non-financial reporting or <IR> could turn into a prerequisite to bid for contracts, and anecdotal evidence suggests that this is already starting to happen. It remains to be seen whether this forced compliance will help reap the promises of <IR>, or turn it into a mere box-ticking exercise.

5 Conclusion and Remarks

The cross-cutting analysis of the experience of Italian firms with <IR> raises important questions to be addressed.

The first question is "*Who are the intended readers of integrated reports?*". In some cases (e.g. *Stafer*), by reading an integrated report one gets the feeling it has been designed primarily to please the Evaluation Board of the Balance Sheet Oscar, and receive an award. In other words, should an integrated report provide detailed technicalities or an inspirational storytelling?

The second question is "*How much standardization is required in <IR>?*" Translating <IR> into checklists to be adhered to makes it simpler to disseminate the practice, but there is a serious risk of "boilerplate", extremely detrimental to credibility. Spontaneous expression and lack of standardization, on the contrary, make the report credible, especially when the company admits that they may fail to achieve their intended objectives, at least from time to time (e.g. *GUNA*), but at the price of little or no comparability of performance information.

The third question is "*Which balance should we strike between a backward-looking and a forward-looking perspective in <IR>?*" This is a difficult choice: hard facts or sense of purpose? The "National observatory on non-financial reporting" points out that very few Italian companies set quantitative objectives on material sustainability topics, so that future reporting exercises can help stakeholders track their ability to deliver on their commitments (Osservatorio Dichiarazioni Non Finanziarie, 2020: 16). Is <IR> meant primarily to facilitate corporate reporting on multiple performance dimensions, or to provide a framework helping managers refine their value creation process?

The fourth question is "*What balance in focus should we strike between market and non-market environment?*" This is a simpler question, because both can be accommodated, but the mix of market vs. non-market stakeholders determines whether we are looking at <IR> from the standpoint of homo oeconomicus or of a corporate citizen.

The final and most important question is "*Why should SMEs adopt <IR> after all?*" Is it about cultural change? Or external accountability? Or "window dressing"? The integrated reports we reviewed seem primarily designed for external accountability, but the information that they provide is very skewed, especially in the reports of larger firms. Is <IR> about providing an objective view of corporate performance, or is it a way to frame the messages the company wishes to pass on to its stakeholders, so ultimately a matter of storytelling (Gumb, 2007; Boiral, 2013)? The evidence from Italy points towards the latter answer, but deep-seated suspicion and mistrust by public opinion towards the claims of private firms raise doubts as whether this attempt at "window dressing" would prove effective, or on the contrary it would backfire (assuming someone would bother to read an integrated report). This leaves us with cultural change as the ultimate rationale for <IR>. At this point, one more question surfaces: "Do firms have a strategy?" We are convinced that <IR> does not get very far as a tool to "make believe", but—if intended correctly—it can serve as a powerful "thinking hat" for inner search.

References

Amelio, F., et al. (2018). *Osservatorio Nazionale sulla Rendicontazione Non Finanziaria ex D.Lgs. 254/2016, 1° Report*. Milano: Deloitte & Touche.

Amelio, F., et al. (2021). *Osservatorio Nazionale sulla Rendicontazione Non Finanziaria, 3° Edizione*. Milano: Deloitte & Touche. Retrieved August 21, 2021, from https://www2.deloitte.com/it/it/pages/audit/articles/osservatorio-nazionale-sulla-rendicontazione-non-finanziaria-2020.html

Aureli, S., Magnaghi, E., & Salvatori, F. (2018). The transposition of the non-financial reporting directive in the UK, France and Italy. *Symphonya Emerging Issues in Management, 1*(1), 48–67.

Bocchi, F. M., & Venier, S. (2019). Misurare il valore condiviso: l'evoluzione necessaria nel reporting delle imprese. *Harvard Business Review Italia, 3*, 70–77.

Boiral, O. (2013). Sustainability reports as simulacra? A counter-account of A and A+ GRI reports. *Accounting, Auditing & Accountability Journal, 26*(7), 1036–1071.

Capodaglio, G., Semprini, L., & Dangarska, V. S. (2016). *Il nuovo bilancio d'esercizio*. Santarcangelo di Romagna (RN): Maggioli.

Caputo, F., et al. (2020). The non-financial reporting harmonization in Europe: Evolutionary pathways related to the transposition of the Directive 95/2014/EU within the Italian context. *Sustainability, 12*(1), 92.

Coda, V. (1984). La valutazione della formula imprenditoriale: come si apprezza e si analizza il grado di successo di un'impresa. *Sviluppo & Organizzazione, 82*, 277–291.

Commissione Bilancio Integrato. (2016). *Il bilancio integrato per le PMI*. Milano: Ordine dei Dottori Commercialisti e degli Esperti Contabili.

Contraffatto, M. (2014). The institutionalization of social and environmental reporting: An Italian narrative. *Accounting, Organizations and Society, 39*(6), 414–432.

Cortesi, A., Mancini, C., & Tettamanzi, P. (2017). *Contabilità e bilancio*. Milano: IPSOA.

Del Baldo, M. (2019). Small and medium-sized organisations: Why and how do they implement integrated reporting. In S. O. Idowu & M. Del Baldo (Eds.), *Integrated reporting. Antecedents and perspectives for organizations and stakeholders* (pp. 95–121). Cham: Springer.

De Luca, F. (2020). *Mandatory and discretional non-financial disclosure after the European Directive 2014/95/EU: An empirical analysis of Italian listed companies' behavior*. Bingley: Emerald.

DESI. (2019). *Digital Economy and Society Index (DESI) 2019 Country Report Italy*. Retrieved August 21, 2021, from https://digital-strategy.ec.europa.eu/en/policies/desi-italy

Deloitte. (2015). *<IR>: how does it fit into the UK corporate reporting landscape?*. Retrieved February 17, 2021, from https://www.iasplus.com/en/publications/uk/other/ir-uk-landscape

Directive 2013/34/EU of the European Parliament and of the Council of 26 June 2013 on the annual financial statements, consolidated financial statements and related reports of certain types of undertakings, amending Directive 2006/43/EC of the European Parliament and of the Council and repealing Council Directives 78/660/EEC and 83/349/EEC Text with EEA relevance. Retrieved March 20, 2021, from https://eur-lex.europa.eu/legal-content/EN/TXT/?uri=CELEX%3A32013L0034

Directive 2014/95/EU of the European Parliament and of the Council of 22 October 2014 amending Directive 2013/34/EU as regards disclosure of non-financial and diversity information by certain large undertakings and groups. Retrieved March 20, 2021, from https://eur-lex.europa.eu/legal-content/EN/TXT/?uri=CELEX%3A32014L0095

EC. (2019). *2019 SBA Fact Sheet Italy*. Belgium: European Commission.

Eccles, R. G., & Krzus, M. P. (2016). *Il viaggio verso la rendicontazione integrata*. Forlì: Edizioni Philanthropy.

Edelman. (2020). *Edelman trust barometer 2020*. Retrieved August 21, 2021, from https://cdn2.hubspot.net/hubfs/440941/Trust%20Barometer%202020/2020%20Edelman%20Trust%20Barometer%20Global%20Report.pdf?utm_campaign=Global:%20Trust%20Barometer%202020&utm_source=Website

Gazzola, P., et al. (2020). Non-financial information disclosure in Italian public interest companies: a sustainability reporting perspective. *Sustainability, 12*, 1–17.

GBS. (2005). *Il bilancio sociale. Standard di base e documenti di ricerca*. Milano: Giuffrè.

GBS. (2007). *Il bilancio sociale, Reporting ambientale e valore aggiunto*. Milano: Giuffrè.

GBS. (2013). *Principi di redazione del bilancio sociale*. Milano: Giuffrè.

Gesuele, B., & Pozzoli, M. (2017). L'utilizzo del integrated reporting in Italia: stato dell'arte. *Economia Aziendale Online, 8*(2), 119–129.

Giovannoni, E., & Maraghini, M. P. (2013). The challenges of integrated performance measurement systems: Integrating mechanisms for integrated measures. *Accounting, Auditing & Accountability Journal, 26*(6), 978–1008.

Girella, L., Zambon, S., & Rossi, P. (2019). Reporting on sustainable development: A comparison of three Italian small and medium-sized enterprises. *Corporate Social Responsibility and Environmental Management, 26*(4), 981–996.

Gumb, B. (2007). What is shown, what is hidden: Compulsory disclosure as a spectacle. *Critical Perspectives on Accounting, 18*(7), 807–828.

Ianniello, M. & Fedele, P. (2011). Teoria degli stakeholder: Tra internazionalizzazione e tradizione aziendale. *Rivista Italiana di Ragioneria e di Economia Aziendale*, 111 (5–6).

Maraghini, M. P., & Tommasiello, S. (2008). Rappresentazione integrata delle performance aziendali: il caso Monnalisa S.p.A. *Amministrazione, Finanza e Controllo*, 305–329.

Mio, C., Fasan, M., & Pauluzzo, R. (2016). Internal application of IR principles: Generali's internal integrated reporting. *Journal of Cleaner Production, 139*, 204–218.

Mion, G., & Adaui, C. R. L. (2020). The effect of mandatory publication of nonfinancial disclosure in Europe on sustainability reporting quality: First insights about Italian and German companies. In L. Songini et al. (Eds.), *Non-financial disclosure and integrated reporting: Practices and critical issues* (pp. 55–80). Bingley: Emerald.

Ortiz-Martinez, E., & Marin-Hernandez, S. (2020). European financial services SMEs: Language in their sustainability reporting. *Sustainability, 12*(20), 8377.

Osservatorio Dichiarazioni Non Finanziarie. (2020). *Osservatorio DNF Report 2019*. Milano: Osservatorio DNF. https://www.osservatoriodnf.it/doc/report-2019-it.pdf.

Panizza, A., et al. (2018). *Integrated reporting for SMEs: Implementation guidance*. Retrieved August 21, 2021, from https://integratedreporting.org/wp-content/uploads/2019/05/NIBR_IR_for_SMEs_ENG_final.pdf

Paolucci, G., & Cerioni, E. (2017). Integrated reporting and Italian companies: An empirical investigation. *International Journal of Business and Management, 12*(9), 221–230.

Provasi, R., & Sottoriva, C. (2015). Preliminary considerations about the transposition of Directive 2013/34/EU into Italian accounting system. *Journal of Modern Accounting and Auditing, 11*(6), 302–312.

Quagli, A. (2018). *Bilancio di esercizio e principi contabili* (9th ed.). Torino: Giappichelli.

Rubino, M., & Garzoni, A. (2018). Il *reporting* integrato: l'influenza del capitale intellettuale sulla *performance* aziendale. Un'analisi empirica delle imprese italiane. In S. Corbella et al. (Eds.), *Nuove frontiere del reporting aziendale* (pp. 1294–1312). Franco Angeli: Milano.

Rusconi, G. (2021). Dai bilanci sociali alla dichiarazione non finanziaria: alcune riflessioni. *Impresa Progetto Electronic Journal of Management, 1*, 1–13.

Rusconi, G., & Dorigatti, M. (2004). *Teoria generale del bilancio sociale e applicazioni pratiche*. Milano: Franco Angeli.

Santesso, E., & Sostero, U. (2016). *I principi contabili per il bilancio d'esercizio. Analisi e interpretazioni delle norme civilistiche*. Milano: EGEA.

Signori, S., & Rusconi, G. (2009). Ethical thinking in traditional Italian Economia Aziendale and the stakeholder management theory: the search for possible interactions. *Journal of Business Ethics, 89*, 303–318.

Sorrentino, M., & Smarra, M. (2014). The burden of accounting standards for small and medium enterprises. *Corporate Ownership and Control, 11*(4), 223–232.

Sottoriva, C. (2015). Il recepimento della Direttiva 2013/34/UE in Italia: annotazioni a margine del Decreto Legislativo n. 139 del 18 agosto 2015. *Rivista Italiana di Ragioneria e di Economia aziendale, 3*, 315–331.

Venturelli, A., et al. (2017). Directive 2014/95/EU: Are Italian companies already compliant? *Sustainability, 9*(8), 1385.

SMEs and IR: Evidence from Poland

Joanna Dyczkowska, Tomasz Dyczkowski, Bartłomiej Nita, Piotr Oleksyk, and Katarzyna Piotrowska

1 The SME Sector in Poland

In 2017, about 2.08 million non-financial companies were registered in Poland, including 2.0 million micro-enterprises, 53.8 thousand small enterprises, 15.3 thousand medium enterprises and 3.6 thousand large companies (PARP, 2019). Considering the "non-financial business economy" with its the most influential sectors such as industry, construction, trade and services (NACE Rev. 2 sections B to J, L, M and N), the structures of the number of enterprises, the number of persons employed and value added generated by particular groups of companies are as follows (see Figs. 1, 2 and 3).

Figure 1 shows that the dispersion of enterprises in Poland is comparable with companies' structure in the EU. There existed only slight differences while considering micro- and small companies.

Firstly, a share of micro-enterprises was a little higher in Poland than in the EU (95.7% and 93.1%, respectively). PARP (2019) notices that micro-companies are characterized by a positive development trend in Poland, reflecting an observable growth in the number of such entities, their production value, revenues, investment outlays and the number of persons employed over the past years. However, micro-enterprises are distinguished by the lowest value added growth rate while comparing to the larger entities.

Secondly, small enterprises' share was a little bit lower in Poland than in the EU (3.2% and 5.8%, respectively). Over the years 2015–2017, a decrease in the number of small enterprises has been observed in Poland. In 2017, there were 6% less small

J. Dyczkowska (✉) · T. Dyczkowski · B. Nita · P. Oleksyk · K. Piotrowska
Wroclaw University of Economics and Business, Wroclaw, Poland
e-mail: joanna.dyczkowska@ue.wroc.pl; tomasz.dyczkowski@ue.wroc.pl; bartlomiej.nita@ue.wroc.pl; piotr.oleksyk@ue.wroc.pl; katarzyna.piotrowska@ue.wroc.pl

J. Dyczkowska et al. (eds.), *Development of Integrated Reporting in the SME Sector*, CSR, Sustainability, Ethics & Governance,
https://doi.org/10.1007/978-3-030-81903-3_5

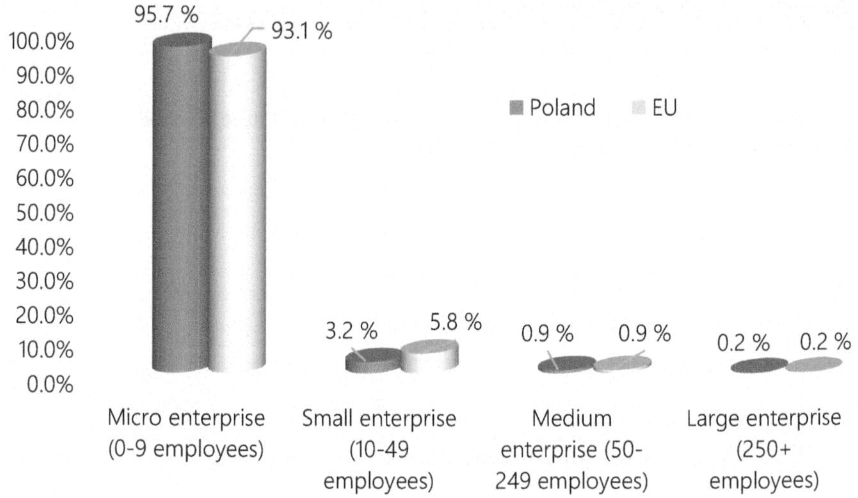

Fig. 1 Structure of the number of enterprises in 2017 (Poland vs EU). Source: Own presentation based on EUROSTAT (2020a)

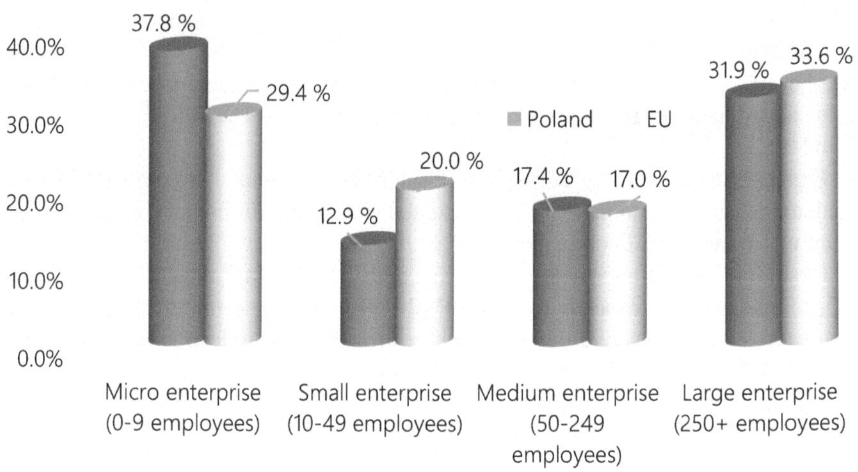

Fig. 2 Structure of the number of persons employed in enterprises in 2017 (Poland vs EU). Source: Own presentation based on EUROSTAT (2020a)

companies than a year earlier. PARP (2019) emphasizes that small enterprises have the lowest share in the GDP and job creation among all groups of companies (11% and 12.2%, respectively). Polish small enterprises are also characterized by low innovative activity both in the group of industrial and service companies. However, they are more profitable, have better financial liquidity than medium and large entities and are characterized by high export dynamics (PARP, 2019).

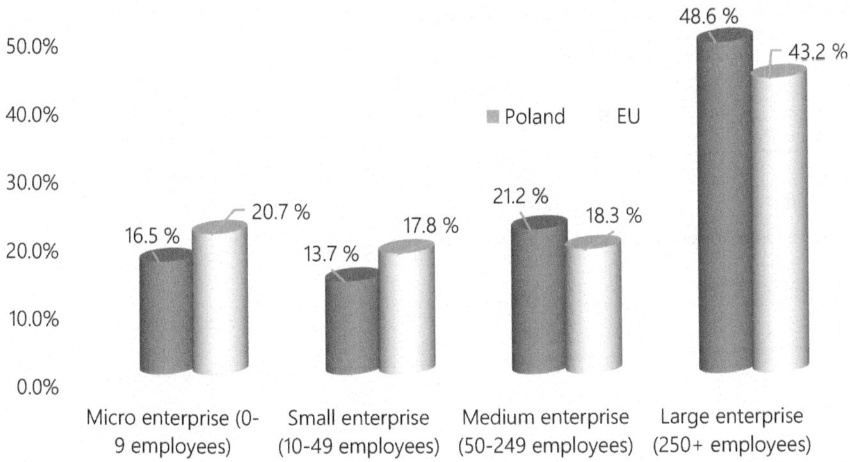

Fig. 3 Shares of value added generated by particular groups of companies in 2017 (Poland vs EU). Source: Own presentation based on EUROSTAT (2020a)

Interestingly, in 2017 shares of medium-sized and large enterprises in the whole population of companies were the same while comparing Polish and EU markets (0.9% and 0.2%, respectively). However, Polish medium-sized enterprises' growth dynamics have been negative since 2011 (Statistics Poland, 2019), which means that the number of these entities has been shrinking regularly. It is worth remarking that medium-sized enterprises generated more jobs than small companies, whereas micro-enterprises prevailed in this matter (see Fig. 2). Almost every third medium-sized company was innovatively active and financed this type of activity for the most part from its own resources. In recent years, medium-sized enterprises have grown dynamically in terms of the value of exports of both products and services per enterprise, although there was a small drop (−2.9%) in value dynamics among product exporters in 2017 (PARP, 2019).

Polish large companies had quite a high share in the GDP creation (32% while assuming the value of GDP generated by the whole enterprise sector). However, micro-enterprises prevailed in this respect since they had the largest share in the GDP creation (41%) among all enterprises' groups. Large companies also had a significant share in the job creation (31.9%) in the enterprise sector, but again micro-enterprises prevailed in this respect (37.8%) (see Fig. 2).

Another interesting point is that large companies actively developed innovations and eagerly cooperates in innovative projects (PARP, 2019). Finally, a group of large companies generated 99.1 billion EUR value added that was only slightly less than the whole group of MSMEs[1] (see Fig. 3: 48.6% vs 51.4%).

Likewise, Polish also EU SMEs faced several problems and tried to overcome various barriers. Since 2008, the European Commission and the European Central

[1] MSMEs—Micro-, small- and medium-sized enterprises.

Table 1 Structure of surveyed SMEs in Poland and EU28

Categories	Enterprise size (number of employees) 1–9 (%)	10–49 (%)	50–249 (%)	Sectors Industry (%)	Construction (%)	Trade (%)	Services (%)
EU28	44	30	26	17	10	24	49
Poland	55	19	26	22	11	29	38

Source: Own presentation based on EC (2019a)

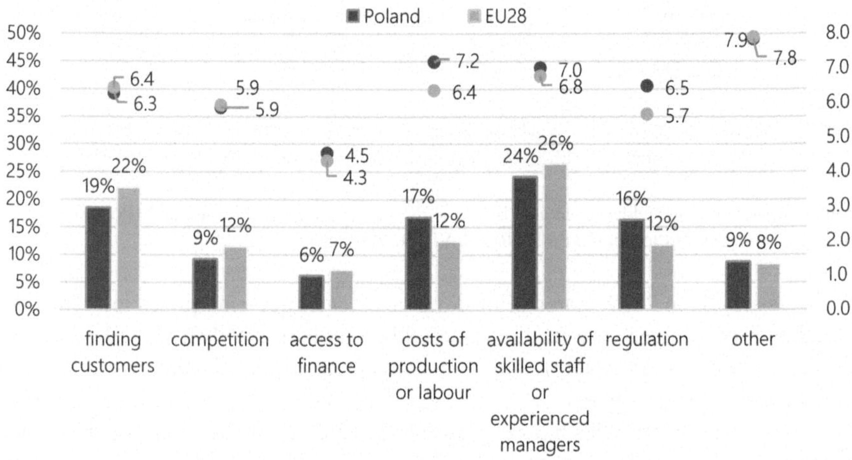

Fig. 4 Most important problems SMEs in Poland and EU28 have been facing. Source: Own presentation based on EC (2019a)

Bank (ECB) have collaborated on the SAFE survey dedicated to SMEs. In 2019, the research covered over 15.000 SMEs in EU28 (EC, 2019a) (see Table 1).

The general topic of the survey regarded the enterprise access to financial sources. The commission formulated several dozen questions. For instance, they asked:

- "*What is currently the most important problem your firm is facing?*" (the problems were classified for each country according to the categories listed in Fig. 4)
- "*How important have the following problems been for your enterprise in the past six months?*" (please answer using a scale of 1–10, where 1 means "*no it is not at all important*" and 10 means "*it is extremely important*").

The bar chart shows the most important problems indicated by SMEs in Poland and EU28 (Fig. 4). It can be seen that there was a consensus on the type of problems SMEs had to face. The largest group of SMEs in Poland and in the EU28 described "*availability of skilled staff or experienced managers*" and "*finding customers*" as the most prominent current challenges. These problems were related to building, maintaining or developing human capital and social and relationship capital in SMEs.

In response to the question, how important have the following problems been for an enterprise in the past 6 months, SMEs in Poland and EU28 indicated 7.0 and 6.8 points, respectively, for problems with "*availability of skilled staff or experienced managers*"; 6.3 and 6.4 points, respectively, for problems with "*finding customers*". However, it should be noted that "*costs of production or labour*" apart from the other non-identified problems were indicated as the most important in the past 6 months in Polish SMEs. Inculcation of integrated thinking in SMEs can help them in overcoming all these problems. Due to integrated thinking, SMEs can better understand the connectivity and interrelations between the range of factors that affect an ability to create value over time. Moreover, integrated thinking may increase the quality of dialogue with providers of financial capital and other stakeholders. It is particularly crucial for SMEs to continually develop their relation network, though their position is often dependent on other market players' power.

2 Overview of Reporting Regulations with Potential Impact on IR

In Poland, corporate reporting is regulated or supported by:

- Polish Accounting Act of 29 September 1994 (Journal of Laws of 2016, item 1047, as amended)—mandatory regulation.
- Regulation of the Minister of Finance of 29 March 2018 on current and periodic information provided by issuers of securities and conditions for recognizing as equivalent information required by laws of a non-member state (Journal of Laws of 2018, item 757)—mandatory regulation.
- National Accounting Standard No. 9: "Management activity report" (here NAS No. 9)—voluntary regulation.
- Non-Financial Information Standard (2017) (here NFI standard)—voluntary regulation.

Furthermore, NAS No. 9 recommends entities committed to compiling a statement (report) on non-financial information to adhere to standards, frameworks, concepts, norms and guidelines included in Table 2.

The use of recognized standards facilitates the interpretation and assessment of information and ensures its comparability. If the entity decides to directly apply any of the principles, standards, norms or guidelines or use them to develop its own principles, it should indicate them in the said statement. In Poland, GRI standards are the most commonly used guidelines by the large public interest companies. GRI standards are universal, which means that they are suitable for all organizations regardless of their size or industry type. Both experienced and non-experienced organizations may cope with an application of GRI guidelines.

Table 2 Standards, frameworks, concepts, norms and guidelines in preparing a statement on NFI

I. Standard of Non-Financial Information (2017)	**XII**. AccountAbility AA1000 Standards
II. Global Reporting Initiative	**XIII**. Standards of Climate Disclosure Standards Board
III. Eco-Management and Audit Scheme together with related sector reference documents	**XIV**. Product and Organisation Environmental Footprint Guides
IV. ISO 26000—Social responsibility	**XV**. Carbon Disclosure Project
V. UN Global Compact Initiative	**XVI**. Natural Capital Protocol
VI. Guidelines for Multinational Enterprises of the Organisation for Economic Cooperation and Development	**XVII**. OECD Due Diligence Guidance for Responsible Supply Chains from Conflict-Affected and High-Risk areas
VII. Tripartite Declaration of principles concerning multinational enterprises and social policy of the International Labour Organisation	**XVIII**. UN Sustainable Development Goals, Resolution of 25 September 2015 transforming our world: the 2030 Agenda for Sustainable Development
VIII. Standards of Sustainability Accounting Standards Board (SASB)	**XIX**. Guidance for Responsible Agricultural Supply Chains of FAO-OECD
IX. International Integrated Reporting Framework	**XX**. Guidance on the Strategic Report of the UK Financial Reporting Council
X. Model Guidance on reporting ESG information to investors of the UN Sustainable Stock Exchanges Initiative	**XXI**. Guiding Principles Reporting Framework on Business and Human Rights
XI. European Federation of Financial Analysts Societies' KPIs for Environmental, Social, Governance	**XXII**. Sustainability Code of the German Council for Sustainable Development

Source: Own presentation based on National Accounting Standard No. 9

Polish Accounting Act as Mandatory Corporate Reporting Regulation

The Directive 2014/95/EU has brought changes to Polish accounting regulations. As a result, on 26 January 2017, the amended Accounting Act entered into force.[2] It imposed on selected entities an obligation to publish reports to the extent beyond previously published financial information. It was established that large companies (public interest entities) meeting the legislator's criteria were committed starting from the financial year beginning on 1 January 2017 or during the calendar year 2017 to report on non-financial information issues.

Under the Accounting Act (§ 3 clause 1e points 1–6), entities classified as public interest entities and covered by the requirement to report non-financial information include:

- organizational units operating based on the Banking Law Act, the Financial Instruments Trading Act, the Investment Funds Act, the Act on Insurance and Reinsurance Activities, and provisions on the organization and functioning of pension funds,

[2]Polish Accounting Act of 29 September 1994 (Journal of Laws of 2016, item 1047, as amended).

Table 3 Recognition criteria for large companies in Poland

Criteria	Threshold
Average annual employment in full-time equivalents	>500 persons
Total assets at the end of the financial year	>85,000,000 PLN
Net revenues from the sale of products and goods for the financial year	>170,000,000 PLN

Source: Own presentation based on Polish Accounting Act

- entities intending to apply or applying for permission to carry out activities based on specific provisions indicated by the Accounting Act,
- issuers of securities admitted, intending to apply or applying for their admission to trading on one of the regulated markets of the European Economic Area,
- issuers of securities admitted to trading on an alternative trading system,
- national payment institutions,
- electronic money institutions.

The above-mentioned entities have to meet some criteria in the financial year for which they prepare the financial statements and in the year preceding that year, they must include the statement on non-financial information within the management activity report (here MAR)[3] (see Table 3).

The MAR should provide material information about the property and financial standing of the company. The said report is supposed to include an assessment of the effects achieved, the indication of risk factors and a description of the threats. In particular, the following list of aspects should be covered by the MAR (§49 clause 2):

- events that significantly affect the entity's operations that took place in the financial year, as well as after its end, until the date of approval of the financial statements,
- the anticipated development of an entity,
- major R&D achievements,
- current and anticipated financial standing,
- own shares,
- branches (factories) owned by the entity,
- financial instruments.

[3]The MAR is a descriptive and numerical report. It is prepared by the head of the entity together with the annual financial statements. §49.1 of the Polish Accounting Act clearly states which group of entities should prepare the MAR. This group cover limited liability companies, limited joint-stock partnerships, mutual insurance companies, mutual reinsurance companies, cooperatives, state-owned enterprises, partnerships and limited partnerships whose all partners with unlimited liability are limited liability companies, limited joint-stock partnerships, companies from other countries with similar to the above-mentioned companies in legal form, specialist open-ended investment funds, closed-end investment funds and alternative investment companies [National Accounting Standard (NAS) No. 9, Part III, point 3.1].

Table 4 Recognition criteria for micro- and small-sized entities

Recognition criteria	Micro-entity	Small-sized entity
Average annual employment in full-time equivalents	≤ 10 persons	≤ 50 persons
Total assets at the end of the year	≤ 1,500,000 PLN	≤ 25,500,000 PLN
Annual net revenues from the sale of products and goods	≤ 3,000,000 PLN	≤ 51,000,000 PLN

Source: Polish Accounting Act, § 3, clauses 1a and 1c

The MAR should include if it is relevant for the assessment of the entity's development, results and situation, at least (§49 clause 2):

- key financial performance indicators related to the entity's operations,
- key non-financial performance indicators related to the entity's operations and information on employee issues and the environment.

In Poland, corporate reporting in MSMEs is simplified in comparison with reporting obligations of large enterprises.

The Polish Accounting Act defines both micro- and small-sized entities and establishes quantitative recognition criteria for these two groups. In order to be recognized as micro- or small entity, an enterprise cannot exceed at least two of three thresholds in the financial year for which it prepares the financial statements and in the year preceding this financial year (whereas in the case of entity starting operations—in the financial year in which it started operating) (see Table 4).

Micro-entities in Poland (§ 3 clause 1a) apply the template of the financial statement according to Annex No. 4 of the Accounting Act, i.e. they prepare an introduction, called general information, balance sheet in which they do not distinguish between short- and long-term liabilities, profit and loss account (by nature of expense) with limited information and additional information and clarifications to a limited extent.

Small entities (§ 3 clause 1a) use the template of the financial statement according to Annex No. 5 of the Accounting Act and prepare, introduction, balance sheet, profit and loss account (by nature of expense or by a function of expense), additional information and clarifications. The information presented in all parts of the report is moderately limited.

Both micro- and small audited entities may use reporting templates following Annex No. 1 of the Accounting Act. It means that they prepare an introduction, balance sheet, profit and loss account (by nature of expense or by a function of expense), additional information and clarifications, statement of changes in equity (fund) and cash flow statement. However, they may limit the scope of information according to the rules for micro- and small entities and opt-out of preparing the statement of changes in equity (fund) and cash flow statement.

It should be emphasized that the written decision of the approving body about preparing the annual financial statement under the proposed templates (Annexe No. 4 or 5 of the Accounting Act) or combinations of the reports' elements from various Annexes (Nos. 1, 4 and 5) is a condition for using simplifications in the preparation of the annual financial statements.

There are also other possibilities for reporting simplifications. For instance, entities that are subject to the mandatory annual audit (e.g. a joint-stock company that is also a micro-entity, or an entity that meets both the thresholds for mandatory audit and being recognized as a small entity) may opt-out of preparing the statement of changes in equity (fund) and cash flow statement.

Micro- and small entities obligated to draw up management activity reports may opt-out to prepare it, providing that information on acquiring own shares will be disclosed in the additional notes (§ 49 clauses 4 and 5). Moreover, entities with a micro- or small enterprise status may not include key non-financial performance indicators related to business operations, employee and environmental issues in the management report. However, following this path may disrupt the communication of an entity with the business environment.

Regulation of the Minister of Finance of 29 March 2018

The Regulation of the Minister of Finance of 29 March 2018 specifies the type, scope and form of current and periodic information passed by stock issuers for which the Republic of Poland is the home country and who admitted to trading on the official listing market in Poland or on a regulated market of a Member State other than the Republic of Poland. The regulation also indicates the frequency and deadlines for providing the above-mentioned information.

Voluntary Corporate Reporting Regulations in Poland that May Impact IR

In Polish organizations, no matter whether they are large, medium, small or micro-enterprises, both NAS No. 9 and NFI standard may constitute a good foundation for the development of non-financial or integrated reporting. Micro- and small companies do not need a general panacea but rather complex and sometimes tailor-made solutions adjusted to their size, activity scope and expectations of their major stakeholder groups. These solutions should have clear objectives and be easy to implement.

National Accounting Standard (NAS) No. 9

The Polish Accounting Act is supported by the National Accounting Standard No. 9: “Management activity report”. The NAS No. 9 was updated in 2018. It applied for the first time to financial statements prepared for the year starting from 1 January 2017. This standard aims to assist in compiling the MAR under §49, §49b and §55 items 2 and 2a of the Polish Accounting Act.

The said standard consists of eight sections of which the last refers to the content of the statement on non-financial information. However, the significant part of the standard is dedicated to the MAR indeed. It describes the purpose, nature and qualitative characteristics of the activity report, rules for preparing and presenting the said report and its content.

Following NAS No. 9, the statement on non-financial information should constitute a separate part of the management activity report or be a separate report published on the entity’s corporate website no later than 6 months from the balance sheet date.

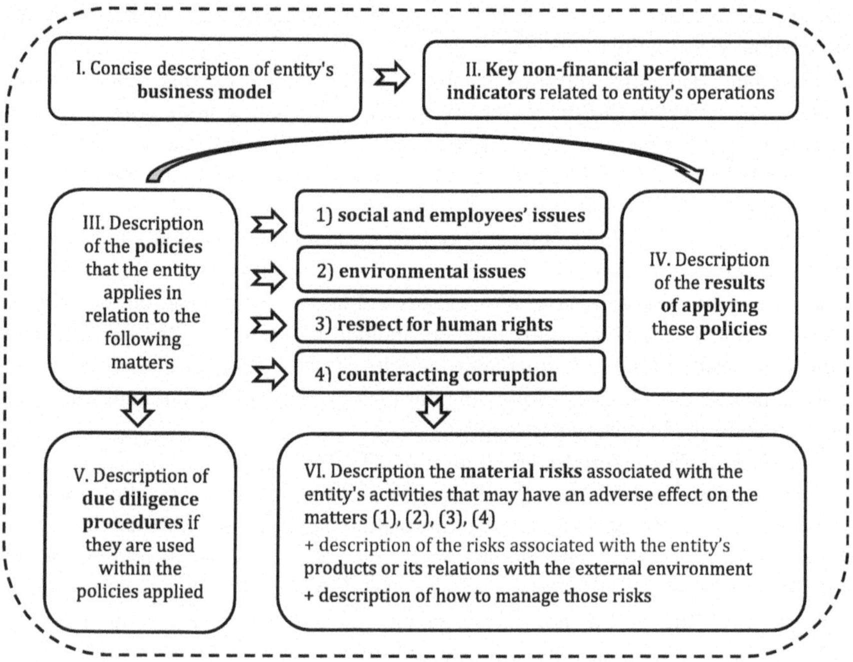

Fig. 5 Structure of the statement (report) on non-financial information. Source: Own presentation based on National Accounting Standard No. 9 (part VIII, point 8.2)

It is worth noticing that non-financial information should be presented to the extent that it is necessary to evaluate the entity's development, performance and situation. The information included in the statement should also enable to assess impacts of activities undertaken by the entity on social and employees' and environmental issues and matters related to respect for human rights and counteracting corruption (see Fig. 5).

Business Model (*NAS No. 9*, points 8.5–8.6)

The entity is expected to report significant changes in the business model, policies or main risks and appropriate explanations in the statement if such appeared in the reporting period.

The description of the business model should cover:

- a general outline of how the entity operates;
- the value offered to various customer segments through its products, goods or services, relationships with contractors, communication channels, distribution and sales, internal organization and key operating procedures;
- key resources and activities implemented in the reporting period aimed at transforming expenditure into results;
- relationships with other stakeholders enabling value creation.

Key Non-financial Performance Indicators (NAS No. 9, points 8.8–9.9)

The statement on non-financial information also presents key non-financial performance indicators useful for measurement, monitoring and assessment of development, results and progress of the entity, and its environmental impact. Moreover, it is necessary to include a balanced combination of qualitative and quantitative information and the relationships between them since this enables an entity to develop a comprehensive picture of its business activity. It is also useful to present both general performance indicators and measures specific to a sector or thematic issues. The entity should present the same performance indicators in subsequent statements enabling the assessment of trends and progress in achieving specific goals. It is particularly beneficial to present key performance indicators about the objectives set, volumes considered to be desirable, historical data and in comparison with other entities or sector averages.

Policies and Results of Their Application (NAS No. 9, points 8.10–8.17)

It is expected that the entity describes the policies applied to environmental, social and employees' issues and respect for human rights and counteracting corruption. The policies indicate approaches, goals and ways in which they are to be achieved. The statement on non-financial information is supposed to provide a useful, reliable and balanced picture of the policies' results. The policies may also refer to management principles, responsibilities, oversight and how resource allocation relates to objectives, risk management and intended results.

Due Diligence Procedures (NAS No. 9, point 8.18)

Due diligence procedures relate to policies, risk and performance management, and aim to ensure that a specific goal is achieved within the policies applied. They help to identify current and potential negative impacts and to prevent and mitigate their effects. The entity should present information regarding its due diligence procedures regarding preventing and mitigating adverse impacts, setting policy objectives and measuring progress in their implementation.

Material Risks (NAS No. 9, point 8.19)

The entity is expected to provide information on the main risks related to its operations and the manner (principles, methods) and the effects of managing them. It should particularly explain the impact the main types of risk had on its business model, operations, market and financial results, and its environment, regardless of whether it results from decisions or actions of the entity or external factors. It is advisable to describe the procedures used to identify and assess these types of risks.

Non-Financial Information Standard (NFI Standard)

The Reporting Standards Foundation published the Non-Financial Information Standard (here the NFI standard) in cooperation with the Polish Association of Listed Companies.

The NFI standard helps Polish companies meet their reporting obligations for non-financial information under the Directive, 2014/95/EU. It discusses the importance of measures and their selection from the perspective of capital markets and provides a detailed description of areas that require reporting, including proposals for key measures and their potential significance for entities representing different sectors. The standard is accepted and supported by many institutions and organizations closely related to the capital market. These are represented by the Polish

Association of Listed Companies, Association of Individual Investors in Poland, Association of Brokers and Advisors, Responsible Business Forum, Chamber of Brokerage Houses and Polish Chamber of Statutory Auditors.

The NFI standard reflects three areas regarding governance, environmental, social and employee issues. Interestingly, it proposes the extent of narrative disclosures or indicators within every single item of a particular area.

The NFI standard includes five annexes that provide a practical basis for implementing non-financial reporting in companies.

Annex 1 elaborates on legal interpretations of the Directive, 2014/95/EU. It provides answers to the following set of questions:

1. Which entities will be covered by reporting?
2. Do the reporting requirements apply to the issuer or subsidiaries together?
3. What will companies exceeding 250 employees have to report?
4. What will companies exceeding 500 employees have to report?
5. How to determine the number of employees in a company?
6. What rules and criteria should be used when subsidiaries of a capital group are based in countries other than the parent company?
7. What is the scope of the capital group?

Annex 2 provides an illustrative materiality matrix focusing on particular areas and indicators and indicates their importance for industries and their subsections.

Annex 3 explains who is a stakeholder and indicates various stakeholder groups. It is also underlined that stakeholder relationship management constitutes a fundamental management practice for quality-conscious enterprises operating following corporate social responsibility principles.

Primary activities in the field of stakeholder relationship management according to the NFI standard cover:

- identifying stakeholders and assessing the importance of individual stakeholder groups,
- identifying essential issues raised by stakeholders, in particular, those key to the organization's activities,
- analysing the issues raised by stakeholders in terms of their impact on the business, including the opportunities and risks they generate. Any issue relevant to the stakeholder concerning the organization should be considered,
- including responses to issues important to stakeholders in reports.[4]

The NFI standard recommends to include a list of stakeholders indicating which of them are critical to the organization. The easiest method is to pay attention to which stakeholders have the most significant impact on the organization and are most interested in it and on which stakeholders the company has the most significant

[4]It is worth noting that the organization should answer all the most important issues signalled by stakeholders, which is not synonymous with meeting all their expectations, because the stakeholders are a diverse group and their expectations may be contradictory.

impact and is most interested in them. Moreover, it suggested to reflect the essential issues and expectations of stakeholders and related activities undertaken in the reporting period or planned to be undertaken in the non-financial report. This information can be obtained from many sources, i.e. customer satisfaction or employee involvement research, market and competition analysis, press monitoring, helpline applications, special surveys, interviews, meetings, panels or dialogue with stakeholders.

Annex 4 puts attention on the importance of KPIs and their selection from the viewpoint of capital markets. It is recommended that when developing a set of non-financial KPIs, an organization should follow the principles of non-financial reporting developed worldwide, especially the GRI guidelines. Furthermore, when assessing which indicators are important for a proper representation of the environmental impact in a given sector or industry, sectoral reference documents developed by the European Commission for the EMAS system's purposes may be used. The NFI standard stresses that the KPIs should be accurate and comparable over time to show trends of changes in the company's results and (if possible) the industry. When defining a set of indicators specific to a given company, the first step should be to pay attention to their business context and, where possible, to the aspect of efficiency.

Annex 5 includes a detailed description of governance, environmental, social and employee areas in terms of policies applied, results of these policies and risk categories associated with each area, outcome indicators and supply chain. The NFI standard stipulates that the accounting principles should also be observed in non-financial reporting. The NFI standard lists materiality, comparability, credibility, completeness, transparency, documentation, timeliness and punctuality principles among the primate ones. In conclusion, the standard recommends companies to report specific social and environmental aspects, and non-financial data, including numerical indicators, analysing the scope of the information provided precisely in terms of the specificity of the industry they represent and current socio-economic aspects, and emphasizing critical issues.

3 National Factors Enabling or Constraining IR

3.1 *Political Factors*

The amendment of the Accounting Act in January 2017 implemented the Directive 2014/95/EU into national legislation within extended non-financial information reporting. The first mandatory reporting of non-financial information took place for the financial year starting on or after 1 January 2017.

The Ministry of Finance, particularly the Accounting and Auditing Department, supported the idea of non-financial reporting in many different ways. The department created a special tab on the Ministry of Finance website dedicated to frequently asked questions regarding reporting of extended non-financial information and diversity policy. The Ministry of Finance has undertaken many educational activities in this area, consisting of thematic conferences and seminars in cooperation with, the Ministry of Development, the Association of Stock Exchange Issuers, the Polish Chamber of Statutory Auditors, the Responsible Business Forum and CSR Info. These activities were intended not only for persons who dealt with non-financial reporting but also for management and supervisory boards. The latter two groups decided on company policy in a given area, which may directly impact the content of non-financial information that the company presents.

One of the very well-evaluated initiatives was implementing a free online educational seminar on non-financial reporting that attracted over 300 spectators (Janczyk, 2018). Moreover, in March 2019, the Ministry of Finance organized a conference to summarise companies' compliance with the obligation to report extended non-financial information for 2017. The panel of experts who assessed the extent to which the new reporting obligations were met consisted of representatives of the following bodies, institutions and associations: Ministry of Finance, Ministry of Investment and Development, Polish Financial Supervision Authority, Polish Chamber of Statutory Auditors, Association of Accountants in Poland, Accounting Standards Committee, Responsible Business Forum, Polish Association of Listed Companies and Reporting Standards Foundation.

3.2 Economic Factors

Polish economy belongs to the most dynamically growing ones that had developed sustainably even at the times of the global financial crisis 2008–2009 (INVESTIN, The Ministry of Economic Development, 2017). Over the last 30 years, the Polish economy doubled in size in terms of real GDP growth. It created many opportunities for both internal and foreign investments. However, still, the GDP gap exists while comparing real labour productivity in Poland with EU-28. Labour productivity reflects *"(...) how well human and technical resources are configured in the production of goods and services. At a national level, this depends on the efficiency with which available resources are utilized, including raw materials, labour, skills, capital equipment, land, intellectual property, managerial capability, and financial capital*" (McKinsey and Company, 2015, p. 13). Based on EUROSTAT data, in 2018, the labour productivity levels (expressed in thousand EUR per person employed) were equal to 25.6 and 54.5 for Poland and EU-28, respectively[5] (EUROSTAT, 2020b). One of the reasons for existing that gap was that Poland's capital-intensive sectors did not finish their transformations, still, sustained inefficient employment levels and used outdated operating practices (McKinsey & Company, 2015, p. 13).

[5]Romania and Hungary had lower real labour productivity levels in comparison with Poland (17.3 and 22.5, respectively), whereas Italy, Germany and UK exceeded real labour productivity level of EU-28 (57.8, 59.6 and 59.8, respectively).

Polish business sector that includes a large number of SMEs can contribute to greater prosperity of the country, resolution of social and local problems and attainment of EU-15 economic level by joint activities in the following challenging areas (McKinsey & Company, 2015, p. 9):

- productivity improvement (by process standardization and moving up the value chain in each sector)
- development of relationships with emerging markets (by attracting new capital investors)
- growth of process manufacturing scale (by consolidating companies on the domestic market and acquiring foreign partners in order to win well-known brands and enter new markets)
- innovations in technology-intensive industries (by establishing high-tech clusters and increasing targeted R&D investment)
- problems with the shrinking workforce (by boosting productivity and opening jobs for women, youth, disabled people and immigrants)
- employee skills development and enhancement of labour force competitiveness (by creating curricula that are calibrated to the expectations on the job market by universities and training centres)

The above-listed challenges are also critical issues on micro-level and as such should be addressed in the integrated reports of economically and socially responsible companies since all of these challenges require actions engaging resources within six capitals framework (see Fig. 6).

3.3 Social Factors

The emergence of the first index of socially responsible companies (here called RESPECT Index) in the Central and Eastern Europe in 2009 has increased interest in the sustainable and responsible investment (SRI) market in Poland. As a result, many large public companies were induced to revise the current rules for reporting non-financial data. It should be noted that the RESPECT Index not only aims at the selection of companies managed responsibly and sustainably, but also highlights the investment attractiveness, which may be characterized by both reporting and investor relations' quality and the existence of good practices of corporate governance. Interestingly, the RESPECT index uses a liquidity parameter among the eligibility criteria to recognize socially responsible entities. It means that potential companies are selected from the portfolio of WIG20, mWIG40 and sWIG80 indices, which suggest a good reference base for professional investors. In 2018, the RESPECT index included 31 organizations in total, of which 12 companies prepared integrated reports (*Bogdanka, Budimex, Grupa Azoty, Lotos Group, ING Bank Śląski, JSW, KGHM Polska Miedź, mBank, Orange, PGE Group, PGNIG, PKN Orlen*).

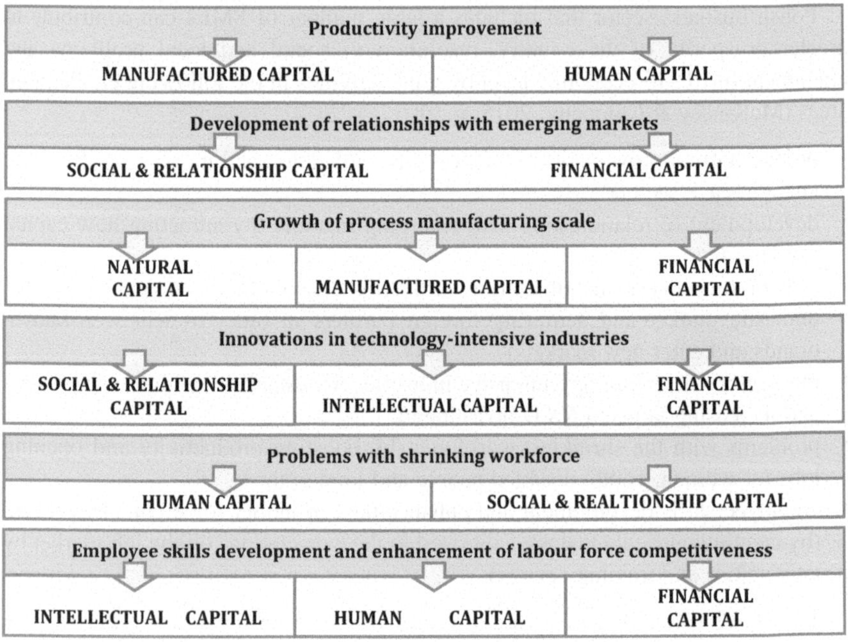

Fig. 6 Challenging areas of economic prosperity in the context of six-capital engagement. Source: Own presentation.

Other social factors that positively impact IR development in Poland are associated with two national contests that select distinctive reports according to various categories, including the best integrated reports category. The first one is the best report contest on CSR and sustainable development organized by the Responsible Business Forum Association and Deloitte Poland. There have been 13 editions of that competition so far (http://raportyzr.pl/edycje/raporty-spoleczne-2019/). The PricewaterhouseCoopers, ACCA Polska, Responsible Business Forum and CSR Consulting were the initiators of this idea addressed to all companies and organizations operating on the Polish market for whom social and environmental issues were close and important. The reports collected in the competition were analysed and evaluated by a panel of judges according to the assessment methodology modelled on similar initiatives in Europe. The criteria for assessing social reports in the first edition of the contest were considered in three areas: completeness, reliability and communication. The Institute of Accountancy and Taxes organized the second contest, and there have been 14 editions of that competition so far (https://irip.pl/poprzednie-edycje).

It is worth noting that it is becoming increasingly common to invite experts and other stakeholders to assess social reports or integrated reports.

3.4 Cultural Factors

Over the last decade, social activities for sustainable development and engaged social participation have become highly visible in Poland. Cultural changes in thinking about common goods and the need for conscious using natural resources can also be observed. The development of civil society has caused that topics related to human rights and adverse environmental impact started to be included in corporate social reports. Nowadays, citizens expect self-regulation of business towards higher transparency and good relationships with stakeholders based on trust and credibility (Żelazna-Blicharz, 2013). Civil society's task, which creates a specific ecosystem, enforces beneficial changes in the public interest. NGOs and informal groups operating in the real and virtual world play an important role in this respect. It should be noticed that their activities may contribute to building social capital. Civil society uses social expression and language, and therefore, it can influence institutional processes and politics (cf. Scholte, 1999, 2007). In democratic states, civil society can control and evaluate the effects of authorities' actions and indirectly influence the decision-making process using social expression tools.

It should be emphasized that in Poland, a significant cultural factor positively influencing the evolution of non-financial reporting and justifying the idea of IR is the development of the CSR concept. Over the past two decades, it has been observed how various activities, pressures and impacts changed business managers' awareness and shaped a new culture of integrated thinking about business (see Fig. 7).

Likewise, civil society's attitude also the cultural environment is changing in Poland. There appear a growing number of public debates in which representatives of various institutions and non-governmental organizations advocate for sustainable development of business organizations and the necessity of their transparency. For 3 years, *Rzeczpospolita*—Polish national economic and legal magazine, has published annual supplement (*Responsible Business in Poland. Benefits for Companies, Economy and Society*) in which the above-mentioned representatives share their opinions, and companies present experiences and benefits deriving from non-financial reporting.

The factor discussed above is a positive one in the context of creating space for IR development. However, there is a dark point in Polish culture that may affect IR development badly. That is bureaucracy. Poland has been overwhelmed by a bureaucracy culture—a relic of past communist times over several decades. The problem of bureaucracy has been evolving even during the political transformation in Poland after 1989. Kieżun (2018, p. 7) stressed that in Poland, gigantomania, luxuryomania, corruption and the arrogance of power have become horsemen of the bureaucracy apocalypse in the 90s. They should be considered as very pathological phenomena. Gigantomania, for instance, reflected in an enormous increase both in the central administration (the number of employees in public administration grew almost threefold in the period from 1990 to 1998) and in the local government (an increase from 83,400 employees in 1990 to 142,100 in 1997) (Kieżun, 2018).

1997-1999: Maximising the value of the company for the owners as the sole purpose of the business (a resounding discussion in literature)

↓

2000-2001: Criticism of the CSR concept by business representatives and some publicists (principles of the free economy as canons of entrepreneurship). Nevertheless, in 2000 the Responsible Business Forum (RBF) has been established (an expert organization, which remains the initiator and partner of key projects for Polish CSR).

↓

2002-2003: Increasing interest in the CSR concept, both among the representatives of business, science and media. (growth of the number of enterprises with foreign capital in Poland, appearance of the first declarations of large and mainly foreign enterprises about their ethical and social activities)

↓

2004-2005: The time of Poland's accession to the European Union that resulted in even greater involvement of companies in sponsorship and charity actions (They were treated, however mainly as marketing activities).

↓

2006-2007: Publicising and demonstrating the implementation of CSR principles by firms. Analysing the environment in terms of learning about stakeholders' expectations and combining social responsibility with charity actions.

↓

2008-2013: Further promoting the idea of social responsibility in press articles, specialist journals and during scientific conferences. In 2009 the CSR Team was established as an auxiliary body of the Prime Minister to ensure consistency and coordination of initiatives in promoting CSR in Poland. In 2010 the World Business Council for Sustainable Development issued a document which inspired Polish institutions, including the Ministry of Economy, the RBF and PwC to prepare a sustainable development vision for Polish business organizations. The new "2050 Vision" stressed the needs of supplementing the existing governmental strategic documents with business perspective and building collaboration in-between public, business and non-governmental sectors towards sustainable development. In 2012 *Lotos Group* publishes the first integrated report in Poland for the year of 2011. The next year *Scanmed Multimedis* publishes its first integrated report.

↓

2014-2017: Between 2014 and 2017 another 14 Polish large companies joined to the group of organizations preparing the integrated reports. Many of them was awarded for the best or distinguished integrated report in national contests. More and more companies preparing integrated reports have begun to involve stakeholders in the materiality determination process The amendment of the Accounting Act in January 2017 implemented the Directive 2014/95/EU into national legislation within extended non-financial information reporting.

↓

2018-2019: The Directive 2014/95/EU in Polish practice. In 2018 public interest companies have published their first mandatory statements on non-financial information.

Fig. 7 Changes in the way of thinking about the business and its impacts. Evidence from Poland. Source: Own presentation based on Adamczyk (2009) and Żelazna-Blicharz (2013)

Interestingly enough, these phenomena have continuously been affecting the Polish economy.

In February 2020, Grant Thornton published a report, which presents the scale of reporting obligations for companies in Poland (see Figs. 8 and 9). Not only the overwhelming number of reports and forms that companies must submit in

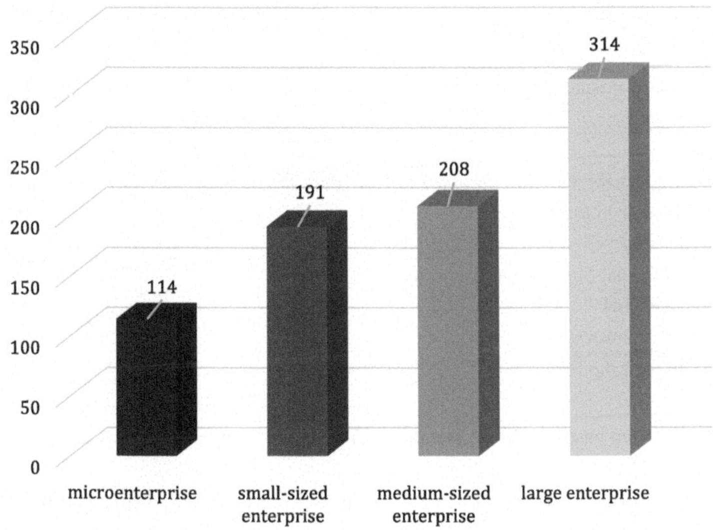

Fig. 8 Average number of reporting elements (prints, forms, reports, etc.) that a statistical company in a given category had to submit to public authorities in 2019—evidence from Poland. Source: Presentation based on Grant Thornton (2020, p. 5)

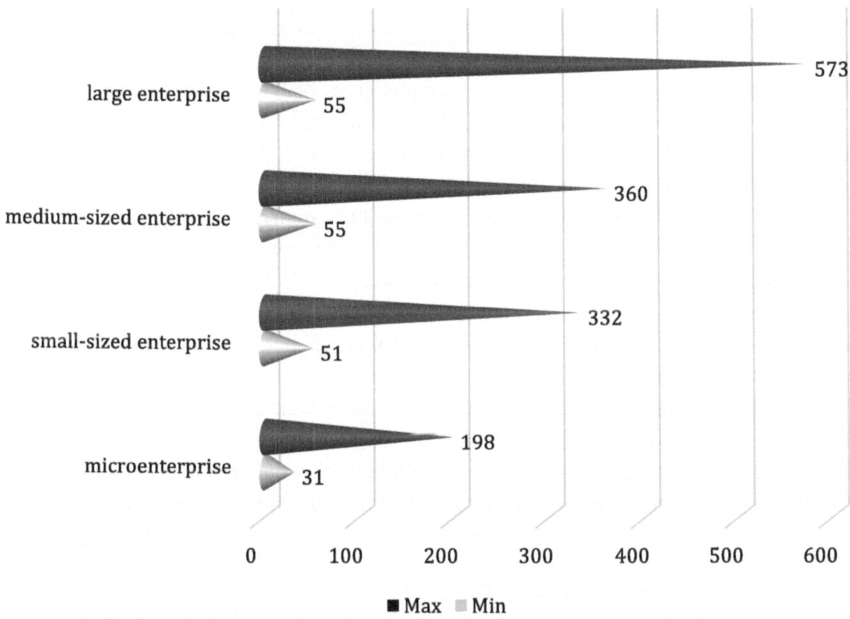

Fig. 9 Minimum and the maximum number of reporting elements in 2019 (depending on the form of business, industry, location, assets, type of employment). Source: Presentation based on Grant Thornton (2020, p. 6)

Table 5 Average number of reporting elements to public institutions for large companies

Public institution	2014	2019	Change (%)
National Bank of Poland (NBP)	132	151	14
General Statistics	77	72	-6
Tax Office	78	50	−36
State Fund for Rehabilitation of Disabled People (PFRON)	50	13	−74
The Social Insurance Institution (ZUS)	12	12	0
Customs Chamber	12	6	−50
The Polish Financial Supervision Authority (KNF)	5	5	0
Voivodship Marshal	6	3	−50
Community Administration	2	2	0
Starost's Office of the Poviat	3	1	−67
Other	11	2	−82

Source: Presentation based on Grant Thornton (2020, p. 12)

government offices is worrying, but also the degree of detail. Filling in reports and forms often requires a lot of work, time and deep specialist financial or accounting knowledge.

What are the reasons why Polish companies have to fill out so many forms? Grant Thornton (2020) indicates that it is associated with the authorities' overzealousness, lack of cooperation between public offices and low social capital (see Table 5).

It is emphasized in the Grant Thornton (2020) report that employees of public authorities often do not realize that reporting obligations are a heavy burden for companies. Public authorities require companies to provide a lot of data of which only a few are potentially useful. Authorities should instead use a minimalistic approach and collect the data they really need. It should be noticed that public administration in Poland does not sufficiently monitor the scale of reporting. Officials of individual institutions are not aware of how many forms and data are often requested by entrepreneurs by other offices. If databases were exchanged to a greater extent, the number of forms that companies have to fill out would decrease significantly. Finally, it is remarked that the multitude of reporting forms filled in by companies is also a symptom of low social capital, i.e. a low level of mutual trust in society both between citizens and between the state and citizens. As a rule, officials do not trust entrepreneurs and therefore impose an excessive, strict control system on them, which results in a large number of reports that the entrepreneur must submit. To sum up, the problem of the overgrown bureaucratic machine may to some extent discourage SMEs in Poland from preparing additional non-financial reports.

3.5 Technological Factors

The technological development in Poland may constitute a foundation of growth not only for the SME sector but also for the entire economy and society. In the report prepared by INVESTIN and The Ministry of Economic Development (2017), it is highlighted that nowadays Poland "*faces the challenge of replacing present growth drivers, such as low cost of labor, EU subsidies and increase the rate of productivity*" with novel technological solutions. They are related to opportunities ingrained in cloud technologies, Big Data, the Internet of Things and cybersecurity. The analysis of the statistical data shows that the number of high-technology SMEs in manufacturing industry and knowledge-intensive services more than doubled over the last decade in Poland (see Fig. 10).

Interestingly, also the number of IPOs registered at the Warsaw Stock Exchange (WSE) is higher than at any other financial market in Europe. In this context, growth dynamics in other EU countries, such as Germany, Hungary, Italy, the UK or Romania, was significantly lower. It should be stressed that the fast-growing sector of high-tech SMEs may become a vital factor enabling and justifying the development of IR in such entities. Some arguments are supporting that statement. Firstly, high-tech SMEs are often start-up companies that have not already established or expanded the stakeholder landscape. In order to find traction with the innovators, early adopter customers or investors, they need to initiate a dialogue with them.

IR may be an excellent start to present a new product or service and business model to explain to potential stakeholders how a company creates value. Secondly, when high-tech SMEs enter into relationships with the innovator having vital research and scientific background, the next step may become more challenging, i.e. building international the base for more efficient technology transfer at the European level. The integrated report, in that case, may play the role of the visiting card of the company. Finally, high-tech SMEs may be naturally open to new technologies and solutions they bring within in the area of information flow.

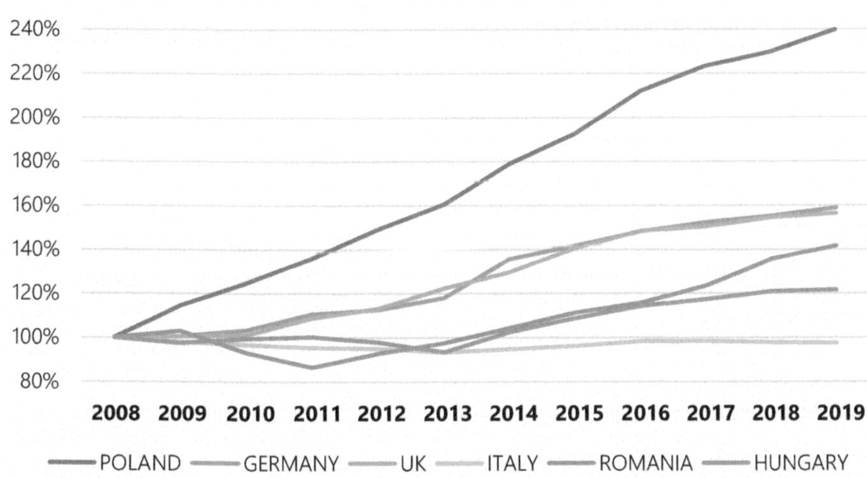

Fig. 10 Growth dynamics of the number of high-technology SMEs in the manufacturing industry and knowledge-intensive services. Comparison between six EU countries (index: 2008 = 100, estimates as from 2016 onwards). Source: Own presentation based on EC (2019b)

Therefore, they may be interested in using the online option of the integrated report where data are interconnected, easily comparable and quickly available to stakeholders.

4 Empirical Evidence on IR in Poland

This chapter presents and analyses the best practices of IR in Poland with reference to Polish large and SME companies. It focuses on companies' adherence to <IR> guiding principles and <IR> content elements.

The development of IR is progressing in Poland in response to changing expectations of interest groups. We identified about 23 Polish large companies that have prepared integrated reports over the last years. They represent various branches, such as the oil industry, chemicals, power industry, mining, financial sector, healthcare services, telecommunication, construction sector, services and transport, textile clothing and commerce sector (see Fig. 11).

Almost a half of the analysed companies were awarded for the best or distinctive integrated report. Interestingly, 65% of the examined companies developed online versions of the integrated reports that in most cases were interactive and interconnected (see Fig. 12).

Experience of Polish SMEs in Non-financial Reporting

In order to identify Polish SMEs, the Amadeus database has been searched. As a result, 114 thousand MSMEs operating in Poland have been sorted out. Then, 369 reports have been extracted from the library of social report contest and matched

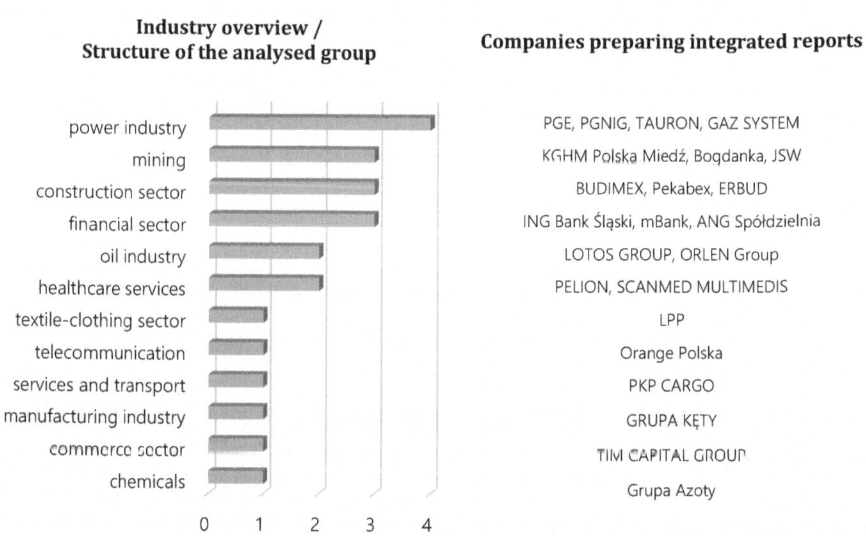

Fig. 11 IR in Poland—information panel. Source: Own presentation

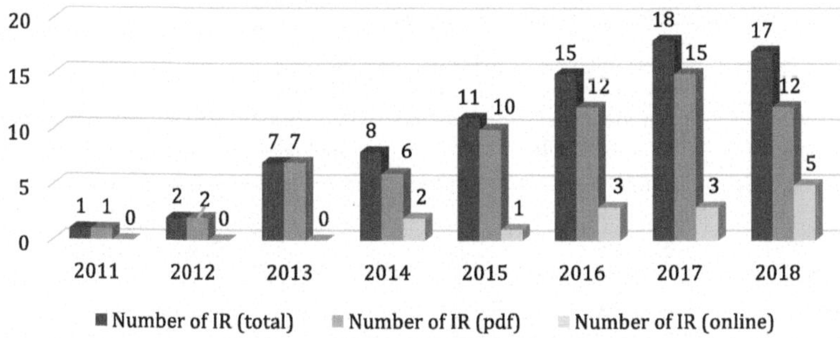

The total number of annual integrated reports in Poland (2011-2018):	78
The total number of annual integrated reports available both as pdf and online	29
The total number of integrated reports available in pdf format (exclusively) (2011-2018):	62 (33)
The total number of integrated reports available online (exclusively) (2011-2018):	45 (16)
Number of companies that prepared at least one integrated report between 2011-2018	23
The company that published the first integrated report in Poland	Lotos Group (Integrated report for the year of 2011)
The company that has published the most integrated reports	LOTOS Group (8 integrated reports: 2011, 2012, 2013, 2014, 2015, 2016, 2017, 2018)
The company that published the longest integrated report	ORLEN Group (521 pages: Integrated report for the year 2016)
The company that published the shortest integrated report	Gaz System (20 pages: Integrated report for the year 2015)
The number of companies adhering to GRI Standards	All 23 companies analyzed in this report (applies only to the reports examined)
The number of companies adhering to IIRC framework	16 companies analyzed in this report (approx.. 70%) (applies only to the reports examined)

Fig. 12 Number of companies preparing integrated reports in Poland between 2011 and 2018. Source: Own presentation

with Polish MSMEs identified in the Amadeus database to find SMEs that prepared the integrated reports. Actually, **only five entities drawn up various social reports**, and **no organization prepared the integrated report** (see Table 6).

Signal Group prepared its 60-page CSR report for the period of 2013–2017. The CSR report consisted of five major parts: social commitment, natural environment protection, development of new technologies, investments in human resources and fair business practices. The company described its understanding of the above-mentioned areas and defined goals for each of them.

The social commitment included supporting the community and building relationships with employees, associates, families, foundations and non-profit organizations, sports organizations and associations. The goals of this area were as follows: (1) strengthening the image of a socially responsible company supporting local initiatives; (2) enhancing employees' loyalty and commitment; (3) integrating employees; (4) building relationships with the community; (5) helping those in need; and (6) promoting a healthy lifestyle.

Table 6 List of Polish SMEs preparing social reports

Company name	Operating revenue (turnover) in thousand EUR	Total assets in thousand EUR	Number of employees	NACE Rev. 2, the main section
SIGNAL GROUP	465.49	2883.36	5	J. Information and communication
MARGOSTAL REWOLIŃSCY	2153.95	2032.05	n.a.	C. Manufacturing
PROFES	1284.75	507.77	13	P. Education
GRUPA ATERIMA	2413.10	1537.44	82	N. Administrative and support service activities
EKO CYKL ORGANIZACJA ODZYSKU OPAKOWAŃ	2486.63	1689.53	27	E. Water supply; sewerage, waste management, and remediation activities

Source: Own presentation

Natural environment protection was about building ecological awareness among stakeholders and creating environmentally friendly technological solutions. The goals of this area were as follows: (1) ensuring long-term and sustainable development; (2) promoting technology solutions as environmentally friendly; and (3) strengthening the image of an environmentally friendly company.

The development of new technologies consisted in supporting scientific research on modern technologies in electricity, technics, IT, electronics, software and automation. The goals of this area were as follows: (1) strengthening the image of a group of technology companies; (2) increasing product competitiveness; (3) obtaining the possibility of using the know-how of new technological solutions; (4) designing and using solutions that taking care of the environment; and (5) strengthening the image of an environmentally friendly company offering solutions that ensure sustainable development.

Investments in human resources were based on creating a friendly workplace for people who passionately pursued their objectives. The goals of this area were (1) strengthening the image of the company as a responsible employer; (2) being an attractive employer for people with a commitment to pursuing goals; (3) creating jobs and developing employees' competencies and individual career paths; (4) promoting an organizational culture based on the idea of people to people; and (5) extending the competences of employees and associates based on individually tailored value paths.

Fair business practices were a means of increasing the organization's ability to act in a socially responsible manner. It enabled the supervision and practical implementation of CSR principles. The goals of this area were as follows: (1) acting following business ethics, according to the principles and values reflected in the mission and strategy; (2) strengthening employees' awareness of the company's development direction and strategic goals; (3) strengthening long-term and trust-based relationships with contractors; and (4) promoting fair play and fair competition. *Signal*

Group also determined the beneficiaries of all actions conducted within the above-mentioned areas.

The next company—*Margostal Rewolińscy*—is a family business. Although the company prepared a concise social report for 2016 (only 9-pages long), it included references to GRI G4 guidelines. The social report of *Margostal Rewolińscy* presented how the company built its competitive advantage by (1) investing in new technologies and equipment to increase efficiency and minimize negative environmental impact; (2) caring for employee development, their safety and satisfaction; (3) implementing global solutions in the manufacturing process; and (4) acting for the benefits of the local community.

The company also emphasized that its corporate social responsibility priorities were focused on achieving sustainable UN goals. *Margostal Rewolińscy* conducted a dialogue with customers, suppliers, business partners and local leaders to collect information about the most critical issues from the stakeholders' perspective. The social report revealed key aspects addressed by interest groups showing their opinions concerning the report's content.

The company reported on human capital, indicating the number of employees, the number of hours spent on raising qualifications and these dedicated to training on work safety improvement. Moreover, *Margostal Rewolińscy* cited employees and other external stakeholders' opinions about the company's activities in the social report. The report ended with an index of GRI indicators.

Another small entity who prepared the sustainability report is *PROFES*—an enterprise in the education sector. In its 28-page report, the company highlighted corporate governance and organizational culture, which were considered strategic success factors. In everyday work, the company was guided by values that complemented its mission, goals, strategies and plans. *PROFES* listed and described its management systems that supported operational business activities, optimized processes and eliminated waste. The enterprise was socially committed and described a variety of social initiatives. The sustainability report also presented environmental activities and defined a term and types of eco-waste. The company emphasized that by undertaking actions to eliminate waste and eco-waste, limiting the negative impact on the natural environment and creating a platform for several initiatives in social involvement, it has achieved many measurable and non-measurable benefits. The sustainability report described anti-eco-behaviours and good practices in various areas.

The 33-page social report of the next enterprise—*Grupa ATERIMA*—was prepared based on the GRI G3.1 guidelines. The report presented CSR activities run by the company and listed key stakeholder groups. It also described employment matters and related diversity policy, indicated employee communication channels, presented the training scope for employees, and elaborated on marketing communications and priorities on relations with competitors. Within environmental issues, *Grupa ATERIMA* emphasized its role in minimizing the negative impact of business activity on the environment. The report ended with an index of GRI indicators.

Interestingly, the enterprise subjected its CSR activities to an audit and assessment of the Coalition for Responsible Business. The main goal was to assess an implementation degree of CSR principles and a level of implemented CSR projects. The auditors also examined areas as (1) relationships with employees, partners, customers, suppliers, competition and the local community; (2) attitude to the natural environment; (3) reliability of marketing communications; and (4) contribution to education and setting standards in the recruitment area.

The last examined small enterprise—*Eko Cykl Organizacja Odzysku Opakowań*—deals with the recovery and recycling of waste from other companies, so in principle, it promotes an ecological style of operation. In its short 13-page CSR report (2011), the company presented environmental policy and quality policy regarding the improvement of customer service processes, information flows, skills and knowledge of employees, staff motivation and ecological education. The company also stressed that employees were their most valuable capital. Moreover, the company set out the mission, strategic goals and tasks in the environmental area and developed non-financial environmental performance indicators.

Although Polish SMEs do not have any experience in preparing integrated reports, it should be noted that two out of five companies referred to GRI standards in their social reports. None of these entities elaborated on six capitals directly; however, all of them referred to some capitals indirectly. The analysed SMEs reported mostly environmental, human and social aspects. Due to the lack of evidence on IR in SME sector, we decided to present the experience of large companies in IR since they may constitute a good benchmark for SMEs who will decide to implement IR in the future.

Adherence to <IR> Guiding Principles: Evidence from Large Polish Companies

Strategic Focus and Future Orientation

The principle of strategic focus and future orientation requires from organization preparing the integrated report to provide "*insight into the organization's strategy*" and show "*how it relates to the organization's ability to create value in the short, medium and long term and to its use of and effects on the capitals*" (IIRC, 2013, p. 16).

ORLEN Group representing the oil industry discussed its strategy in a separate chapter of the integrated report titled "*Our strategy*". Strategy focus was combined with a future orientation. The group started by presenting the update of the strategy for 2019–2022. It emphasized that macroeconomic volatility enforced regular revision of business goals. Therefore, the group conducted macrotrend analyses in such areas as new energy sources, climate and environment, groundbreaking technologies, new business models and consumer behaviour. *ORLEN Group* also made insight into the regulatory framework. These actions had two purposes: setting development directions and defining targets for the two subsequent years (ORLEN Group 2018, p. 2).

It should be noticed that the *ORLEN Group* created value by its operational activities in downstream, retail and upstream segments. These segments could have operated effectively due to the involvement of manufactured capital and social and relationship capital. There was also a positive impact of other factors on value creation. These included human capital underpinning future sustainable growth of group, intellectual capital reflecting a culture of innovation and finally financial capital strengthening the group in terms of diversified funding sources and comfortable debt levels (ORLEN Group 2018, p. 50).

ORLEN Group presented value levers, goals and financial targets for each segment for 2019–2020 systematically and delivered information about strategy implementation for the reporting year. It also provided some narrative description of plans/goals regarding human capital, a culture of innovation and financial strength. Interestingly, the group disclosed key success factors for the strategy in the form of a table with key performance indicators in three segments and financial areas. KPIs were presented on an annual basis for the reporting year and 2 years back. Moreover, *ORLEN Group* listed the most significant investments realized by three segments (ORLEN Group 2018, pp. 174–188).

A value added of the integrated report constituted a part that reflected how the company monitored its strategy implementation. *ORLEN Group* adopted a uniform system of regular tracking of the strategy implementation progress. This system engaged corporate bodies in three stages. The first phase focused on the strategy review carried out by the management and supervisory boards. The second phase was dedicated to reviewing sub-strategies or strategic projects, and it was a Corporate Strategy Committee task. The last stage reflected KPIs' monitoring by key managers in day-to-day business (ORLEN Group 2018, p. 189).

The chapter "Our strategy" was concluded with a part concerning the short-term market outlook. The group presented market prospects in 2019 through the expected macroeconomic environment's prism, projected market trends and legislative changes.

In its sustainability report, *KGHM Polska Miedź* explained its strategy very extensively and well-structured. The report clarified the Strategy Committee's role in supervising the implementation of the company's strategy and long-term operating plans. According to the report, the committee assessed these documents' coherence and provided its opinions on draft strategies and their amendments presented by the Management Board to the Supervisory Board, and on the Company's annual and long-term operating plans. Interestingly, the corporate social responsibility strategy was an integral part of *KGHM's* Business Strategy for 2017–2021 with the outlook until 2040. The authors of the report emphasized the fact that the strategy was subject to monthly monitoring during the financial year. Although *KGHM Polska Miedź* is a huge business organization, the entire group's strategy was presented very clearly using a diagram. An additional distinctive feature of the report was the overview of strategy execution as the report described how successfully the group implemented strategic projects relating to the exploration, the main process line, the development of assets and production (KGHM 2018, pp. 89–96).

Connectivity of Information

The principle of information connectivity requires an organization to prepare the integrated report which reflects "*a holistic picture of the combination, interrelatedness and dependencies between the factors that affect the organization's ability to create value over time*" (IIRC, 2013, p. 16).

The integrated report of *ORLEN Group* provided key functionalities indicating availability and connectivity of information. First, the report was available online with the possibility to generate a pdf file. Second, it contained interactive infographics, including the business model, the value creation model and the market map. Current and historical data were presented using interactive key performance indicators. All information had its place. For instance, the integrated report's multimedia contents were available in the Multimedia Centre, key publications relating to the company's operations were downloadable from the Document Centre, and selected figures were included in the Charts and Tables Centre. *ORLEN Group* also provided an instructional video in the Help section on how to navigate an integrated report.

Moreover, to properly understand the report's content, the glossary of financial and industry-specific terms was presented. Users of the report might also complete an interactive questionnaire to provide feedback on it. Concluding, the content of *ORLEN Group's* integrated report was not static. The pages were interlinked and constituted a unique chain-like structure (ORLEN Group 2018, pp. 5–6).

Orange Polska integrated report is an excellent example of the report that offers high-quality adherence to connectivity principle. It was available online and could be easily converted to the pdf format. The online version of the report was easily navigated, giving immediate access to individual parts and attachments. The report emphasized the relationships and links between the various factors that determined value creation. In addition to the traditional descriptive part, the report included many diagrams, infographics and tables explaining the most critical information to stakeholders in an integrated way, synthetically and without lengthy texts (http://raportzintegrowany.orange.pl/raport2018/en/index).

Stakeholder Relationships

The principle of stakeholder relationships requires an organization to prepare the integrated report, which provides "*insight into the nature and quality of the organization's relationships with its key stakeholders*" (IIRC, 2013, p. 17). Therefore, the reporting organization should indicate how and to what extent it understands, considers and responds to legitimate stakeholder needs and interests.

Grupa Azoty from the chemicals industry emphasized the role of dialogue with stakeholders in its integrated report. The company adjusted the form and frequency of the dialogue to the characteristics of a given stakeholder group and the expectations and issues that were material to both parties. Interestingly, the group also assigned responsibility for the two-way communication to the heads of individual functional areas of the group companies, who were most acquainted with individual stakeholder groups' expectations. As a result, a stakeholder map was developed. It covered the following aspects: list of stakeholders groups, methods and frequency of engagement.

Moreover, the company collected the most frequent questions asked by particular stakeholder groups. It helped in recognizing the areas of their interests. *Grupa Azoty* stressed that regular and fair communication might constitute a base for mutual understanding. It might also contribute to the update of CSR strategy priorities that could translate into better business performance (Grupa Azoty 2016–2017).

In the same vein, LOTOS Group also highlighted the role of dialogue with social and market stakeholders. The company remarked that the form and frequency of the dialogue varied depending on the stakeholder group. In order to recognize the needs and expectations of its stakeholders, *LOTOS Group* took several initiatives. Firstly, it conducted regular surveys to gauge the level of satisfaction among customers and trading partners. Secondly, it ensured a regular exchange of information with capital market participants through the Investor Relations site and roadshows. Thirdly, it maintained contacts with regulatory, inspection/audit and monitoring bodies. Finally, it communicated with employees during day-to-day work and through trade unions, and regular job satisfaction surveys (LOTOS Group 2018, p. 17).

Budimex Group, which represents the construction industry, mapped its stakeholders and distinguished six major groups that impacted the organization. They covered (1) employees and social partners (full-time employees, students and potential employees, former employees, trade unions, employees of subcontractors and suppliers, labour inspection and other similar supervision authorities); (2) investors (strategic investor, institutional investors, individual investors, Warsaw Stock Exchange, brokerage houses, banks); (3) customers (GDDKiA, institutional customers, individual customers, business partners, key suppliers, subcontractors, local government and government administration); (4) society (local communities within the investment area, residents and community leaders, universities and academics/students, technical and professional organizations); (5) natural environment (environmental organizations, environmental supervision inspectors, state forests); and (6) media and public opinion. Furthermore, *Budimex Group* applied the principle of decentralized dialogue (direct relations with stakeholders prevailed). Channels of communication with stakeholders (surveys for suppliers, meetings, conferences, social media, chatbots and social projects) carried the communication department, the spokesperson and the strategic analysis office (Budimex 2018, pp. 8–9).

Materiality

The principle of materiality is about disclosing information about "matters that substantively affect the organization's ability to create value over the short, medium and long term period" (IIRC, 2013, p. 18).

TAURON Group from the power industry identified material issues in extensive consultations with key stakeholders through the dialogue broken down into stages. It enabled obtaining a full and clear picture of the external and internal environment's expectations regarding the report's contents and the business.

The dialogue covered (http://en.raport2017.tauron.pl/o-raporcie/):

- face-to-face interviews with experts (representatives of HEIs, organizations supporting responsible business and non-governmental environmentally focused organizations),
- expert online survey—distributed, among others, to representatives of industry organizations, the regulator, non-governmental organizations and the social partner,
- online survey—a questionnaire distributed electronically and completed by a record number of over 12,000 employees and customers.

- workshops with *TAURON Group* managers, where the topics covered include strategy, customer, distribution, human resource management and compliance.

Initially, the analysis covered 41 issues broken down into four thematic groups: market, environment, workplace and society. However, finally, 16 topics were identified to be depicted in the integrated report. They were picked after comparing the results of each stage of the dialogue with the external environment and the employees' perspective.

PKP CARGO—a company representing the services and transport sector—enabled all stakeholders to express their opinion on the extent to which their information needs were met. Stakeholders could assess the quality of information presented on a 5-point scale. At the same time, they indicated the critical aspects of the company's functioning by selecting a maximum of 4 out of 13 elements. Stakeholders could also assess the areas of the integrated report that should be developed. The last opportunity was to indicate the missing information and ways to improve the report in the future.

Budimex Group started defining important aspects in 2012 as part of a comprehensive audit among key managers. The group applied the standard PN-ISO 26000 while conducting the audit and identifying critical areas of interest. The selected issues were verified on an annual basis in terms of environmental and financial impact. Interestingly, the group took into account feedback from the Ministry of Finance and the Association of Issuers while determining essential non-financial report issues. It should be noticed that media information and the current company's position on the market could also influence the identified areas' significance. Finally, the group conducted surveys among stakeholders to test the importance of non-financial issues from their point of view. Those surveys enabled identifying key non-financial risks in the social and environmental areas regarding employment conditions, occupational health and safety, impact on the local environment, biodiversity and unethical conduct prevention (Budimex 2018, pp. 6–9).

Conciseness

The conciseness principle requires organization preparing the integrated report to provide "*sufficient context to understand the organization's strategy, governance and prospects without being burdened by less relevant information*" (IIRC, 2013, p. 21).

An excellent example of conciseness in integrated reports of Polish companies is that of *Pelion* from healthcare services. The report was available in the online format, where the main page referred directly to the six-capital model (every capital was depicted as a triangle—one of six parts of the equilateral triangle) (http://raport2016.pelion.eu/en/schemat-tworzenia-wartosci.html). In each capital case, the management objective was shortly described, and the primary metrics visualized. Each capital was then further described in detail in three subsections. It gave a perfect overview of the organization's strategy and performance.

Consequently, stakeholders obtained access to the following qualitative information.

- Pelion believes in people.
  The company emphasized employee roles, competencies, openness to teamwork in their day-to-day work. It developed a dialogue culture, which involved listening to employees' opinions and supporting their engagement.
- Pelion protects lives.
  The company remarked the need to promote disease prevention and make patients aware of their physical and mental well-being, which positively affected social capital management.
- Pelion builds trust.
  Within its manufactured (operating) capital, the company used innovative solutions and expanded the warehouse infrastructure and distribution networks to allow patients to order and collect the medicines they need quickly.
- Pelion sets standards.
  As a result, the company managed its intellectual capital by conducting in-house research and clinical trials and providing opportunities to bring together the academic community and market practitioners.
- Pelion aims to maintain the balance.
  Within this area, managing natural capital was to mitigate the adverse environmental impact of the company's production, distribution, and other operational processes.
- Pelion makes responsible investments.
  While managing its financial capital, the company maintained financial liquidity through cooperation and honest communication with capital market participants and lenders.

In quantitative form, the primary metrics of the six capitals included, respectively, the number of employees (9400), editions of Łódź marathon sponsored (6), patients served in pharmacies each month (4.000.000), patents and patent applications based on 1-MNA molecule (28), year of presence in the RESPECT index (5) and revenue growth (8.5%).

A good practice of conciseness in Polish companies' integrated reports is presented by *Bogdanka* from the mining industry (Bogdanka 2018). The structure of the report was strictly adjusted to the six-capital model without offering burden and unnecessary information. The company presented the achieved financial results at the end of the reporting year, compared with the social, environmental and management results. In the report, *Bogdanka* used six capitals: financial, manufacturing, intellectual, human, social and natural, indicating the risks for each of them and amounts spent illustrating the scale of engagement. Each chapter of the report was devoted to discussing one of the capitals transparently and well-structured.

PKP CARGO introduced content in the integrated report in a sequential manner. The company's strategy, challenges and plans were clearly described. Transparent illustrations supplemented narrative information. Stakeholders could benefit from the detailed information, which developed the basic data. Important aspects of governance and outlook were supplemented with additional information that was presented outside the integrated report. Another advantage was the indication of future development directions against the background of changes in the geopolitical situation.

Reliability and Completeness

IIRC expects that the integrated report is reliable and complete, which means that it will include "*all material matters, both positive and negative, in a balanced way and without material error*" (IIRC, 2013, p. 21).

ANG Spółdzielnia is a perfect example of adherence to reliability and completeness principle while preparing the integrated report (ANG Spółdzielnia 2018). On the one hand, the entity reported that 2018 was a good year for the cooperative since the cooperative achieved excellent financial results. On the other hand, the entity pointed out that it failed in some areas, including volunteering, environmental impact, revenue sources diversification, humanities education and community involvement in joint matters. Therefore, *ANG Spółdzielnia* determined what it planned to do in order to overcome deficiencies. The entity paid attention to employee volunteering and financial education programmes for children and youth within volunteering. It wanted to engage more people in the programme and offer them more support. *ANG Spółdzielnia* also planned to decrease its negative impact by reducing paper and plastic consumption and continuing waste segregation within the environmental impact. Within revenue source diversification, the entity intended to diversify its revenue structure favouring cash loans and insurance. Within humanities' education, *ANG Spółdzielnia* wanted to increase training in this area in the next years. Finally, to involve the community in joint matters, the entity intended to strengthen an internal dialogue and organize joint work in the cooperative.

Business activities of *Budimex Group* had a direct impact on the environment in given local communities. It was always a matter of trade-offs. The group reported: "*On the one hand, new investments improve the quality of life of the residents—new roads, culture centres, modern hospitals, new jobs, but the construction process itself, often lasting many months, may be disruptive to the environment*" (Budimex 2018, p. 55). Therefore, in 2018 the group decided to conduct five resident satisfaction surveys regarding projects carried out in their surroundings. An independent research agency conducted surveys. *Budimex Group* showed the results of that survey in a reliable and balanced way. It disclosed the title of the project, population size in the vicinity of the project, number of persons who read the survey on the corporate website, number of persons who took part in the initial evaluation with the results of the assessments and number of persons who took part in the detailed assessment. It worth mentioning that the group indicated the structure of positive, neutral and negative ratings.

Orange Polska is a perfect example of adherence to reliability and completeness principle. The company received the Best Integrated Report 2017 Award in the 12th edition of the Social Reports Competition. The award was given for presenting the approach to management and business in a way that integrated the financial prospect and ESG (environment, social, governance), comprehensive display of risks, a reliable, accurate and trustworthy report, showing both the strengths and weaknesses of the organization, subject to external verification. In addition, the company received a special award from the Warsaw Stock Exchange for maintaining high standards of non-financial reporting and contributing to the credibility of listed companies among investors. The Responsible Business Forum and Deloitte organize the Social Reports Competition.

The example of a reliable and complete presentation of essential matters to stakeholder was *PGE Group* report. The group presented both positive and negative facts on its activities without prioritizing the first in the report part related to natural capital metrics. Thus, stakeholders could see that, unfortunately, the emission of CO2 over one year grew by 1/6 to over 70 million tons. Also, the emissions of SO2 and particulate matter increased. The company showed that the quantity of hazardous and other waste grew significantly over a year time. The reduction in negative environmental impact was observed in NOx emission and wastewater produced (PGE Group 2018).

Consistency and Comparability

The consistency and comparability principles require organization preparing the integrated report to ensure "*consistency over time*" and enable "*comparisons with other organizations to the extent material to the organization's own ability to create value*" (IIRC, 2013, p. 23).

PGNiG, in its online report, provided stakeholders with comprehensive information on performance presented consistently and comparably. There were three main pages with key economic metrics included under the "*interactive data*" section. The first presented "*operating highlight*"; the second, "*financial highlights*"; and the last, "*stock market indicators*". Up to 50 metrics were presented on each page, and every metric included levels of the five recent years. The users could also pick any of the metrics for visualization, selected the required data and exported them to an Excel file. It should be pointed out that financial highlights for years 2016 and 2017 were restated in the "*financial highlights—restated data*" tab. In the first case, this was due to the new segmentation of the PGNiG Group's operations and the other one connected with the application of the new IFRS 15 Financial Reporting Standard with effect from 1 January 2018. Consequently, besides original levels, the restated data guaranteed consistent and comparable view of financial operations over time (PGNIG 2018).

ING Bank Śląski is involved in projects related to cash flow minimization. It was described in detail in the integrated report. The data were consistent with *the Cashless Poland Program's* provisions, focused on the development of card and mobile payments. The bank's performance against the background of the sector and the entire economy was also consistent with the National Bank of Poland (NBP), Ministry of Finance and the Polish Financial Supervision Authority reports (ING Bank Ślaski 2018).

Observance of <IR> Content Elements: Evidence from Large Polish Companies

Organizational Overview and External Environment

IIRC expects that an integrated report within the section of organizational overview and external environment shall provide the answer to the following question: "*What does the organization do and what are the circumstances under which it operates?*" (IIRC, 2013, p. 24).

The *KGHM Polska Miedź* is one of the best examples of a report that discusses the functioning of the organization and its environment in an almost perfect way. The company provided a concise context for its activities as the largest company in Poland and one of the leading companies in the world active in the exploration and extraction of non-ferrous metals. Because *KGHM Polska Miedź* is a global company, it presents itself as an organization with nearly 60 years of experience in the mining and processing industry. It operates one of the largest copper deposits globally, thereby ensuring continuity of production for many upcoming decades. The report discussed group's business activities in Europe, North America and South America on copper, silver, gold, molybdenum, lead and rock salt production. In the integrated report, there was a whole chapter on organizational overview of the external environment. It clearly explained what *KGHM Polska Miedź* did, the scope of operations, the most crucial business lines, and copper's application from a global perspective. For example, the group argued that copper was indispensable to live. It helped supply electricity and pure water to homes and residential units and made a material contribution to sustainable development. For centuries, this metal has been present in the history of human progress. In the *KGHM Polska Miedź,* they are confident that copper's unique properties make it an invaluable part of the future, while its significance for global development is growing. Energy efficiency, renewable energy sources, smart power grids and electrification of transport are merely some of the areas in which copper's role will expand, simultaneously make it possible to pursue sustainable development in the global economy (KGHM 2018).

LOTOS Group provided a clear organizational overview and described its external environment in details. The group is the second-largest fuel producer in Poland operating in the crude oil and natural gas production and selling quality petroleum products. The company emphasized that its activities were driven by sustainable development. The group indicated its companies' locations in four countries and presented organizational structure and areas of competence of the individual *LOTOS Group* companies. Two segments of operations—(1) exploration and production and (2) refining and marketing—were described. The company pointed out that people were at the centre of *LOTOS's* business. Therefore, the group made efforts to enhance a dialogue with them. In particular, the company tried to discover customers' opinions about the *LOTOS Group* and its subsidiaries. Therefore, it used the classification proposed by the Apostle model developed in the Harvard Business School. This approach distinguishes between four types of customers: Terrorists, Hostages, Mercenaries and Apostles. Terrorists are customers, who had a bad experience with the brand, which incline them to complain about it publicly. Hostages are those customers who are not satisfied, but they continue to purchase from the company because of the monopoly situation on the market or high switching costs. In turn, Mercenaries are satisfied customers, but they are not attached to one particular branch and tend to switch between them as a result of impulse or some fashion trends. The LOTOS Group reported that almost half of their customers were the Apostles. They were the most loyal group, emotionally attached to the brand about which they disseminated positive opinions (LOTOS Group 2018,

p. 18). In the organizational overview, the group mentioned memberships in industry associations, awards and distinctions.

Description of the external environment provided information about the challenges of the oil market. The group listed critical drivers of oil and gas prices and connected the population growth with the increase in crude oil consumption. The company also presented future challenges and global forecasts for its segments of operation: production and refining.

The *LOTOS Group* noticed that the profitability of production operations was affected by numerous legal regulations. These were the Polish Geological and Mining Law, EU regulations and international conventions, particularly those on environmental protection. However, the company also predicted the other issues that could arise and became crucial soon, such as planned amendments to tax regulations applicable to hydrocarbon production or continued tightening of environmental protection regulations. Likewise, the refining segment was under various external impacts. In this segment, macroeconomic factors could drive a situation of the sector. One of the key threats to oil refining was growing competition from refineries in the Middle East and Russia. The group foresaw that the Mediterranean could become the primary market for these refineries, which would change the fuel supply demand balance across Europe. The other arising opportunity was related to implementing the IMO (International Maritime Organization) regulations in 2020 that would tighten the sulphur content standards for bunker fuel and lead to higher demand for middle distillates.

The example of *LOTOS Group* shows that the company perceived its business activity in narrower and broader contexts reflected in the stakeholder map. The group distinguishes between internal and external stakeholders as well as the market environment.

Business Model

The description of a business model constitutes a pillar of IR. It explains how inputs are transformed into outputs and outcomes by conducting business activities and how these contribute to the fulfilment of the organization's strategic objectives and value creation over the short, medium and long term (IIRC, 2013, p. 25).

The perfect example of how to present a business model of a company is that of *PGNiG* Group. It is worth noting that the business model was the starting point of the company's annual report. It was visualized with clear and convincing graphics, which covered the four main areas of operations: exploration and production, trade (wholesale and retail) and storage, distribution and generation. The complete explanation of the business model was included in the online version of the report and presented with four videos, including main figures related to the business's four areas.

From these sources, stakeholders could learn that in the first domain, the company was involved in the entire oil and gas production process, from geological analyses, via drilling to field development and hydrocarbon production. It was responsible for 90% of the domestic gas production. The trade included sales of natural gas to large industrial customers, the Polish Power Exchange (PPX), SMEs, households, the Ukrainian market and West European customers. Apart from the domestic gas and delivered by pipelines, the company operated the LNG terminal in Świnoujście. The storage business was related to maintaining seven underground gas storage facilities. The distribution network providing gas to companies and households had 186.000 km in length and served 1510 municipalities and communes. Within the joint production of heat and electricity, the company operated 17 units with the total thermal power of 5.3 GW and electricity power of 1.2 GW. The business's primary beneficiary is Poland's capital—Warsaw—with 70% of its heating demand and 65% of that for electricity covered by the company (PGNIG 2018).

PKP CARGO based its business model on shaping lasting relationships with key stakeholders, including suppliers and customers. The company consciously used the advantage of having the most extensive transport fleet in the country. Constant, partnership-based cooperation with suppliers of electricity, diesel and railway infrastructure managers allowed for cost discipline. Durable relations with the large customers of the heavy industry sector (steel mills and mines) were developed thanks to the early negotiation of contract extensions for future years. These contracts took into account the assumed level of service quality.

Risk and Opportunities

Risk and opportunity description is vital for an integrated report. The content of the report should provide an answer to the following question: "*What are the specific risks and opportunities that affect the organization's ability to create value over the short, medium and long term, and how is the organization dealing with them*?" (IIRC, 2013, p. 27).

PGNiG may serve as a perfect example of how to present risks in an unbiased form. First of all, the company listed the risks related to the achievement of its strategic goals. Altogether, there were 12 key risk factors identified, including delay in exploration and production, disruptions to gas supplies, negative impact on the natural environment, unfavourable relations with local communities, poor relations with customers, departure of qualified staff, problems with occupational health and safety, ineffective dialogue with trade unions, misconduct at work, corruption, irregularities in the public procurement process and unfavourable relations to suppliers. The company then presented 45 risk management measures (the majority related to employee-related risks and ethics-related ones).

Further on the company addressed operational risks related to the regulatory area and the four pillars of its business model, i.e. exploration and production, trade and storage, distribution and generation. Throughout the whole discussion on various risk factors, the same visual code was applied. It consisted of three elements: risk materiality level (1–3 blue bullets indicating low, medium and high materiality), probability level (1–3 orange bullets reflecting low, medium and high probability) and year-on-year change in risk level (indicated with arrows for the increase, no change or decrease).

Four risks were considered highly material (3 related to EU legislation) and one very probable within the regulatory area. Four risks were considered highly material (all related to operations in Norway) and two as highly probable in the exploration and production domain. Trade and storage business area was exposed to four risks of the highest materiality (all risks disclosed) and two being very probable (influence on prices by Polish regulators and competition). Two risks were highly material and one very probable (the main concern being lack of long-term regulatory policy) within the distribution area. Finally, generation was considered a perilous domain, where three of the four risks identified were both highly material and probable (they included CO2 emission allowances, fuel prices and coal supplies) (PGNIG 2018).

PKP CARGO identified risk groups in detail. Each significant risk was assigned to a risk leader who took care of accurate measurement and implementation of hedging methods (see the link). The company prepared separate reactive actions to threats of macroeconomic, market and financial nature. Significant risk factors related to key customers were analysed on an ongoing basis. It was a pre-emptive action, which allowed adjusting plans to long-term threats. *PKP CARGO* also presented areas of future opportunities. These included:

- development of new communication routes ("Tricity" and "New Silk Road");
- alignment with the governmental and European transport development strategy;
- mergers and acquisitions of key carriers in the region.

It should be stressed that the plans in the *PKP CARGO* strategy included the need to develop rolling stock resources in order to take advantage of the opportunities mentioned above effectively.

Budimex Group presented the main risks concerning the supply chain (occupational health and safety, terms and conditions of employment, environmental protection, timeliness and quality of works performed, finance) for each of the six capitals (FC: foreign exchange risk, price risk, credit risk, liquidity risk; HC: risk of an increase in employment costs, risk of lack of a sufficient number of qualified employees; MC: risk of delay in timely performance or insufficient quality of the subcontractors' work, risk of delay in obtaining relevant administrative decisions; IC: risk of change in the scope of works or technologies agreed in agreements; SC: risk of delay in obtaining relevant administrative decisions; and NC: risk of delay in obtaining relevant administrative decisions, risk of adverse weather or soil conditions) (Budimex 2018, p. 32).

Pekabex described in great detail significant risks related to its operations that could impact the policies applied for an employee, social and environmental issues, and risks related to products and relations with the external environment, together with a description of the management of all these risks. The group described risks using materiality (1–5, where 5 is the maximum materiality) and presented countermeasures for each risk type. It is worth noting that the auditors applied a similar methodology when auditing companies. They identified the type of risk within the selected areas, assessed these risks and valued them according to the adopted scale and proposed control mechanisms for each risk (countermeasures). This way of presenting information about the type of risk seems clear and understandable for the stakeholders (Pekabex 2018, pp. 114–125).

Strategy and Resource Allocation

Within the strategy and resource allocation, an integrated report should provide an answer to the following question: "*Where does the organization want to go and how does it intend to get there?*" In order to achieve that an integrated report is expected to include four elements in its content: (1) an organization's short-, medium- and long-term strategic objectives; (2) the strategies it has in place or intends to implement, to achieve those strategic objectives; (3) the resource allocation plans it has to implement its strategy; and (4) measurement of achievements and target outcomes for the short, medium and long term (IIRC, 2013, p. 27).

TAURON Group presented in its online report the way it outlined the strategic objectives. The company stressed that the strategy laid down the roadmap indicating how to attain the intended targets. Such a roadmap included tasks, responsible persons, required resources and expected effects. *TAURON Group* was aware that it was not plausible to develop plans without considering favourable and unfavourable factors affecting strategy implementation. Thus, the approach to strategy execution was regularly revised and adjusted to new circumstances. *TAURON Group* remarked that it was also essential to measure outcomes and compare them against the competitors' activities (TAURON Group 2018).

TAURON Group distinguished from the other Polish companies preparing the integrated reports since it outlined the strategic planning process. The process was composed of eleven key elements (http://raport2018.tauron.pl/en/strategia/jak-wyznaczalismy-cele-strategii/):

- diagnosis and monitoring of the environment;
- identification of risks, opportunities and threats;
- assessment and estimation of the impact exerted by risks, opportunities and threats on the business;
- preparation of priorities and definition of objectives;
- matching resources (budgets, capital) to the execution of strategic objectives, allocation of capital;
- cascading quantified aims into individual business areas;
- identification of the tasks/initiatives/projects making it possible to attain our targets;
- execution of adopted tasks/initiatives/projects;
- measurement/monitoring the effects and adjustment of actions, if any, on the business areas and group level;
- monitoring the changes in the external environment and assessment of their impact on the group;
- adjustment/update of strategic priorities in response to the challenges stemming from the environment's changes (opportunities and threats).

The other interesting thing is that the *TAURON Group* set three strategic priorities (financial stability; operational and investment efficiency; capital partnerships) and necessary related actions. The company also referred to short-, medium- and long-term challenges and described them across a particular function, including mining, generation, heat, renewable energy sources, sales and distribution.

Orange Polska presented a report that discussed its strategy and resource allocation originally. The first part of the chapter devoted to the strategy was the interview with Jean-François Fallacher (*Orange Polska* CEO). He discussed 5G as the technology that became the key topic for the telecom industry for the coming years.

Moreover, he explained how their customers would be able to benefit from it. The most important part of the chapter concerned the strategy's presentation in a well-structured way in connection with the allocation of resources (Orange 2018, pp. 40–49).

ING Bank Śląski subordinated all activities of its innovation development strategy. The bank attempted to stay ahead of the competition with new technological solutions and social innovations. The bank's goal was to inspire customers and employees to provide new ideas of which each was carefully analysed. If it was positively assessed, the bank took action aimed at its implementation. A vital element of each new action was the analysis of the impact on natural resources. Moreover, innovative projects which supported environmental protection were strongly encouraged and promoted.

Governance

The integrated report should clarify: "*How does the organization's governance structure support its ability to create value in the short, medium and long term?*" (IIRC, 2013, p. 25).

Budimex Group was boasted its high management culture, which was based on operating in compliance with top management standards. The group implemented management systems that enabled transparent decision-making processes. The company emphasized that while any irregularities were identified, corrective measures were immediately taken. The company also notified its stakeholders about critical issues in a material and timely manner. Furthermore, it applied the software supporting the risk identification and management.

It should be noted that the parent company of the group adhered to a set of corporate governance rules called "*Best Practice for Companies Listed on the WSE 2016*". Observance of the corporate governance rules aimed to eliminate risks in the management area since the principles regulated the way of communication policy with investors, internal systems and functions, and relations with shareholders (Budimex 2018, p. 33).

Budimex Group also presented its authorities, including management board, supervisory board and general meeting of shareholders. Those bodies' roles were determined, and the changes in the structures of the management and supervisory boards were disclosed.

It worth mentioning that Budimex S.A. (parent company) had the "*Integrated Management System Policy*" which provisions related directly to CSR and liabilities of *Budimex Group*. The policy aimed at minimizing the adverse effects of business activity while maintaining top-quality customer services at the same time. Interestingly, the group set up the CSR Committee, which was accountable for a comprehensive approach to social responsibility management and assurance that decisions made complied with the Integrated Management System Policy (Budimex 2018, pp. 34–35).

Budimex Group also listed the international management standards of which the organization implemented norms and certificates. They covered PN-ISO 26000: 2012 (management system of the company's social and environmental responsibility); ISO 9001:2015 (quality management system); ISO 14001:2015 (environmental management system); PN-N-18001:2004 and OHSAS 18000:2007 (occupational health and safety management system); ISO/IEC 27007:2013 (information security management system); AQAP 2011:2009 (quality management system); ISO 14001:50001 (power management system); ISO 10001 (system for managing the codes of conduct connected with customer satisfaction); ISO 20000-1 (IT service quality management system); and NATO Commercial and Government Entity Code (NCAGE2)2 (Budimex 2018, pp. 34–35).

mBank accurately described governance principles applied by the management and supervisory boards and about shareholders and employees. The bank also presented information policy principles and methods of financial statement assurance. Moreover, a code of conduct shaping relationships between employees and business partners was developed. The code was a key element of building mutual trust. The internal control rules and the principles of appointing and dismissing board members were examples of monitoring function realized by the bank (mBank 2018).

Performance

The companies who draw up an integrated report should respond to the following question: "*To what extent has the organization achieved its strategic objectives for the period and what are its outcomes in terms of effects on the capitals?*" (IIRC, 2013, p. 28).

KGHM Polska Miedź presented a report, which described its performance in various dimensions almost exhaustively. Generally, the performance information was described in three sections. The first one referred to business results closely linked to production results. There were a lot of detailed tables displaying major reporting segments of the *KGHM Group*. The second section was devoted to financial results referring to financial stability, sales results, cost efficiency, financial liquidity, group's net debt and capital expenditures. The most crucial section on GRI G4 indicators presented a non-financial performance that complemented the previous sections' financial and production content. The company emphasized how it achieved its strategic objectives and its performance metrics regarding effects on the capitals, considering corporate social responsibility (KGHM 2018).

PGNiG holistically presented its performance both in the printed and online versions of its reports. The first included a summary of performance metrics in the form of a 2-page dashboard including 36 metrics broken into six categories: "*the PGNiG Group*" (8 measures), "*PGNiG* on the Warsaw Stock Exchange (WSE)" (8), and those related to the four pillars of its business model "exploration and production" (8), "trade and storage" (4), "distribution" (4) and "generation" (4). The online version included close to 150 metrics related to operational activities, financials and performance on WSE—all with levels for the recent 5 years, with a possibility to visualize selected data in a chart or export them to Excel (PGNIG 2018).

Outlook

The content of the integrated report in part concerning outlook should answer the following question: "*What challenges and uncertainties are the organization likely to encounter in pursuing its strategy, and what are the potential implications for its business model and future performance*?"(IIRC, 2013, p. 28).

The chief economist in *PKN Orlen* supplemented the integrated report 2018 with far-reaching Outlook 2019+. This part included bright and bold ideas about the future of energy markets. The chief economist highlighted the most pressing challenges facing business, such as the necessity of changing the approach to energy efficiency improvements. The focus was put on strategic thinking that should have prepared the company for uncertain times. The company made efforts to put its strategy dynamics into practice. Therefore, it identified five leading megatrends which probably would impact its business in 2040 and beyond, including (ORLEN Group 2018, p. 425):

- "*customers and their changing preferences and behaviours: remote sales, increase in production on-demand, using rather than possessing, conscious consumption with due consideration for human rights, natural environment and climate;*
- *new mobility developing in four dimensions: autonomous driving, use of 4G and 5G networks, electrification of drives and shared mobility;*
- *e.0 economy—digital, electrical, smart, efficient, renewable (circular);*
- *sustainable development: climate and environmental pressures, renewable (circular) economy;*
- *the new geography of demand, supply and influence: water, food, minerals*".

Further, the chief economist determined how companies and their leaders should respond to new arising opportunities. There appeared a suggestion to design business in a way enabling to meet customer needs with the consumption of raw materials limited to a necessary minimum. The sustainable approach requires not to manufacture products that customers will quickly use, discard and replace with new ones. The other thing is that companies should be more responsive to changes. Therefore, they are expected to spin off entities that operate under more flexible rules, based on new business models. There was a suggestion that companies should eliminate myopia by devising strategies expected to be successful over a few decades. Simultaneously, long-term visions should be implemented by the subsequent development of small scale, regenerative by design innovative projects.

The way how the outlook for the *ORLEN Group* was presented in the integrated report proved consciousness and foresight of the managers and their advisors. The chief economists of the group, who was a narrator of this part of the report referred several times to external sources of knowledge such as Mc Kinsey and Company report, press releases or well-known persons such as George P. Mitchell (a pioneer in the economic extraction of shale gas) or Professor Richard Rumelt (professor of strategy at UCLA's Anderson School of Management) (ORLEN Group 2018, pp. 424–428).

Basis of Presentation

IIRC requires preparers of the integrated report to answer the following question: "*How does the organization determine what matters to include in the integrated report and how are such matters quantified or evaluated?*" (IIRC, 2013, p. 29). Thus, it is expected that companies will summarize the organization's materiality determination process, a description of the reporting boundary and how it has been determined, and a summary of the significant frameworks and methods used to quantify or evaluate material matters.

PKP CARGO announced that it had published the integrated report for 2018 in the online version (https://raportzintegrowany2018.pkpcargo.com/en/#podsumowanie). The company stressed that this was the second publication of this type. In this way, the company wanted to familiarize the readers of the report with the entire group's activities in a holistic way, combining financial and non-financial aspects to show how the company value was built for all stakeholder groups. *PKP CARGO* indicated that the integrated report was based on the *IIRC framework* and *GRI guidelines*. The company decided to implement *GRI indicators* in compliance with the core option. *PKP CARGO* also introduced markings to the content of the report under the six-capital concept.

Budimex Group distinguished from the other companies in terms of the basis of presenting the integrated report. The group emphasized that the presented report was the eleventh consecutive annual report on sustainable development and the third integrated report. *Budimex Group* highlighted that each of the reports published included data concerning business activity and associated risks, environmental protection, employee and social issues. Furthermore, data were presented in a way that enabled their verification and year-over-year comparison. The group informed that it had developed the content of the integrated report in compliance with the guidelines of the *GRI standards* in the basic Core option, *ISO 26000 Standard*, principles of the *Global Compact*, Polish and European legal regulations within the scope of reporting non-financial data, *the Directive 2014/95/EU* and the *IIRC guidelines*. *Budimex Group* also disclosed that the report's reliability and compliance with the GRI standards were verified and acknowledged by an independent auditor. In 2017, non-financial report was awarded in the competition "*Social Reports*" in the category "*Award of the Stock Exchange*" and in 2018 in the plebiscite of Company Bulletins in the category "*Corporate One-Off Project*". *Budimex Group* also clearly explained how the process of defining important aspects looked like over the years (Budimex 2018, p. 6).

5 Conclusion and Remarks

IR in SMEs should take a simplified form in comparison with the requirements for large companies. The reason is that the scale of reporting obligations for SMEs in Poland is massive. The average number of reporting elements (prints, forms, reports, etc.) that a statistical SME had to submit to public authorities in 2019 was 191 and 208, respectively. Therefore, our proposition for SMEs is to determine which of the six capitals are the most crucial. Figure 13 presents the relevance of particular capitals to SMEs considering their business sector.

We propose solutions that large companies have already adopted to apply them, of course, in a modified scope to SMEs.

SIX CAPITALS	High relevance	Low relevance
HC	professional, scientific & technical activities (knowledge-intensive services); legal & expert services (specialized services); biotech (R&D); information & communication	distributive sales (within unspecialized services & sales); construction; manufacturing
S&RC	professional, scientific & technical activities; legal & expert services (specialized services); start-ups (market network); biotech (cooperation with academics, R&D labs); accommodation & food services (customer relationships)	distributive sales (within unspecialized services & sales)
FC	start-ups, manufacturing, logistics, mining & quarrying	administrative & support services (standard services), legal services (specialized services)
MC	construction, manufacturing, R&D (biotech), mining & quarrying	administrative & support services (standard services), legal & expert services (specialized services)
IC	information & communication, R&D (biotech), start-ups (IP protection)	Standard services, unspecialized sales and services
NC	manufacturing (i.e. chemicals production); transportation and storage (fuel, packaging); distributive trades (waste, packaging), electricity & gas; water supply, sewage & waste management; mining & quarrying	real estate (standard services), administrative & support services (standard services), legal & expert services (specialized services)

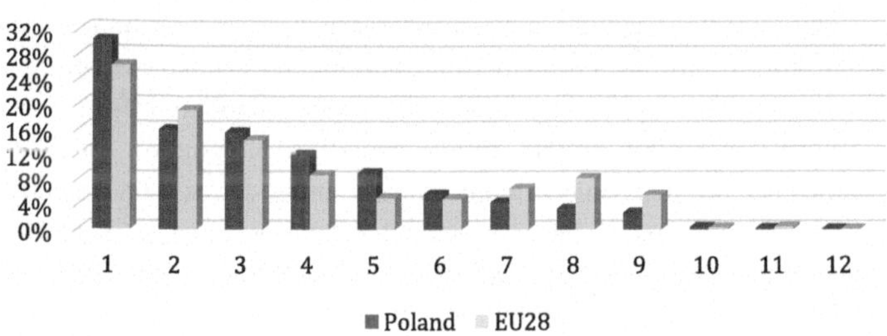

1	Distributive trades	7	Administrative & support services
2	Professional, scientific & technical activities	8	Accommodation & food services
3	Construction	9	Real estate
4	Manufacturing	10	Water supply, sewage, waste management
5	Transportation & storage	11	Electricity, gas
6	Information & communication	12	Mining & quarrying

Fig. 13 Relevance of six capitals in particular business sectors. Source: Own presentation

Firstly, we recommend SMEs to identify stakeholders, preferably in the form of a stakeholder map, considering economic, technological and political environment with its competitors and complementors [cf. with the model proposed by Cummings and Doh (2000)]. Before creating the map, it is necessary to analyse potential stakeholders that [cf. Neil (2009)]:

- directly affect the company's operations positively or negatively,
- are under the direct influence of the company's operations and have or not knowledge about this impact,
- have a direct interest in the company's operations,
- collaborate the company on joint projects,
- are a part of the broader community (local, regional, national or international) and are indirectly interested in the company's operations,
- regulate business activity of the company at an international, national, regional or local level, control or issue licences or permits to operate,
- exercise control over a particular sector or industry,
- are responsible for social and economic development, infrastructure and service provision, town or regional planning.

Afterwards, SMEs should prioritize stakeholders and categorize them into specific groups.

Secondly, we suggest SMEs select information corresponding to the identified stakeholders' needs, i.e. material information. G. Niekerk (Director of Global Citizenship Intel Corporation) said that "Materiality is like packing a backpack for a hike: you can only bring the supplies that are absolutely critical, otherwise the weight will slow you down and eventually bring you to your knees" (Murninghan, 2013). This can be seen in the LPP report in which information is addressed to the individual client (simple language, numerous graphics, more non-financial information), while Budimex addresses information to contractors (business entities), banks from which it acquires capital and investors (more financial information, fewer drawings, graphics and photographs, more specialized language). In general, also large companies use the materiality determination method based on a dialogue with stakeholders. It takes forms of face-to-face interviews with experts, expert online surveys, questionnaires directed at employees and customers, and workshops with managers, where the topics covered include strategy, customer, distribution, human resource management and compliance.

In literature, we may find an interesting proposition—five-part materiality test—that links together a spectrum deriving from classical, narrow approaches to interpreting materiality through far more inclusive, and arguably complex approaches. In this test, five drivers are under consideration while determining materiality: direct short-term financial impacts, policy-related performance, business peer-based norms, stakeholder behaviour and concerns and societal norms (Zadek & Merme, 2003). However, the above-mentioned approach seems to be too broad from the viewpoint of SMEs. Therefore, we postulate that only primary stakeholders should determine the relevance of critical issues in SME case.

Thirdly, it is essential to determine the type and scope of financial and non-financial information (in the context of establishing <IR> content elements suitable for SMEs) and how it should be presented (graphically, descriptively, in a simplified manner, in the appropriate language) concerning the identified group of stakeholders (this involves adapting the form of the report, i.e. graphics, illustrations, photographs, icons), the type of language, the type of information, the narrative, the choice of relevant concepts, etc., to the specific group of stakeholders).

Fourthly, we propose a presentation of the business model, e.g. in a simplified graphic form based on six capitals (of course, the formula should be simplified, as well as selecting the capitals that a specific SMEs manages and describing them in simple and comprehensible language), indicating the company's objective, mission, vision, expected results and future plans. The structure of this section should be clear and uniform to some extent in order to enable the implementation of the consistence and comparability principle.

Finally, we suggest that SMEs should identify the type of risk, assess it (one measure can be taken for the SME sector), its probability and propose remedies (control mechanisms).

References

Adamczyk, J. (2009). *Społeczna odpowiedzialność przedsiębiorstw (Social responsibility of enterprises)*. Warszawa: PWE.

Azoty, G. (2016–2017). *Integrated report 2016–2017*. Retrieved February 11, 2020, from http://raport.grupaazoty.com/en/

Budimex. (2018). *Integrated report 2018*. Retrieved February 11, 2020, from http://annualreport.budimex.pl/2018/

Bogdanka (2018). Integrated report 2018. Retrieved February 11, 2020, from http://ri.lw.com.pl/czytaj-aktualnosc/2742/lwbogdanka-publikuje-raport-zintegrowany-za-2018-r-/

Cummings, J. L., & Doh, J. P. (2000). Identifying who matters: Mapping key players in multiple environments. *California Management Review, 42*(2), 83–104.

Directive 2014/95/EU of the European Parliament and of the Council of 22 October 2014 amending Directive 2013/34/EU as regards disclosure of non-financial and diversity information by certain large undertakings and groups. Retrieved March 20, 2021, from https://eur-lex.europa.eu/legal-content/EN/TXT/?uri=CELEX%3A32014L0095

EC. (2019a). *Survey on the Access to Finance of Enterprises (SAFE)*. Retrieved February 3, 2020, from https://ec.europa.eu/growth/access-to-finance/data-surveys_en

EC. (2019b). *SME Performance Review*. Retrieved February 10, 2020, from https://ec.europa.eu/growth/smes/business-friendly-environment/performance-review_en

EUROSTAT. (2020a). *Structural business statistics*. Retrieved 31.01.2020 from https://ec.europa.eu/eurostat/web/structural-business-statistics/data/database

EUROSTAT. (2020b). *Real labour productivity, 2008, 2013 and 2018*. Retrieved February 2, 2020, from https://ec.europa.eu/eurostat/statistics-explained/index.php?title=File:Real_labour_productivity,_2008,_2013_and_2018_FP19.png

Grant Thornton. (2020). *Sprawozdawczość firm 2019. Badanie obowiązku sprawozdawczego przedsiębiorstw wobec instytucji publicznych w Polsce (Reporting of companies 2019. Examination of the reporting obligation on enterprises to public institutions in Poland)* (2nd ed.). Retrieved February 14, 2020, from https://grantthornton.pl/wp-content/uploads/2020/02/sprawozdawczosc-firm-2019-RAPORT-Grant-Thornton-Lewiatan-11-02-2020.pdf

IIRC. (2013). The International framework. International integrated reporting council, Retrieved January 30, 2020, from www.theiirc.org/international-irframework/

ING Bank Śląski. (2018). *Integrated report 2018*. Retrieved February 11, 2020, from https://raportroczny.ing.pl/en/

INVESTIN & The Ministry of Economic Development. (2017). *Growth perspectives for Polish ICT sector by 2025*. Retrieved February 2, 2020, https://en.parp.gov.pl/storage/publications/pdf/2017_ict_sector_by_2025_en.pdf

Janczyk, W. (2018). *Raportowanie informacji niefinansowych. Jaka jest sytuacja po roku od wejścia w życie zmian w prawie?* (Reporting of non-financial information. What is the situation one year after the changes in the law come into force?). Supplement to '*Rzeczpospolita*' and '*Parkiet*' – 'Responsible business in Poland', p. 7.

Kieżun, W. (2018). Four riders of the apocalypse of the Polish bureaucracy. *Foundations of Management, 10*, 7–12.

KGHM. (2018). *Sustainable annual report 2018*. Retrieved August 12, 2018, from https://kghm.com/en/archive/csr-reports

LOTOS Group. (2018). *Integrated report 2018*. Retrieved February 11, 2020, from https://raportroczny.lotos.pl/en/downloads

mBank. (2018). *Integrated report 2018*. Retrieved February 11, 2020, from https://www.mbank.pl/en/annual-report/2018/ogrupie-mbanku/mbank/

McKinsey & Company. (2015). *Poland 2025: Europe's new growth engine*. Retrieved February 2, 2020, from https://www.mckinsey.com/~/media/mckinsey/business%20functions/economic%20studies%20temp/our%20insights/how%20poland%20can%20become%20a%20european%20growth%20engine/poland%202025_full_report.ashx

Murninghan, M. (2013). *Redefining materiality II: Why it matters, who's involved, and what It means for corporate leaders and boards*. In T. Grant (ed.) *AccountAbility*. Retrieved February 17, 2020, from https://www.accountability.org/wp-content/uploads/2017/02/Redefining-Materiality-2.pdf

Neil, J. (2009). *Stakeholder engagement: A road map to meaningful engagement*. Doughty Centre, Cranfield School of Management.

Orange. (2018). *Integrated report 2018*. Retrieved February 11, 2020, from http://www.orange-ir.pl/results-center/annualreports (access 11.02.2020)

ORLEN Group. (2018). *Integrated report 2018*. Retrieved February 11, 2020, from https://www.orlen.pl/EN/InvestorRelations/AnnualReport/Pages/default.aspx

PARP. (2019). *Raport o stanie sektora małych i średnich przedsiębiorstw w Polsce*. Retrieved May 25, 2020, from https://www.parp.gov.pl/storage/publications/pdf/2019_07_ROSS.pdf

Pekabex. (2018). *Integrated report 2018*. Retrieved February 11, 2020, from https://pekabex.pl/pl/582-zintegrowany-raportpekabex-za-2018-rok

PGE Group. (2018). *Integrated report 2018*. Retrieved February 11, 2020, from https://raportzintegrowany2018.gkpge.pl/en/

PGNIG. (2018). *Integrated report 2018*. Retrieved February 11, 2020, from http://pgnig2018.pl/en/

Scholte, J. A. (1999). *Global Civil Society: Changing the World?*, CSGR Working paper, 31/99. Retrieved February 10, 2020, from https://www.unicef.org/socialpolicy/files/Global_Civil_Society_Changing_the_World.pdf

Scholte, J. A. (2007). Civil society and the legitimation of global governance. *Journal of Civil Society, 3*(3), 305–326.

Spółdzielnia, A. N. G. (2018). *Integrated report 2018*. Retrieved February 11, 2020, from http://www.raport2018.angkredyty.pl/

Statistics Poland. (2019). *Atlas of enterprises*, Warsaw.

TAURON Group. (2018). *Integrated report 2018*. Retrieved February 11, 2020, from https://raport.tauron.pl/en/

Zadek, S. & Merme, M. (2003). Redefining materiality. *Practice and public policy for effective corporate reporting, accountability*.

Żelazna-Blicharz, A. (2013). *Społeczna odpowiedzialność w procesie gospodarowania a zrównoważona produkcja i konsumpcja (Social responsibility in the management process and sustainable production and consumption)*. Lublin: Monografie, Politechnika Lubelska.

SMEs and IR: Evidence from Romania

Gianluca Zanellato and Adriana Tiron-Tudor

1 The SME Sector in Romania

According to the European Commission, the Romanian economic fabric is mainly composed of SMEs, with an overall number of companies of 480.791 represent 99.8% of the total number of private organizations operating in Romania. Table 1 represents in figures the number of MSMEs and large organizations.

Even though many SMEs are composing the Romanian economy, their share in total structure is lower than the European Union. The share of large organizations is higher in Romania in comparison with European countries.

Moreover, despite the overwhelming number of SMEs compared to large enterprises, it is worth noting that the impact of SMEs, in terms of number of employees and added value, is lower compared to large organizations and compared with other European countries. Table 2 outlines the differences in terms of employees' number and added value by comparing SMEs and large companies and providing statistics on a European level.

The sectors of activity involving SMEs are multiple. In this sense, Table 3 presents the number of SMEs involved in a wide variety of sectors.

G. Zanellato · A. Tiron-Tudor (✉)
Faculty of Economics and Business Administration, Babeş-Bolyai University, Cluj-Napoca, Romania

J. Dyczkowska et al. (eds.), *Development of Integrated Reporting in the SME Sector*, CSR, Sustainability, Ethics & Governance,
https://doi.org/10.1007/978-3-030-81903-3_6

Table 1 Number of enterprises in Romania and the EU

Class size	Romania	Share (%)	EU Share (%)
Micro	426.629	88.4	93.0
Small	45.731	9.5	5.9
Medium-sized	8.431	1.7	0.9
SMEs	**48.0791**	**99.7**	**99.8**
Large	1.664	0.3	0.2
Total	482.455	100.0	100.0

Source: EC (2019)

Table 2 Number of employees employed and value added: Romania and EU

	Number of persons employed			Value added		
	Romania		EU	Romania		EU
Class size	Number	Share (%)	Share (%)	Billion €	Share (%)	Share (%)
Micro	917.449	22	29	11.04	17	21
Small	912.188	22	20	11.04	17	18
Medium-sized	870.977	21	17	11.79	18	18
SMEs	**2.700.614**	**66**	**66**	**33.87**	**51**	**57**
Large	1.402.445	34	34	32.10	49	43
Total	4.103.059	100	100	65.97	100	100

Source: EC (2019)

Table 3 Number of SMEs per sector

Sectors	Romania	%	EU28	%
Mining and quarrying	1.060	0.22	19.423	0.08
Manufacturing	49.716	10.34	2.144.237	8.76
Electricity, gas	1.325	0.28	106.869	0.44
Water supply, sewerage, waste management	2.913	0.61	79.221	0.32
Construction	50.939	10.59	3.511.210	14.34
Distributive trades	181.067	37.66	6.439.747	26.30
Transportation and storage	44.776	9.31	1.253.219	5.12
Accommodation and food services	27.834	5.79	2.030.535	8.29
Information and communication	24.128	5.02	1.215.104	4.96
Real estate	12.840	2.67	1.370.485	5.60
Professional, scientific and technical activities	62.955	13.09	4.695.465	19.18
Administrative and support services	21.238	4.42	1.617.980	6.61
Manufacturing	49.716	10.34	2.144.237	8.76
Construction	50.939	10.59	3.511.210	14.34
Trade	181.067	37.66	6.439.747	26.30
Services	193.771	40.30	12.182.788	49.76

Source: EC (2019)

2 Overview of Reporting Regulations with Potential Impact on IR

Romanian regulation does not provide a mandatory framework for corporate reporting in small and medium enterprises (SMEs). Nowadays, SMEs are reporting financial information in accordance with the Ordinance of the Public Finances Ministry (OPFM) Nr. 10/2019 of 3 January 2019, which foresees the main aspects of the preparation and submission of the annual financial statements and the annual accounting reports of the economic operators at the Ministry Public Finance territorial units and for regulating some accounting issues.

The previously mentioned law regulates the methods, schedule and set of principles organizations have to comply with. Accordingly, the law presents a long list of requirements for legal entities based on their characteristics. In this vein, legal entities corresponding to the EU criteria for determining SMEs are required to comply with the following obligations:

1. Balance sheet (code 10), in the structure provided in point 598 of the accounting regulations;
2. Profit and loss account (code 20) in the structure provided in point 600 of the accounting regulations;
3. The situation of the changes in the own capital;
4. The cash flow statement;
5. Explanatory notes to the annual financial statements.

These will be accompanied by the form "Informative data" (code 30) and the form "Statement of fixed assets" (code 40), included in the structure provided in points 7, respectively, 8, of Annex No. 4.

2.4. For the unitary reporting of information, the shortened balance sheet/balance will bear the "code 10" symbol, and the profit and loss account/shortened profit and loss account, the "code 20" symbol.

2.5. In the case of newly established entities, they may prepare for the first financial year of reporting the annual financial statements provided either under section 20 or section 21 of the regulations.

2.6. (1) For the financial year of 2018, the entities prepare annual financial statements corresponding to the category in which they fall according to point 9 of the approved accounting regulations

(2) "For the preparation of the annual financial statements as of 31 December 2018, [. . .], as the case may be, is made at the end of the financial year, based on the indicators determined from the annual financial statements related to the previous financial year and of the indicators determined on the basis of the accounting data and the balance of verification completed at the end of the current financial year. Entities that have chosen a financial exercise different from the calendar year determine the respective criteria based on the indicators determined from the annual financial statements related to the previous financial year and the indicators

determined based on the accounting data and the verification balance drawn up at the end of the financial year" (Ministry of Public Finance, 2019, p. 6).

The corporate reporting landscape in Romania has moved towards a mandatory regulation of non-financial information. The change is brought by the Directive 2014/95/EU that has been transposed into national regulations through the OPFM 1802/2014 and successively modified with the OMFP 1938/2016. Despite the inclusion in national laws of the Directive 2014/95/EU, the Romanian government did not enlarge the requirements also to include organizations with less than 500.

Corporate reporting in Romania is regulated through the recent regulation on non-financial information, derived from the Directive 2014/95/EU. The directive has been adopted with few changes. By introducing the OPFM 1802/2014 and successively modified with the OPFM 1938/2016, the Romanian government slightly enlarged the organizations that comply with the regulation. In this sense, according to the Global Reporting Initiative (GRI) report entitled Member State Implementation of Directive 2014/95/EU, Romania added the following aspects: "Comply and explain the principle, Safe harbour principle, Diversity statement, Auditor's involvement: the presence of statement and consistency check of disclosures as part of the review of the management report and Fines: specified in the Accounting Law no.82/ 1991" (CSR Europe and GRI 2017). Despite the modification brought by the government, there is no mention concerning the Integrated Reporting Framework in the OPFM.

Any law does not regulate SMEs' corporate reporting practices in Romania. It leads to a shortcoming in SMEs' corporate reporting practices. The only reporting practices Romanian SMEs are adopting are those mandatory and some attempts to produce corporate social responsibility reports.

3 National Factors Enabling or Constraining IR

3.1 Political Factors

Romania does not emphasize the non-financial information relevance. Indeed, the lack of regulation may lead to a shortcoming in SMEs' corporate reporting, but in the National Sustainable Development Strategy 2013–2020–2030 document, it is expressed the willingness to move towards a more European philosophy of development. Although, in the mentioned document, none of the existing reporting frameworks, for non-financial reporting, are mentioned to direct organizations to adopt corporate reporting practices. Moreover, according to Soflan (2016), Romanian companies listed in the Bucharest Stock Exchange (BSE), which are trying to emerge as international players, are already providing some of the IR requirements without acknowledging it.

Given the Romanian economic position, IR adoption may not only affect listed companies positively, but also it could bring benefits to SMEs as well. Accordingly, the lack of a prevailing reporting framework can result in an advantage for the future development of the IR.

3.2 Economic Factors

The Romanian economy, based mainly on consumption, provided high GDP increase in the latest years. Although the previously mentioned expansion is reaching its end as, according to Standard & Poor's, the growth will decrease below 4% falling towards 3–3.5%, driven by the fiscal impulse, wage increase and external demand will decrease.

In addition to the economic issues affecting the Romanian economic development, another issue is the limited the economic growth possibilities of Romanian enterprises of all sizes. According to Roman and Voicu (2010), the labour migration, mainly composed of youngsters, represented an emerging issue and authors considered the link between migration flows with national economic growth. To this extent, Anghel et al. (2016), in a more recent study, outline that about three million Romanian citizens migrated abroad and at least 10% of the Romanian adult population participated in one or more episodes of temporary labour migration.

Thus, the lack of qualified labour prevents Romanian SMEs from reaching the development and/or the strength of other European competitors. In this sense, the application of IR by Romanian SMEs can lead to multiple benefits such as attracting foreign investors and attracting qualified labour.

3.3 Social Factors

Social interests in organizations activities are very limited in Romania. To this extent, an exemplification of social issues, which can benefit Romanian companies by adopting the IR, is mainly theoretical. Based on some social expectations emerging from a survey provided by E-ON Romania, in 2018, it is possible to derive some assumptions in relation to the possible benefits the IR may bring to Romanian SMEs. The survey finds that 1 out 4 Romanians consider the "climate change" a relevant issue. The top of the ranking of a social issue that may affect the country, according to the previously mentioned survey, is "poverty". In addition, the survey demonstrates that Romanians are ready to change their consumption behaviours and would buy more expensive products if these are made in a sustainable way. Therefore, the adoption of IR, by SMEs, may give the possibility to such organizations to demonstrate how their business model meets such expectations (see the link https://www.eon-romania.ro/ro/despre-noi/media/comunicate-de-presa/2018/181204.html).

3.4 Cultural Factors

The Romanian legal system is based on civil law, deriving from the Roman law. Thus, the system follows a series of complex written laws.

Moreover, according to the cultural dimensions developed by Hofstede, Romania represents a country with an elevated level of power distance, which outlines a general acceptance of the hierarchical order. Yet, Romania is considered a collectivistic society rather than individualistic, outlining particular importance of relationships and membership to a group. Moreover, Romania emerges to be a feminine society, which values the quality of the working life. The uncertainty avoidance dimension outlines a society that there is a need for rules, and innovation may be resisted as also Romanian society presents a low score in indulgence, exposing a tendency towards pessimism and cynicism.

3.5 Technological Factors

Recently, many information technology organizations moved to Romania, attracted by Romania's Internet infrastructure, which is highly developed, and the large pool of talented developers. To this extent, it can be noted that Romania has raised technological potential (see the link). Accordingly, many start-ups have emerged in the recent period. Consequently, Romanian SMEs could benefit from the adoption of IR to further develop their start-ups by demonstrating the potential of the technological infrastructure to a wide range of stakeholders.

4 Empirical Evidence on IR in Romania

According to the IIRC database, no Romanian company have adopted IR. To this extent, providing an example of how the principles or contents are currently disclosed might result misleading in the development of the research. However, due to the Directive 2014/95/EU several organizations have been improving their reports.

Adherence to <IR> Guiding Principles: Evidence from Romanian Companies

Strategic Focus and Future Orientation

The strategic focus and future orientation are observable in the report prepared by *OMV Petrom* (2017), which has dedicated an entire section on the company's future prospects, although notions are mainly related to expected growth in demand.

Connectivity of Information

Among the best reporters in Romania (OMV Petrom, Romgaz, Nuclearelectrica S.A.), there is no trace of connectivity. Such an issue can be reconducted to the fact that Romanian organizations are not entering the IR journey, rather are applying the traditional annual report to disclose non-financial information.

Stakeholder Relationships

The same issue emerges also in relation to the stakeholders' relationships and interdependencies. Stakeholders are not acknowledged in the reports, and it is not expressed their role in relation to the value creation of the company.

Materiality

The materiality assessment as required by the IIRC is yet to be implemented in the case of Romanian SMEs, yet the same perspective occurs in the case of listed companies, which are disclosing annual reports. The materiality assessment emerges in the case of the only organization complying with the GRI guidelines, which disclose in a comprehensive manner the materiality assessment (Ursus Sustainable Development Report, 2019, p. 12).

Conciseness

Among the listed companies, in Romania, the trend in relation to reports length demonstrates a decrease from 2016 to 2017 (Tiron-Tudor et al., 2019). The average number of pages for the largest Romanian companies is 167, which, according to KPMG (2016), is enough to present an IR. Therefore, the principle of conciseness is respected, even if the IR framework is not used.

Reliability and Completeness

As regards completeness, the reports available in the Romanian case, considering the lack of a consolidated framework, do not allow any consideration on the completeness of their reports. In Romania, some listed organizations are assuring their report providing some reliability to the issued reports, and in 2017, the following companies assured their reports: *Banca Transilvania, OMV Petrom, Societatea Energetica Electrica, Biofarm, TeraPlast, Turbomecanica, Oil Terminal, Patria Bank, Turism Hoteluri Restaurante Marea Neagra, CEMACON, Romcarbon and AAGES*. Besides, most of the assurance services are provided by one of the Big 4 organizations.

Consistency and Comparability

The reports of the listed companies over the years follow the same structure, although the structure is a part per each organization. In this vein, reports are consistent over the years but present difficulties when comparing the reports.

Observance of <IR> Content Elements: Evidence from Romanian Companies

Given the similarities of the content elements foreseen by the International Integrated Reporting Framework with other traditional reports, an inclusion of the current state of the art of Romanian corporate behaviour can be better captured.

Organizational Overview and External Environment

Romanian listed companies are describing the environment and what are the circumstances under they operate. In this vein, a good example is represented by *OMV Petrom*. In the introduction, it is mentioned about how *OMV Petrom* develops its activity and further deeps the discussion about the Romanian potentiality for exploitation. The section answers the requirements of the IIRF regarding the general information of the organization (Organizational overview and external environment) Answering in this sense to the requirements of the IIRF, although information is at a general level (OMV Petrom Annual Report, 2017; p. 7).

Business Model

For disclosing the business model of the organizations, and how this creates value, two main trends were found in the case of Romanian companies: first, through a graphical model (see the Annual Report, 2017; p. 8), following other reporters, which are adopting the IR framework; and second, a discursive prospect of how the organization creates values (see the Annual Report, 2017; p. 24).

Risks and Opportunities

Most of the Romanian companies are disclosing information about the risks the company may encounter in the course of its activity, but they merely disclose opportunities that can be generated from those risks, or opportunities that can emerge from the development of the context in which the organization operates. Accordingly, a Romanian organization producing wine includes in its section of risks some opportunities through which the organization may be able to respond to risks (Purcari Wineries Annual Report, 2019; p. 27).

Strategy and Resource Allocation

According to the IIRF requirements, for the strategy and resource allocation content, it should demonstrate how the organizations are developing its activity in order to reach their goals. In this vein, organizations are not demonstrating how these are organizing their activity in order to pursue the company mission.

Governance

Vrancart section of corporate governance discloses all the information related to the administrators of the organization (see the Board of the Administrator Report, 2017; p. 10), although it does not describe how governance is supporting the organization's ability to create value over time. In this sense, the disclosure provided by Vrancart does not fit with the IIRF requirements.

Performance

The organization's performance, concerning the strategic objective, represents a significant challenge to report, as it requires the use of the key performance indicators oriented to evaluate in terms of number how the organization is reaching the proposed objectives. To this extent, the performances of the organizations are disseminated along with the report and are not connected with other results or performances. In this sense, the reports are not connected and do not mention any of the capitals, foreseen by the IIRF.

Outlook

Among the Romanian listed companies, only one mentions some information about the future of the field and of the organization. Accordingly, *OMV Petrom* outlines in a very synthetic manner what the future of the organization will be (see the Annual Report, 2017; p. 72), although the mentioned information does not reflect the requirements of the IIRF.

Basis of Presentation

Considering the lack of a well-established framework for the development of corporate reporting in Romania, none of the organizations mentioned one of the international frameworks or guidelines for the development of the report. Although due to the introduction of the Directive 2014/95/EU some organizations are mentioning the use of the European Guidelines for what concerns the element that has to be included in the non-financial report, this is done to comply with the law rather than to communicate towards stakeholders.

5 Conclusion and Remarks

The implications for the SMEs are multiple. First, the national context seems that it is not favouring the emergence of IR use for multinational organization and for small-medium enterprises. Second, the national report outlines the Romanian economic backbone as small-medium enterprises, which can provide a significant segment for the development of the IR in SMEs' case. Second, Romanian SMEs are not disclosing any international type of report (sustainability reporting, IR). Romanian SMEs primarily disclose some corporate social responsibility report, which is not following any international guideline or framework. Under a listed companies' perspective, the IIRF is yet to be included in the reporting journey of Romanian organizations. Accordingly, examples coming from the Romanian case are not available to be included in the present report. Although some evidence appears from corporate reporting behaviour, it has been included and demonstrates that Romanian organizations are far from applying the IIRF.

Given the previous assertions, the implications for the current projects are multiple. As none of the international guidelines or framework are adopted, the main aim of the project shall find fertile soil in developing IR in SMEs, although general awareness of the meaning and benefit of the IR should be demonstrated. Moreover, IR examples, from SMEs, shall be given to Romanian SMEs in order to increase the interest surrounding such reporting phenomena.

References

Anghel, R., Botezat, A., Coşciug, A., Manafi, I. & Roman, M. (2016). *International migration, return migration, and their effects: a comprehensive review on the Romanian case*. Retrieved March 20, 2020 from https://mpra.ub.uni-muenchen.de/75528/1/MPRA_paper_75528.pdf

EC. (2019). *2019 SBA Fact Sheet Romania*. Belgium: European Commission.

KPMG. (2016), *Room for improvement-the KPMG survey of business reporting, Second Edition - an Australian perspective*, KPMG.

Ministry of Public Finance. (2019). Order No. 3781/2019 of December 23, 2019, regarding the main aspects related to the preparation and submission of the annual financial statements and annual accounting reports of economic operators at the territorial units of the Ministry of Public Finance and for the regulation of some accounting aspects. Retrieved February 9, 2021 from https://static.anaf.ro/static/10/Anaf/legislatie/OMFP_3781_2019.pdf

OMV Petrom Annual Report. (2017). Retrieved June 30, 2021 from https://www.bvb.ro/infocont/infocont18/SNP_20180427101154_2017-Annual-Report-and-payments-to-governments.pdf

Purcari Wineries Annual Report. (2019). Retrieved June 30, 2021 from https://m.bvb.ro/infocont/infocont20/WINE_20200429161406_Annual-Report-Purcari-Group-2019.pdf

Roman, M., & Voicu, C. (2010). *Some socio-economic effects of labour migration on the sending country. Evidence from Romania.* Retrieved March 20, 2020, from https://mpra.ub.uni-muenchen.de/23527/1/MPRA_paper_23527.pdf

Tiron-Tudor, A., Nistor, C. S., Ştefănescu, C. A., & Zanellato, G. (2019). Encompassing non-financial reporting in a coercive framework for enhancing social responsibility: Romanian listed companies' case. *Amfiteatru Economic, 21*(52), 590–606.

Ursus Sustainable Development Report. (2019). Retrieved June 30, 2021 from https://ursus-breweries.ro/wp-content/uploads/2020/09/Raport_EN_final.pdf

Vrancart, Report of the Board of Administrators for the Financial Year 2017. (2017). Retrieved June 30, 2021 from https://m.bvb.ro/infocont/infocont18/VNC_20180427161544_Raport-CA-2017-En-BVB-v1.pdf

SMEs and IR: Evidence from UK

Fiona Robertson, Brian Jones, and Albana Rasha

Abstract Small Medium Enterprises (SMEs) are integral to a successful, competitive, and dynamic market-based economy. The UK government encourages SMEs as they add value, create employment, help promote a more diverse business base that strengthens local economy resilience to external shocks. Integrated Reporting (IR) has been something that large businesses have engaged with, and it is something that SMEs will need to address to ensure their future success. IR, with its focus on sustainable development in the guise of meeting the needs of the economy, environment, and society, can help businesses with the recruitment and retention of employees, investors, and customers. Corporate reporting regulations are reviewed to inform an understanding of how SMEs might work with IR. One conclusion drawn is that for SMEs IR should be voluntary so as not to add to the burden on business and to encourage the principle and ideals of "Think Small First." Preceded by a discussion of macro-environmental factors, the chapter moves on to consider IR guiding principles that are used to report on evidence from large UK companies. With regards to IR, it can be said with a degree of certainty that SMEs in the UK are at the start of a journey. To encourage engagement, a simplified form of IR guidance with accompanying practice-based examples of what can be achieved is needed. Once SMEs begin to engage with IR and to appreciate the benefits it offers, then uptake can be expected to increase and the benefits of "value creation" and "Integrated Thinking" better realised.

F. Robertson (✉) · B. Jones · A. Rasha
Leeds Beckett University, Leeds, UK
e-mail: F.Robertson@leedsbeckett.ac.uk; B.T.Jones@leedsbeckett.ac.uk;
A.Rasha@leedsbeckett.ac.uk

J. Dyczkowska et al. (eds.), *Development of Integrated Reporting in the SME Sector*,
CSR, Sustainability, Ethics & Governance,
https://doi.org/10.1007/978-3-030-81903-3_7

1 The SME Sector in UK

Of the total number of UK enterprises, 99.7% (micro 90%; small 8.4; medium 1.3%) are SMEs (EC, 2019a). In the UK, "non-financial business economy" SMEs have experienced solid growth in recent years and make a significant contribution to the UK's "non-financial business economy", generating slightly more than half of total employment and value added (EC, 2018, 2019b). Therefore, many sectors in the UK, and indeed the global economy today, rely on intangible non-financial value drivers such as advanced technology, brand and customer loyalty, to a much greater extent than traditional tangible resources, and while some sectors still rely upon the more traditional tangible value drivers, competitive advantage often depends upon how intangible factors are coupled with tangible resources to differentiate organizations from their competitors (Unerman et al., 2007). This provides scope for UK SME organizations to make visible the often-invisible intangible drivers of value to their key stakeholders.

SME employment increased by 10.4% between 2014 and 2018, while SME value added rose by 3.4%, comparable with the 4% value added growth in large firms (EC, 2019b) (see Figs. 1 and 2).

SME employment is projected to increase by 2.1% between 2018 and 2020, estimated to create around 228,400 new SME jobs by 2020. SME value added is also forecast to grow by 10.9% over the same period (EC, 2019b). Future company leaders need to adapt their businesses to respond to the aspirations of millennials, who want their work to be purposeful and to make a contribution in the world if they want to attract talent to their organizations (Parker, 2017). Particularly, prior research has highlighted that IR, with its focus on integrating the three essential elements of sustainable development, the economy, the environment and society, encourages

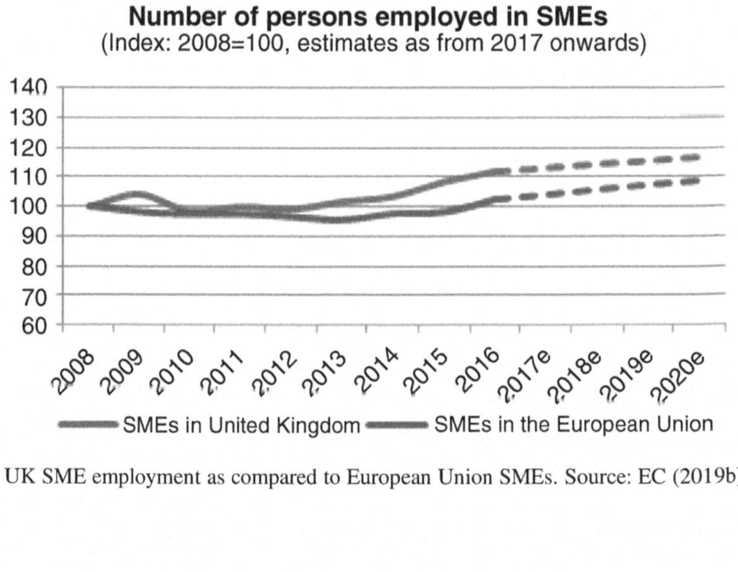

Fig. 1 UK SME employment as compared to European Union SMEs. Source: EC (2019b)

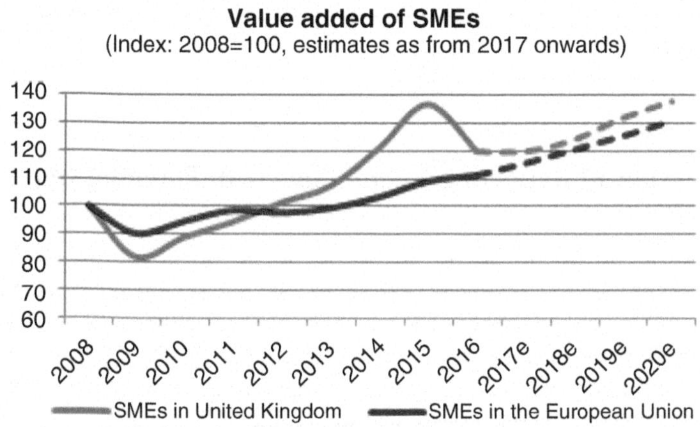

Fig. 2 UK SME value added as compared to European Union SMEs. Source: EC (2019b)

greater internal engagement, including current and prospective employees, which improves attraction and retention of skills (IIRC, 2011).

Particularly, the emergence of the knowledge-based economy highlights the need for a broader information set, which is clearly demonstrated by research on the top 500 US organizations, which finds that a small percentage of organizational market value is now explained by physical and financial assets—down to only 10% in 2015 from 83% in 1975 (Ocean Tomo, 2020). This transformation has been driven by the growth in service-based industries where knowledge-intensive resources constitute the main part of the value creation process (Beattie & Smith, 2013). Therefore, many sectors in the global economy today rely on intangible non-financial value drivers, such as innovation, brand equity, customer loyalty and key stakeholder relationships (IR Technology Initiative, 2016), to a much greater extent than traditional tangible resources.

The biggest SME sector in the UK, in terms of value added, is professional activities, accounting for one fifth of overall SME value added, which is significantly higher than the EU average of 13.8%. In terms of SME employment, wholesale and retail trade is the largest sector followed by professional activities (EC, 2019b).

According to the European Commission (2019b), particular challenges for UK SMEs relate to poor payment practices, uncertainty about regulatory changes, future access to EU markets and potential increases in input costs. Particularly, <IR> is seen by some as a way to gain credibility in international financial markets (Atkins & Maroun, 2015; Macias & Farfan-Lievano, 2017) and/or to attract the growing number of socially responsible investors (Robertson & Samy, 2015). Indeed, Atkins et al. (2015) provide evidence of changing investor expectations due to increasing integration of social and environmental considerations into the mainstream investment process, driven by climate change agendas and increasing legislation. IR can also drive organizational change towards more sustainable outcomes (Eccles & Krzus, 2010), and transform corporate processes (Phillips et al., 2011), resulting in the realization of significant cost savings from issues ranging from systems design to energy expenditure.

2 Overview of Reporting Regulations with Potential Impact on IR

This section provides an overview of the corporate reporting regulations in the UK, external environmental factors in UK which enable and constrain IR and the current reporting behaviour of large public corporations and SMEs. It then concludes by drawing implications of the UK regulatory framework, external environment and current behaviour for the integrated reporting in the SME context.

Based on the development of a worldwide database of the most recent integrated reports drawing on several recognized sources of data (including the GRI, the IIRC example database and the Corporate Register database of integrated reports), Gibassier et al. (2019) find that the majority of integrated reports (43%) are from South Africa and Japan, followed next by 6% (76 reports) from the UK. Industries with high intangibles, such as banking, are among the biggest reporters along with those with high environmental footprints, such as chemicals. Further, this research found that the number of companies with more than 5000 employees represents only 58% of the sample, with medium-sized enterprises accounting for 28% and small enterprises 14%.

As a result of supportive regulatory developments (detailed in Sect. 7.3.1), recent research has shown that many larger UK organizations were starting to address some of the fundamental issues of <IR>, albeit at a broader level (PWC, 2017; Robertson & Samy, 2015). For example, a recent UK annual report survey found that not only 60% of FTSE 100 companies explained the company's key inputs and outputs that create value within their business model, but only 25% clearly integrated this model with other core reporting areas (PWC, 2017).

For SMEs, it is the aim within the UK to simplify reporting and reduce the regulatory burden for SMEs. The "Think Small First" (TSF) principle requires policymakers to take SMEs' interests into account at the early stages of the policy-making process. It is a guiding principle for all policy- and law-making activities, which calls for newly designed legislation, administrative rules and procedures to be made simple and easy to apply for SMEs (EC, 2019b).

Most TSF recommendations have been in place in the UK since 2006. Policy measures implemented in the UK in recent years have largely sought to reduce the burden and cost of regulations on businesses. The launch of the Red Tape Initiative in 2017 by a cross party parliamentary group is the most recent example, which aims to assess how to reduce bureaucracy in nine sectors once the UK has exited the EU (EC, 2019b). However, the TSF principle was not a priority area for UK government policy action in 2018 and in the first quarter of 2019; it did not adopt or announce any significant new measures (EC, 2019b). Based on this initiative, it is expected that

IR would therefore remain voluntary for SMEs. Therefore, clear benefits of IR adoption for SMEs would need to be demonstrated.

3 National Factors Enabling or Constraining IR

3.1 Political Factors

There is a supportive regulatory environment in the UK for IR. A4S, founded in the UK by HRH Prince of Wales in 2004, was an early initiative to develop "connected reporting", which influenced the development of IR (A4S, 2012). The most recent UK regulatory development by the Financial Reporting Council (FRC), the UK independent regulator responsible for promoting high-quality corporate governance and reporting, has been the introduction of the strategic report, which aims to improve the relevance of narrative reports for stakeholders (KPMG, 2014). All companies, except small companies and micro-entities, must prepare a strategic report in accordance with s414A of the Companies Act 2006 (see the link). While the FRC's guidance to the strategic report provides companies with assistance on how to demonstrate a holistic and meaningful picture of an entity's business model, position and prospects in a clear, concise and cohesive manner, the contents of a strategic report alone do not satisfy the content elements of an integrated report (FRC, 2014; Deloitte, 2015). However, additional information required by UK Corporate Governance Code (the corporate governance statement and directors' remuneration) combined with the strategic report broadly match the reporting content elements of the <IRF> (Deloitte, 2015). Despite these similarities, focus in the strategic report remains at disclosure level. <IR> takes things further by providing a basis for linking and telling a connected story, through the process of integrated thinking (Abela, 2016; Deloitte, 2015).

3.2 Economic Factors

Latest data suggest that UK output per worker lags around 10–15% behind Germany, France and Sweden and more than 30% behind the USA. Comparative international evidence suggests that relatively low levels of UK investment and R&D spending and longer tail of companies and workers with relatively low productivity and skills are the main reasons for this productivity shortfall in the UK relative to other advanced economies (UK Economic Outlook June 2021—PwC UK). IR would allow companies to focus on how they can create value in relation to human capital.

3.3 Social Factors

In late July, environmental law firm *ClientEarth* and *YouGov* surveyed more than 2000 UK adults on attitudes across a spectrum of climate-related questions. *ClientEarth* has embroiled the UK government in various legal battles over a perceived lack of environmental stewardship, and it appears that the public agrees that policymakers should be doing more to steer the agenda. For example, 71% believe that fossil fuel companies should help pay for damage caused by extreme weather events (In numbers: the UK public's attitudes towards climate change (edie.net)) IR would allow companies to demonstrate to stakeholders the value they create in relation to environmental issues.

3.4 Cultural Factors

The IR framework is principle-based rather than being founded on a more rigid, rule-based approach. This is compatible with the UK accounting culture where the FRC encourage innovative accounting and reporting by developing principle-based standards and guidance.

3.5 Technological Factors

Technology has been the single biggest change agent in the transformation of business and the finance function. IR allows companies to identify how they can create value using technology and to tell this story to potential investors in an effective way to attract investment. Research shows that UK tech companies secured a record £5.5bn in foreign investment in the first seven months of 2019 (UK sees record foreign investment in tech start-ups—BBC News).

Technological breakthroughs in areas including machine learning, artificial intelligence, natural language coding, robotics, sensors, connectivity, cloud computing, nanotechnology, 3D printing, the Internet of Things (IoT) and biotechnologies are now heralding a Fourth Industrial Revolution, which has the potential to reshape almost every sector across the globe (DBEIS, 2019; Morgan, 2019). In the UK, there is an ambition to becoming a world leader in the Fourth Industrial Revolution by 2030 (Maier, 2017).

At a scale, speed and complexity that is unprecedented, these technological advances are creating new industries, disrupting existing ones and transforming business models leading to new opportunities and challenges for businesses, society, the economy and the environment (DBEIS, 2019; Morgan, 2019; World Economic Forum, 2017). The World Economic Forum (2017) estimates the cumulative value of digital transformation to the UK economy alone to both industry and wider

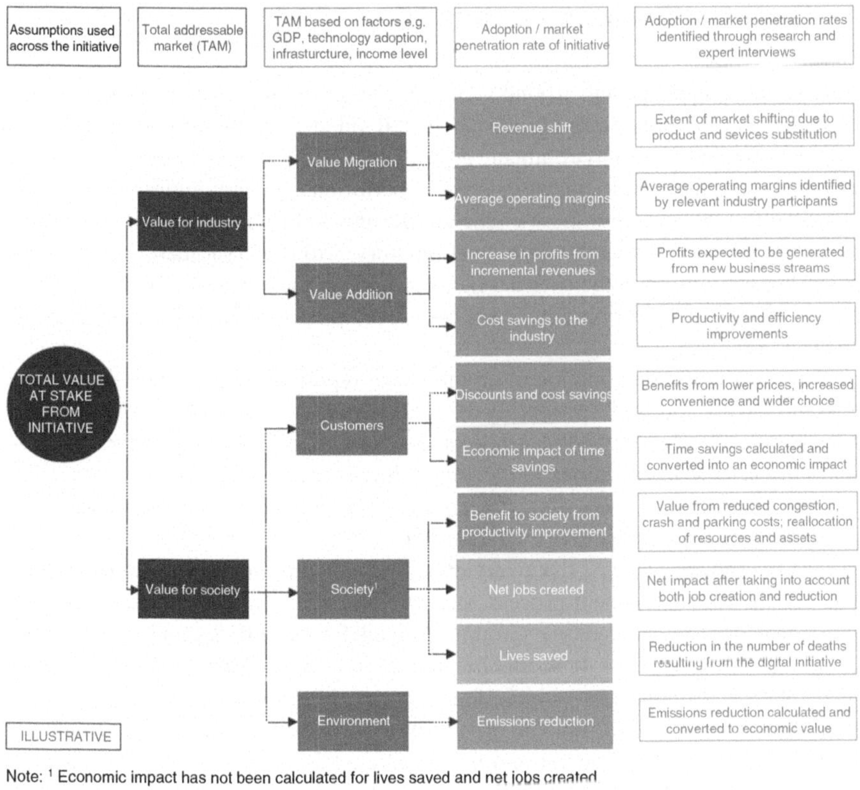

Fig. 3 Societal and business value created through new technologies. Source: World Economic Forum (2017)

society will be more than $1 trillion over the next decade. It is vital that business leaders consider the societal impact of their digital investments, in addition to the value generated for their organizations, as failure to understand their interdependencies and balance these two goals will attract media criticism and societal backlash leading to loss of reputation and market value (World Economic Forum, 2017). Benefits to both business and society identified by the World Economic Forum (2017) are highlighted in Fig. 3.

Particularly, new technologies create the potential to increase economic growth, reduce inequality and address environmental degradation (World Economic Forum, 2017). For example, digital innovations have the potential to drive progress towards realizing the UN Sustainable Development Goals and contribute to the three pillars on which they are built: improving people's quality of life; fostering equitable growth; and protecting the environment (World Economic Forum, 2017). SMEs, therefore, through the use of IR, can demonstrate how their organizations are contributing to these goals (Adams, 2017).

4 Empirical Evidence on IR in UK

An integrated report is built around seven elements, which determine its content and communicate the organization's unique shared value creation story: organizational overview and external environment; governance; opportunities and risks; strategy and resource allocation; business model; performance; and future outlook. By linking information across these elements, IR aims to provide a holistic illustration of an organization's shared value creation story "from a basic description of the business model through the external factors affecting the business, and the management's strategy for dealing with them and developing the business" (Busco et al., 2014, p. 34).

The content and presentation of an integrated report are informed by the guiding principles. This approach recognizes the wide variation in individual organizational circumstances including SMEs, while at the same time facilitating sufficient comparability across organizations to meet the relevant user needs.

Adherence to <IR> Guiding Principles: Evidence from UK Companies

Strategic Focus and Future Orientation

Lloyds Banking Group's risk overview effectively presents the fundamental links between the risk assessment process, strategic planning, mitigation and sustainable value growth (Lloyds Banking Group—Annual Report—Risks and opportunities (integratedreporting.org)). It begins by stating that the business sees the risk management as a differentiator, which demonstrates the importance of the matter. A description is provided of how the organization's governance structure accounts for the risks of the financial sector and the fundamental values that directs it. This is comprehensively illustrated in a hierarchal diagram of the organization's risk framework. The report provides an in-depth table of *Lloyds Banking Group's* principal risks, its mitigating actions, the key risk indicators by which its performance is measured, and the areas on which it will focus for the future. Helpfully, each component of the section is cross-referenced to other areas of relevance in the report.

Connectivity of Information

The 2017 *Marks and Spencer* integrated report "*presents a 'Connected Value' spread which concisely integrates a number of additional factors into the company's business model (thereby complying with paragraph 3.6 of the International <IR> Framework—stating that Integrated Reports should show a 'holistic picture' of the factors that influence a company's value creation ability)*" (Marks & Spencer—Integrated Report—Business model (integratedreporting.org)).

The Marks and Spencer operating model (00_CoverXfile_v48.indd (marksandspencer.com), p. 10) serves to demonstrate the degree of information connectivity within the report and the business. In a section of the report titled "*Connected Value*", they bring together "*Inputs*", "*Core Objectives*" and "*Business Model*". The core objectives are connected to the company's key performance indicators and thereby illustrate another degree of connectedness. The report demonstrates that *Marks and Spencer* take their commitment to the connectivity of information within IR seriously.

Stakeholder Relationships

In their 2017 report, *British Land* identifies 7 stakeholders (investment partners, investors, suppliers, occupiers, local communities, consumers and employees) that have varied roles to play in helping the business deliver on their IR agenda. The integrated report recognizes that stakeholders help the company to create value that is both long term and sustainable. The report identifies aspects of each of the 7 stakeholder relations that contribute to improving sustainability and to business success (British Land AR 2017, p. 15). Local communities include "*places which support local jobs and skills*". Four themed headings run through, inform and help structure the report, and they are (1) customer orientation; (2) right places; (3) capital efficiency; and (4) expert people. In addition to this, governance and remuneration, report of the auditor and sustainability performance measures feature in the report. Stakeholder relationships are fed into different parts of *British Land's* IR and are shown to help them deliver successful business and sustainability outcomes.

Materiality

The 2017 Integrated Annual Report for the *Duchy of Cornwall* looks at material risks to *Duchy's* estate. It also discusses the resources and relationships—in other words, the capitals—that are affected by the integration of information on strategy. The IR identifies 5 material risks, and these are (1) capital cash generation; (2) the state of farming; (3) safe buildings and places; (4) balancing access and protection; and (5) public understanding and perception. The report describes each of the 5 risks, identifies ways in which they might be mitigated and then moves on to consider their effects in terms of the strategic objective, as well as the resources and relationships affected. *Duchy's* material risks are plotted on a chart with two axis being likelihood and impact (duchy-iar-2017.pdf (duchyofcornwall.org), p. 18). *Duchy's* IR states, "*The sustainable, commercial management of our land and property was the primary issue in our stakeholder materiality review. At a minimum, we must ensure that our natural capital is not being depleted*". (2017, p. 20). Acknowledging this as a key priority for the environment is important for the future of the Duchy and in terms of all issues associated with materiality.

Conciseness

The ING Annual Report for 2015 (duchy-iar-2017.pdf (duchyofcornwall.org)) is visually appealing and presented in an accessible yet informative style. There is a high level of detail in this report, and it has a logical structure and a good flow of text and this contributes to its measure of conciseness. Graphs, tables and infographics are integrated well and explained clearly, and this aids reading of the report and the extraction of relevant information in straightforward way. The actual *ING* Report recognizes the importance of the concept "*conciseness*" when it states (ING, 2015, p. 60), "*The data and content in the integrated report and Non-finance Annex aim to provide a concise, accurate and balanced account of ING's economic, social and environmental performance in 2015*". Their commitment to conciseness extends to their online presence (ING, 2015, p. 60): "*we also publish a concise and accessible online overview of our results in 2015 in our Annual Review on ING.com*". The importance of concise communication is mentioned in the Report's Glossary of Terms under IR. It is clear that ING takes the issue of conciseness seriously, and this is evident from the way in which the annual report is written.

Reliability and Completeness

The 2018 *Crown Estates* integrated report emphasizes the positives by looking at the highlights of the business but does not shy away from the negative aspects when discussing for example the risk strategy architecture. The balance between the negatives and positives is best captured in the words of the report (Crown Estates, 2018, p. 45) "*In summary that risk appetite is: to take measured risk to drive outperformance, where we have confidence in our delivery by virtue of our critical mass and expertise in our core markets*".

This report can be said to be reliable and complete in so far as it gives a balanced view and the importance of doing so is acknowledged in the following statement from the report (Crown Estates, 2018, p. 7): "*Public trust in business has been challenged once again this year, with a number of high profile companies facing scrutiny over their corporate responsibility and contribution to society. Our purpose and values-led approach continue to guide us in how we do business. By ensuring that integrity remains the foundation of our business, we protect our reputation and trusted relationships. It also helps us to create and maintain our strategic partnerships with like-minded investors*". It is in the *Crown Estates* own interest to present a balanced, rounded view that is accurate and fair. Inaccurate and misleading statements are not in the *Crown Estates* public or business interest. The Crown Estates integrated report is a reliable and complete as it can be in its reporting of the various capitals. Their business model identifies what the *Crown Estate* does (investment management, development management, asset management and property management); what they rely on (financial resources, physical resources, natural resources, our people, our know-how, our networks); and the value this creates (The Crown Estate Integrated Annual Report and Accounts 2017/18, pp. 10–11). The business model is robust and reliable and serves to illustrate the reliability and completeness of the integrated report in terms of its representation of fairly and finely balanced facts, figures and statements.

Consistency and Comparability

The 2017 Annual Report for *BAE Systems (*BAE Systems, 2017*)* shows evidence of consistency and comparability of issues and matters being reported. Consistency is explicitly addressed at various points throughout the report. On page 63, it states, "*In order to ensure consistency, all businesses are required to comply with our Health and Safety Policy, which outlines and prescribes the responsibilities and arrangements in place for ensuring safety*". Outlining the group's financial statements and the need to make sure they can be understood are clear and being fair and balanced page 84 of the report notes, "*- comprehensive reviews undertaken at different levels in the Group that aim to ensure consistency and overall balance*". Their commitment to consistency and comparability is also evident in their methodology assessment and page 136 of the report states, "*We used our own actuarial specialists to assess the appropriateness and consistency of the methodology applied by management in setting the key assumptions. We challenged the reasons for any* *changes in methodology and considered the presence of indicators for bias*". Finally, to allow for comparability it is stated on page 150 of the report that "*Finance costs and taxation expense of equity accounted investments are excluded for consistency with pre-interest, pre-tax business performance*". The need for a consistent approach to report writing allows for a degree of comparability over time. The Group Strategic Framework shapes and informs a consistent and comparable approach to business and to the writing of the integrated report (LSE_BA_2017.pdf (annualreports.co.uk), p. 18).

Observance of <IR> Content Elements: Evidence from Romanian Companies

Organizational Overview and External Environment

An example of IR good practice is *Mondi's Plc.* Integrated Report and Financial Statements (2018) that bring together the enterprise by showing a general overview of the organization and of the market context in which it operates (mondi_ir_2018_final.pdf (mondigroup.com), p. 3). The report includes appropriate information for internal and external environment highlighting the performance. The integrated report signifies an evolution in their reporting. Using a logical structure which lends itself to being highly accessible, this is a concise report that articulates a strategic story in an effective way.

A review of Mondi's history, mission, vision, culture shows that it delivers sustainable growth and values and that it is founded on integrity, performance and caring for the world and each other. This is supplemented by the following pages, which use the informative titles of "*what we do*", "*where we operate*" and "*how we're managed*" to provide an insight into the scope of operations, the scale of the business and how the business is led.

In the opening pages, a glance of the performance is highlighted. This is followed by a clear content page (p. 3), which is supplemented with a site map, which clearly demonstrates where information can be found online, providing the reader with multi-channel options for their reporting journey. Included is the reporting scope performance measurement financially and non-financially in relation to material financial, economic, social environmental and governance issues. The ensuing pages titled "*about this report*" outlines the scope of the report and how the IR processes supports "*integrated thinking*" in *Mondi*, which in turn provides the basis for the integrated report. Interestingly, the narrative discusses the external acknowledgement which the report has received and how the feedback has been used to develop the report further this year. There is also a transparent discussion of assurance, acknowledging the journey which the business is taking towards full assurance. This sets the scene for the report, while the opposite page provides a summary of performance in numbers, covering financial, economic, social—employees, social—communities and environment.

The overview section provides the reader with a very informative insight into the business and how it operates. The first spread outlines the five material issues "*which stakeholders want to know about*" providing a succinct overview of what the key areas of focus the report will have this year. The following spread then provides a summary of the "value we've created" to demonstrate how *Mondi* is "keeping customers happy" which covers investment in *Mondi*, their people, the countries in which they operate and the providers of capital. The opposite page identifies the five strategic priorities—which *Mondi* then uses to structure the bulk of the report around—clearly signposting the reader to where more detail can be found on customers, growth, operations, people and reputation.

Management is then featured—chairman, CEO and CFO—and through their personal narratives, they tell the company's story, and in particular provide the context for the year's performance. The CEO delves into the future strategic direction of the business, which is particularly insightful.

The following spread reviews what is happening in the industry focusing on both key regulatory changes and customer trends, which provide the reader with the context for *Mondi's* strategy and performance. *Mondi* takes this one step further and provides a five-year outlook, which helps readers gauge the long-term environment of the business.

Other example, as outlined by 4.6 of the <IR> framework, *British Land's* market discussion begins by highlighting five "key long-term trends", which will impact their business (British Land—Integrated Report—Organizational overview and external environment (integratedreporting.org)). Each trend is concisely discussed, with the narrative indicating how the trends have impacted, or will impact, the industry. The market discussion then demonstrates strategic focus and future orientation (3A of the <IR> framework), by highlighting five ways in which the company is responding to these trends. The narrative discussions here regularly reference *British Land's* strategy, thereby demonstrating connectivity (3.6–3.9 of the <IR> framework), and are supplemented by two signposts to the strategy discussion and *British Land's* sustainability section on their website.

Business Model

At the heart of an organization is its chosen business model. Current business model reporting is inconsistent, both in terms of uptake and in terms of scope particularly for the SMEs. Uptake for listed companies appears to be influenced by the presence of regional legislation UK Companies Act, corporate governance codes (principle-based) and listing requirements. Scoping inconsistencies are linked to mixed interpretations of what, exactly, constitutes a business model. *Coca-Cola* Integrated Annual Reports (2018) have a clear distinction made between business model disclosures and other information such as external factors or context, capitals, governance, strategy and resource allocation, opportunities and risks, performance and future outlook. These elements are highly interconnected as shown in *Coca-Cola* Integrated Annual Reports (2018) and clearly interrelated to the business model the chosen system of inputs, business activities, outputs and outcomes that aims to create value over the short, medium and long term (LSE_CCH_2018.pdf (annualreports.com), pp. 14–15).

Consideration of inputs, outputs and outcomes has helped to clarify the organization's positive and negative impacts on six capitals. Such considerations have also encouraged the organization to take a broader view of the concept of value creation. A distinction is made between outputs and outcomes related the key products or services that an organization produces, as well as the waste or other by-products that create or erode value. Outcomes are the internal and external consequences for the capitals as a result of an organization's business activities and outputs. *Coca-Cola* Integrated Annual Report (2018) key outcomes are assessed against actual performance and strategic objectives have prompted changes to the business model to create sustainable shared value.

Risks and Opportunities

An integrated report should answer the question: "*What are the specific risks and opportunities that affect the organization's ability to create value over the short-, medium- and long term and how is the organization dealing with them*" (IIRC, 2015, p. 27). In *Mondi's Plc.* Integrated Report (2018), the disclosure of risks and opportunities influencing value creation is elevated as a specific content element. Included are the specific risks and opportunities that affect the *Mondi's* ability to create value and affect the availability, quality and affordability of relevant capitals. Specific external and internal sources of risk and *Mondi's* assessment of the likelihood that the risk or opportunity will come to fruition and the magnitude of its effect if it does are also highlighted. This is followed by steps being taken to mitigate and manage key risks that are real risks and fundamental to the ongoing ability of the *Mondi* to create value and that could have extreme consequences. The requirements of the content element are regarded as valuable proxy for disclosure guidelines.

Meanwhile, *Coca-Cola* and the *United Utilities* have linked risks and opportunities within the identification of strategic purposes, strategies, politics, targets, related KPIs and bonuses. This provides a complete vision of how internal (strengths and weaknesses) and external (opportunities and threats) factors affect the business activity, resulting in a periodically overhaul of the performance analysis to identify, prevent or limit the impact of its risk factors. In addition, management and functions responsible constantly monitor risk factors in the main exposed units and targets.

Strategy and Resource Allocation

British Land Sustainability Report (2019) clearly indicates where the organization wants to go and how it intends to get there through aligning corporate strategy to build a sustainable strategy around four focus areas, which address major social, economic and environmental trends to create value for their stakeholders and the business (Sustainability-Accounts-2019.pdf (britishland.com), p. 7). The report sets out clearly the organization's short-, medium- and long-term strategic objectives with explanation of the strategies implemented to achieve its strategic objectives. It sets out the resource allocation plans that the organization has in place to support the implementation of its strategy and ensure its financial sustainability in the short, medium and long term with the measurement of its performance to achieve its strategic objectives in the short, medium and long term. Further, the report explains how they differentiate itself in the sector and how this is reflected in its strategy, structure and activities.

Governance

Unilever Annual Report (2018) governance has a strategic focus and future orientation. Connectivity of information includes a "committed to good governance" discussion, which highlights how specific actions taken by the board have impacted the strategic direction of the company in the short, medium and long term. The report provides information in respect of the leadership structure, including the skills and diversity of those charged with governance, explaining the roles of the different elements of the governance leadership structure and how they interact with each other. It explains the differences in roles and responsibilities between executive and non-executive members of the leadership team and how strategic decisions are made across the institution and sets out specific actions that those charged with governance have taken to influence and monitor the strategic direction of the company and its approach to the management of risk. It highlights how those charged with governance, and other members of the leadership team, are remunerated and how the nature and level of their remuneration are determined. This aligns with 4.9 of the IR framework, which calls for insights into how governance activities are linked to the company's ability to create sustainable value. In line with the Unilever sustainable living plan, "*key deliberations*" are then highlighted, with page references linking readers to earlier sections of the report. This shows connectivity between content elements. Succinct explanations give greater insight of each of the deliberations which provide context to "Our response and action" discussions, which themselves cover how the board have acted, or plan to act, in regard to each issue. This section therefore shows alignment with the IR framework strategic focus and future sustainable orientation and indicates strong links between Unilever's governance and sustainable value creation activities.

Performance

Marks and Spencer Annual Report (2019) clearly states the challenges and uncertainties encountered in pursuing its strategy, and what the potential implications are for its business model and future performance. The report sets out the company expectations about the external environment in the short, medium and long term and its ability to achieve company strategic objectives. It also explains how the external environment has impacted on the financial, intellectual, human and natural resources upon which the company depends and provides an assessment of the company's ability to respond effectively to changes in the external environment, which is based on a realistic appraisal of the competitive landscape and of the company's strengths, weaknesses and market positioning.

Marks and Spencer Annual Report (2019) clearly states achieved strategic objectives for the period and its outcomes in terms of effects on resources. It provides a balanced and complete view of the company's performance with information in respect of strategic, financial, people and environmental issues. It also explains the impact of the M&S activities and performance on the financial, intellectual, human and natural resources upon which the institution depends and provides information on the state of relationships with key stakeholders and how the M&S has responded to these stakeholders' legitimate needs and interests. Further, the report discusses the linkages between past and current performance and between current performance and the institution's outlook.

Outlook

British Land Sustainability Report (2019) strategic focus and future orientation are concise and provide an insight into the five-year priorities through to 2019/20. Company has also highlighted the priorities, which will be the focus areas for the coming year in the journey to achieving the overall vision of the business. The upcoming priorities are discussed in more detail, focusing on the future activities, which will be undertaken. It also sets out the challenges and uncertainties in pursuing its strategy and implications of its business model and future performance. It sets out the institution's expectations about the external environment that it is likely to face in the short, medium and long term and explains how the external environment will impact on the institution's ability to achieve its strategic objectives. Their report further explains how the external environment will impact on the financial, intellectual, human and natural resources upon which the company depends and provides an assessment of the company's ability to respond effectively to changes in the external environment, based on a realistic appraisal of the competitive landscape and of the strengths, weaknesses and market positioning.

Basis of Presentation

The ACCA Integrated Report (2019) states clearly what matters to their business model with the connectivity of information and stakeholder relationships quantified and evaluated materiality. *ACCA's* discussion of stakeholder engagement and materiality serves a dual purpose of describing the organization's materiality determination process and evaluating stakeholder feedback in its overall IR process. *ACCA* identifies its key stakeholder groups and provides a brief overview of each group and its relevance to the ongoing viability of the organization. The evaluation of material issues on page 37 uses an innovative spiral graph to highlight the relative importance of each issue to internal stakeholders and external stakeholders. The feedback from this assessment was used to shape the report in terms of content and presentation. *ACCA* also includes feedback from stakeholders regarding the organization's ability to incorporate the guiding principles in the <IR> framework. While the feedback from stakeholders was very positive overall, several suggestions for improvement and related action items are included to underscore the organization's pursuit to improve reporting and address its stakeholders' needs.

5 Conclusion and Remarks

The scarcity in UK SME <IR> is in line with Del Baldo (2017) who highlights that SMEs have only just started to approach IR and that this could be due to the absence of SME guidelines, which consider their unique specificities which are "*mainly related to the different governance (often family-based) and organisational structures, the strategic approach (the logic of the strategic management process is usually incremental-based and process-driven and does not follow an object-driven logic, nor is it formalised) and the limited provision of managerial and financial resources, which mirrors a weak culture of management control and reporting*" (Del Baldo, 2017, p. 511).

Based on our analysis of UK PLCs, IR adoption has not resulted in transformational change, but rather incremental changes to processes and structures over time. These PLCs have adopted a gradual process, by developing <IR> over the course of several years. During this time, these PLCs have been able to operationalize the IR principles, although difficulties were encountered with the IR concepts of materiality, completeness, and connectivity and their ability to adapt the IIRC framework to its specific context and reporting. Indeed, research indicates that difficulties encountered by <IR> adopters include the complexity of <IR> processes (Lodhia, 2015); competing standards (Robertson & Samy, 2015); balancing the interests of multiple stakeholders (Lodhia, 2015; Parrot & Tierney, 2012); and lack of clear guidance on measurement systems and metrics for integrated thinking and reporting (Dumay et al., 2017: Feng et al., 2017; Guthrie et al., 2017; Robertson & Samy, 2015).

For SMEs, we suggest that a simplified and operative guidance for producing an integrated report within SMEs is required together with provision of practical examples and suggestions to reflect the unique nature of SMEs. Indeed, it is the intention of the IR framework to "*strike an appropriate balance between flexibility and prescription which recognizes the wide variation in individual circumstances of different organisations while enabling a sufficient degree of comparability across organisations to meet relevant information needs*" (IIRC, 2013a, b, p.4).

Current UK IR adoption in SMEs is scant with the majority of IR adoption being undertaken by PLCs. There is therefore a need to encourage IR for SMEs in the UK. We argue that IR for SMEs should be voluntary in the UK, due to the regulatory environment that seeks to reduce administrative burden on SMEs. We therefore suggest that clear benefits of IR for SMEs need to be clearly articulated and training for SMEs provided, given the complexity of some of its key concepts and paradigm shift in thinking that IR presents.

Particularly, there is a need for more performative and interventionist research where academics work together with organizations in understanding and applying key IR concepts such as "integrated thinking" and "value creation" in a practical way, which can contribute to both theoretical and SME practice perspectives.

References

A4S. (2012). *The value of extra financial disclosure*. Retrieved February 17, 2021, from https://www.accountingforsustainability.org/en/knowledge-hub/reports/value-financial-disclosure.html

Abela, M. (2016). *Integrated reporting in the UK*. Retrieved February 17, 2021, from http://gather.london/wp-content/uploads/2016/03/8.1.7_White-Paper-Integrated-Reporting_v3.pdf

Adams, C. (2017). Conceptualizing the contemporary corporate value creation process. *Accounting, Auditing and Accountability Journal, 30*(4), 906–931.

Atkins, J., Atkins, B. C., Thomson, I., & Maroun, W. (2015). "Good" news from nowhere: Imagining utopian sustainable accounting. *Accounting, Auditing and Accountability Journal, 28*(5), 651–670.

Atkins, J., & Maroun, W. (2015). Integrated reporting in South Africa in 2012: Perspectives from South African institutional investors. *Meditari Accountancy Research, 23*(2), 197–221.

Beattie, V., & Smith, S. J. (2013). Value creation and business models: Refocusing the intellectual capital debate. *The British Accounting Review, 45*(4), 243–254.

Busco, C., Frigo, M., Quattrone, P., & Riccaboni, A. (2014). Leading practices in integrated reporting. *Strategic Finance, 96*(9), 23–32.

Del Baldo, M. (2017). The implementation of integrating reporting <IR> in SMEs: Insights from a pioneering experience in Italy. *Meditari Accountancy Research, 25*(4), 505–532.

Deloitte. (2015). *<IR>: how does it fit into the UK corporate reporting landscape?*. Retrieved February 17, 2021, from https://www.iasplus.com/en/publications/uk/other/ir-uk-landscape

Department for Business, Energy & Industrial Strategy (DBEIS). (2019). *Regulation for the Fourth Industrial Revolution.* Retrieved February 17, 2021, from https://www.gov.uk/government/publications/regulation-for-the-fourth-industrial-revolution/regulation-for-the-fourth-industrial-revolution

Dumay, J., Bernardi, C., Guthrie, J., & La Torre, M. (2017). Barriers to implementing the international integrated reporting framework: A contemporary academic perspective. *Meditari Accountancy Research, 25*(4), 461–480.

Eccles, R., & Krzus, M. P. (2010). One report. *AFP Exchange, 30*(6), 49–51.

EC. (2018). *2018 SBA Fact Sheet United Kingdom*. Belgium: European Commission.

EC. (2019a). *2018 SBA Fact Sheet Germany*. Belgium: European Commission.

EC. (2019b). *2019 SBA Fact Sheet United Kingdom*. Belgium: European Commission.

Feng, T., Cummings, L., & Tweedie, D. (2017). Exploring integrated thinking in integrated reporting – An exploratory study in Australia. *Journal of Intellectual Capital, 18*(2), 330–353.

FRC. (2014). *Guidance on the strategic report*. London: FRC.

Gibassier, D., Adams, C. & Jerome, T. (2019). *Integrated Reporting and the Capitals' Diffusion*. Retrieved February 17, 2021, from http://www.anc.gouv.fr/files/live/sites/anc/files/contributed/ANC/3.%20Recherche/B_Appels%20à%20projets/2017/First_report_ANC_final_version_GIBASSIER_ADAMS_JEROME_2019-07-24.pdf

Guthrie, J., Manes-Rossi, F., & Orelli, R. L. (2017). Integrated reporting and integrated thinking in Italian public sector organizations. *Meditari Accountancy Research, 25*(4), 553–573.

IIRC. (2011). *Towards integrated reporting. Communicating value in the 21st century*. Retrieved November 3, 2013, from http://theiirc.org/wp-content/uploads/2011/09/IR-Discussion-Paper-2011_spreads.pdf

IIRC. (2013a). *The international <IR> framework*. International Integrated Reporting Council, Retrieved January 30, 2020, from www.theiirc.org/international-ir-framework/

IIRC. (2013b). *Business model background paper for <IR>*. International Integrated Reporting Council. Retrieved April 24, 2021 from https://www.ifac.org/system/files/publications/files/Business-Model-IIRC.pdf

IIRC. (2015). The International Framework. http://integratedreporting.org/wp-content/uploads/2015/03/13-12-08-THE-INTERNATIONAL-IR-FRAMEWORK-2-1.pdf

IR Technology Initiative. (2016). *Technology for integrated reporting: A CFO guide for driving multi capital thinking*. Retrieved February 17, 2021, from http://integratedreporting.org/wp-content/uploads/2016/10/Technology-for-Integrated-Reporting_CFOguide.pdf

KPMG. (2014). *A practical guide to the strategic report*. London: KPMG.

Lodhia, S. (2015). Exploring the transition to integrated reporting through a practice lens: An Australian customer owned bank perspective. *Journal of Business Ethics, 129*(3), 585–598.

Ocean Tomo, L. L. C. (2020). *Ocean Tomo's annual study of intangible asset market value – 2020*. Chicago: Ocean Tomo.

Macias, H. A., & Farfan-Lievano, A. (2017). Integrated reporting as a strategy for firm growth: Multiple case study in Colombia. *Meditari Accountancy Research, 25*(4), 605–628.

Maier, J. (2017). *Made smarter review 2017.* Department for Business, Energy and Industrial Strategy. London: HM Government.

Morgan, J. (2019). *Will we work in twenty-first century capitalism? A critique of the fourth industrial revolution literature*. Economy and Society.

Parker, L. (2017). *Future of the corporation: The voice of business*. Retrieved February 17, 2021, from https://www.thebritishacademy.ac.uk/publications/future-corporation-voice-business

Parrot, K. W., & Tierney, B. X. (2012). Integrated reporting, stakeholder engagement, and balanced investing at American electric power. *Journal of Applied Corporate Finance, 4*(2), 27–37.

Phillips, D., Watson, L., & Willis, M. (2011). Benefits of comprehensive integrated reporting. *Financial Executive, 27*(2), 26–30.

PWC. (2017). *Accountability in changing times. Analysis of FTSE 350 corporate reporting trends in 2017*. Retrieved February 17, 2021, from https://www.pwc.co.uk/audit-assurance/assets/pdf/ftse-350-reporting-opportunities.pdf

Robertson, F., & Samy, M. (2015). Factors affecting the diffusion of integrated reporting – A UK FTSE 100 perspective. *Sustainability Accounting, Management and Policy Journal, 6*(2), 190–223.

Unerman, J., Guthrie, J., & Striukova, L. (2007). *UK reporting of intellectual capital*. London: ICAEW.

World Economic Forum. (2017). *Unlocking digital value to society: A new framework for growth*. Retrieved February 17, 2021, from https://www.accenture.com/_acnmedia/Accenture/Conversion-Assets/WEF/PDF/Accenture-Unlocking-Digital-Value-To-Society.pdf#zoom=50

Integrated Reports

BAE Systems. (2017). *Annual report 2017*. Retrieved February 11, 2020, from https://investors.baesystems.com/~/media/Files/B/Bae-Systems-Investor-Relations-V3/PDFs/results-and-reports/results/2017/annual-report-2017.pdf

Crown Estates. (2018). *Integrated report 2018*. Retrieved February 11, 2020, from https://assets.publishing.service.gov.uk/government/uploads/system/uploads/attachment_data/file/719587/The_Crown_Estate_Integrated_Annual_Report_2018.pdf

Duchy of Cornwall. (2017). *Integrated annual report 2017*. Retrieved February 11, 2020, from https://duchyofcornwall.org/assets/images/duchy-iar-2017.pdf

ING. (2015). *Annual report 2015*. Retrieved February 11, 2020, from https://www.ing.com/Investor-relations/Financial-performance/Annual-reports/2015.htm

Conclusions

The following book provides valuable insight into non-financial reporting practices of SMEs operating in West European countries and CEECS characterized by various regulatory frameworks and differentiated IR implementation progress.

This study indicates a general acceptance of the EU definition of SMEs; however, some occasional national divergence appears in terms of standards used by bodies within specific countries. One example of this is that in Germany, sole proprietors and business partnerships that are not subject to German Commercial Code disclosure rules but match different size criteria (exceeding the EU definition of medium entities) must disclose additional information [§1 Public Disclosure Act (PDA)]. For instance, the Polish Accounting Act distinguishes micro-, small and other entities based on its own criteria to determine their reporting obligations. The Italian legislator has established only three size classes, merging medium enterprises with large ones. It means that, from 2016 onwards, the Italian legal system foresees micro- and small enterprises that can draft financial statements in a simplified format and medium-to-large enterprises, which must provide cash flow statements on a compulsory basis, whereas Directive 2013/34/EU of the European Parliament and the Council of 26 June 2013, which has provided significant amendments to the Italian Legislative Decree No. 139/2015, distinguishes between four separate size classes: micro-, small, medium and large enterprises.

In each analysed country, SMEs formed the backbone of the economy. They constituted more than 99% of all businesses, employed more than 50% of all employees (the most 78.1% in Italy and the least 53.8% in the UK, whereas the EU average was 66.6%) and generated more than 47% of all total value added to the national economy (the most 66.9% in Italy and the least 47.7% in the UK, whereas the EU average was 56.4%) (EC 2019a, b, c, d, e, f).

Each country under examination has specific legislation pertaining to financial reporting requirements that are tailored and specific. For instance, the German Commercial Code requires all businesses to prepare a financial statement consisting

J. Dyczkowska et al. (eds.), *Development of Integrated Reporting in the SME Sector*, CSR, Sustainability, Ethics & Governance,
https://doi.org/10.1007/978-3-030-81903-3

of a balance sheet and a profit and loss statement. By contrast, in Hungary, accounting and bookkeeping are regulated by Act C of 2000 on Accounting and some additional explanatory legal rules issued by the Ministry of Finance. Act C of 2000 shall apply to all economic entities; however, there are some exceptions. It shall not apply to private entrepreneurs (sole proprietors), civil law associations, building groups, the Hungarian commercial representation offices of foreign-registered companies. It makes a point of difference between Germany requiring all businesses to prepare financial statement and Hungary allowing some exceptions.

Sustainability and corporate social responsibility (CSR) are pillars that fall under voluntary corporate reporting regulations. The common aim is to encourage businesses to engage with the sustainability and CSR agenda to give them ownership over what they can do. By definition, this area's reporting is voluntary but is shaped and influenced by country-specific regulatory requirements.

IR should be used to inform the future. Looking forward can help businesses integrate value creation in all its guises to create a more sustainable future for all. It requires, however, political leadership and policy intervention. Political impacts in the different countries vary between supportive, restrictive and permissive. For instance, Hungary's regulatory environment is neither supportive nor restrictive but is best described as permissive concerning IR. Furthermore, a need for a rule-based framework is called (e.g. in Romania), but at the same time, the concern arises that rules should not be too bureaucratic (e.g. in Germany).

There was no evidence of voluntary IR in SMEs concerning all countries under examination, except for Italy. Italy had evidence of IR for SME's, albeit at a minimal level (six organizations). It may be attributed to the practice of Italian SME's having published sustainability reports for many years, and therefore, they have developed capabilities to flexible transition towards IR.

Minimal evidence for sustainability reporting was found in the other countries under examination. In respect of Germany, Hungary and Romania, this was attributed to the compliance-based culture, suggesting that IR adoption for SME may be difficult unless made mandatory. In the UK, where there is a principle-based culture, resistance to sustainability reporting was attributed to cost issues and unfavourable government policies. Development of IR business cases and providing training to overcome stumbling blocks could aid IR adoption in SMEs. In all instances, learning from the IR cases existing in Italy could also facilitate the implementation of the IR concept.

This book includes several recommendations for SMEs regarding IR. It emphasizes the importance of clearly presenting a convincing business base for IR and highlights the possibility of positioning IR as a legal and even ethical or moral imperative essential for longer-term sustainability and better future performance. IR may be an excellent start for SMEs to present a new product or service and business model to explain to potential stakeholders how a company creates value. Further, IR may be perceived as a marketing tool that allows SMEs to reposition their business offer, identify and appeal to new market segments and providers of capital, build relationships with key stakeholders and deliver a more efficient and effective way of doing business. IR in SMEs should take a simplified form in comparison with the requirements for large companies. It is essential to determine the type and scope of financial and non-financial information in the context of establishing <IR> content elements suitable for SMEs and how it should be presented (graphically, descriptively, in a simplified manner, in the appropriate language). This process will involve adapting the report form, i.e. graphics, illustrations, photographs and icons, considering the stakeholders' information needs.

Likewise, as with large companies, SMEs may benefit from IR triggering a more profound managerial process of integrated thinking (Higgins et al., 2019). IR opens an opportunity to understand better the value creation process, identify emerging risks and opportunities and start more collaborative thinking about goals and targets. Greater focus on measuring the business's long-term success that IR offers may contribute to effective decision-making. By presenting a transparent picture of the total value generated for society, IR may enhance SME's reputation (CIMA, 2015).

References

EC. (2019a). *2018 SBA Fact Sheet Germany*. Belgium: European Commission.
EC. (2019b). *2019 SBA Fact Sheet Hungary*. Belgium: European Commission.
EC. (2019c). *2019 SBA Fact Sheet Italy*. Belgium: European Commission.
EC. (2019d). *2019 SBA Fact Sheet Poland*. Belgium: European Commission.
EC. (2019e). *2019 SBA Fact Sheet Romania*. Belgium: European Commission.
EC. (2019f). *2019 SBA Fact Sheet United Kingdom*. Belgium: European Commission.
Higgins, C., Stubbs, W., Tweedie, D., & McCallum, G. (2019). Journey or toolbox? Integrated reporting and processes of organisational change. *Accounting, Auditing & Accountability Journal*, 32(6), 1662–1689.

Integrated Reports

Alteo. (2020). *Integrated report 2019*. Retrieved March 20, 2020, from https://alteo.hu/fenntarthatosag/fenntarthatosagi-jelentesek/
Alteo. (2019). *Integrated report 2018*. Retrieved March 20, 2020, from https://alteo.hu/fenntarthatosag/fenntarthatosagi-jelentesek/
ANG Spółdzielnia. (2018). *Integrated report 2018*. Retrieved February 11, 2020, from http://www.raport2018.angkredyty.pl/
BAE Systems. (2017). *Annual report 2017*. Retrieved February 11, 2020, from https://investors.baesystems.com/~/media/Files/B/Bae-Systems-Investor-Relations-V3/PDFs/results-and-reports/results/2017/annual-report-2017.pdf
Bogdanka. (2018). *Integrated report 2018*. Retrieved February 11, 2020, from http://ri.lw.com.pl/czytaj-aktualnosc/2742/lw-bogdanka-publikuje-raport-zintegrowany-za-2018-r-/
Borsodi. (2019). *Sustainability report 2018*. Retrieved March 20, 2020, from http://www.borsodisorgyar.hu/-/media/global-sites/molson-coors-corporate/hungarian/privacy-and-terms/borsodi_fenntarthatosagi_jelentes_2018_hu.ashx?la=hu-hu
Borsodi. (2020). *Sustainability report 2019*. Retrieved March 20, 2020, from http://borsodisorgyar.hu/-/media/global-sites/molson-coors-corporate/hungarian/privacy-and-terms/20200805_borsodi_fenntarthatosagi-jelentes-mod20201012-01-online.ashx?la=hu-hu
British Land. (2017). *Integrated report 2017*. Retrieved February 11, 2020, from http://examples.integratedreporting.org/fragment/709

J. Dyczkowska et al. (eds.), *Development of Integrated Reporting in the SME Sector*, CSR, Sustainability, Ethics & Governance,
https://doi.org/10.1007/978-3-030-81903-3

CIMA. (2015). *Integrated reporting for SMEs – helping businesses grow. Case studies*. Retrieved October 15, 2021, from https://www.cimaglobal.com/Documents/Thought_leadership_docs/reporting/integrated-reporting/Case_study_IR_SMEs.pdf

Budimex. (2018). *Integrated report 2018*. Retrieved February 11, 2020, from http://annualreport.budimex.pl/2018/

Crown Estates. (2018). *Integrated report 2018*. Retrieved February 11, 2020, from https://assets.publishing.service.gov.uk/government/uploads/system/uploads/attachment_data/file/719587/The_Crown_Estate_Integrated_Annual_Report_2018.pdf

Duchy of Cornwall. (2017). *Integrated annual report 2017*. Retrieved February 11, 2020, from https://duchyofcornwall.org/assets/images/duchy-iar-2017.pdf

Dunacell. (2018). *Sustainability report 2015–2017*. Retrieved March 20, 2020, from http://dunacell.com/letoltheto/Dunacell_Fenntarthatosagi_jelentes_2015_2017%20vegleges.pdf

Gaz System. (2017). *Integrated report 2017*. Retrieved February 11, 2020, from https://www.gaz-system.pl/centrum-prasowe/materialy-do-pobrania/ (access 11.02.2020).

Grupa Azoty. (2016–2017). *Integrated report 2016–2017*. Retrieved February 11, 2020, from http://raport.grupaazoty.com/en/

KGHM. (2017). *Integrated report 2017*. Retrieved February 11, 2020, from https://kghm.com/en/node/4991

ING. (2015). *Annual report 2015*. Retrieved February 11, 2020, from https://www.ing.com/Investor-relations/Financial-performance/Annual-reports/2015.htm

ING Bank Śląski. (2018). *Integrated report 2018*. Retrieved February 11, 2020, from https://raportroczny.ing.pl/en/

LOTOS Group. (2018). *Integrated report 2018*, Retrieved February 11, 2020, from https://raportroczny.lotos.pl/en/downloads

LPP. (2018). *Integrated report 2018,* Retrieved February 11, 2020, from https://www.lppsa.com/wp-content/uploads/2018/02/LPP-raport2018-online.pdf

Marks and Spencer. (2017). *Integrated report 2017*. Retrieved February 11, 2020, from http://annualreport2017.marksandspencer.com/M&S_AR2017.pdf

mBANK. (2018). *Integrated report 2018*, Retrieved February 11, 2020, from https://www.mbank.pl/en/annual-report/2018/o-grupie-mbanku/mbank/

MOL Group. (2018). *Integrated annual report 2018*. Retrieved March 20, 2020, from https://molgroup.info/storage/documents/publications/annual_reports/2018/mol_group_integrated_annual_report_2018.pdf

MVM. (2019). *Integrated report 2019*. Retrieved March 20, 2020, from http://mvm.hu/download/Integralt-jelentes-2019_V10_2.pdf

Orange. (2018). Integrated report 2018, Retrieved February 11, 2020, from http://www.orange-ir.pl/results-center/annual-reports (access 11.02.2020).

ORLEN Group. (2018). *Integrated report 2018*, Retrieved February 11, 2020, from https://www.orlen.pl/EN/InvestorRelations/AnnualReport/Pages/default.aspx

Pekabex. (2018). *Integrated report 2018*, Retrieved February 11, 2020, from https://pekabex.pl/pl/582-zintegrowany-raport-pekabex-za-2018-rok

Pelion. (2016). *Integrated report 2016,* Retrieved February 11, 2020, from http://raport2016.pelion.eu/en/

PGE Group. (2018). *Integrated report 2018,* Retrieved February 11, 2020, from https://raportzintegrowany2018.gkpge.pl/en/

PGNIG. (2018). *Integrated report 2018*, Retrieved February 11, 2020, from http://pgnig2018.pl/en/

PKP CARGO. (2018). *Integrated report 2018*, Retrieved February 11, 2020, from https://raportzintegrowany2018.pkpcargo.com/en/ (access 11.02.2020).

Richter Gedeon Nyrt. (2018). *Sustainability report 2016–2017*. Retrieved March 20, 2020, from https://www.richter.hu/hu-HU/felelossegvallalas/Documents/Richterfenntarthatosagijelentes20162017.pdf

Richter Gedeon Nyrt. (2020). *Sustainability report 2018–2019*. Retrieved March 20, 2020, from https://www.richter.hu/hu-HU/felelossegvallalas/Documents/Richter_Fenntarthatosagijelentes_20182019.pdf
SCANMED MULTIMEDIS. (2013). *Sustainability report 2013*, Retrieved February 11, 2020, from http://raportyspoleczne.pl/wp-content/uploads/raports/30e59bb6c0bcfb15280740fcfae08e90.pdf
TAURON Group. (2018). *Integrated report 2018*, Retrieved February 11, 2020, from https://raport.tauron.pl/en/
Unicredit. (2020). *Integrated report 2019*. Retrieved March 20, 2020, from https://www.unicreditgroup.eu/content/dam/unicreditgroup-eu/documents/en/sustainability/sustainability-reports/2019/IR_ENG2019.pdf

Databases

GRI database: https://database.globalreporting.org/
IIRC database: https://integratedreporting.org/resource/emerging-integrated-reporting-database/
Hungarian Sustainable Reporting Database: www.sustainability.hu

Webpages

Survey of non-financial reporting requirements for SMEs in Europe: https://www.efaa.com/cms/upload/efaa_files/pdf/News/20181119_NFRbySMEsReport-FINAL.pdf
Reporting of non-financial information by SMEs in Europe: https://www.ifac.org/knowledge-gateway/business-reporting/discussion/reporting-non-financial-information-smes-europe
IFRS (incl. IFRS for SMEs) by country: https://www.ifrs.org/use-around-the-world/use-of-ifrs-standards-by-jurisdiction/
NFRD by country https://www.globalreporting.org/resourcelibrary/NFRpublication%20online_version.pdf
Uploading the statements: https://e-beszamolo.im.gov.hu/ebekuldes
http://raportyspoleczne.pl/edycje/raporty-spoleczne-2019/
https://irip.pl/poprzednie-edycje

The manufacturer's authorised representative in the EU is Springer Nature Customer Service Centre GmbH, Europaplatz 3, 69115 Heidelberg, Germany. If you have any concerns regarding our products, please contact ProductSafety@springernature.com

Printed and bound by CPI Group (UK) Ltd, Croydon, CR0 4YY
22/09/2026
02221061-0005